Happyland

THE WEST SERIES

Aritha van Herk, Series Editor

ISSN 1922-6519 (Print) ISSN 1925-587X (Online)

This series focuses on creative non-fiction that explores our sense of place in the West - how we define ourselves as Westerners and what impact we have on the world around us. Essays, biographies, memoirs, and insights into Western Canadian life and experience are highlighted.

No. 1 · **Looking Back: Canadian Women's Prairie Memoirs and Intersections of Culture, History, and Identity** S. Leigh Matthews

No. 2 · **Catch the Gleam: Mount Royal, From College to University, 1910–2009** Donald N. Baker

No. 3 · **Always an Adventure: An Autobiography** Hugh A. Dempsey

No. 4 · **Happyland: A History of the "Dirty Thirties" in Saskatchewan, 1914–1937** Curtis R. McManus

Happyland

A History of the "Dirty Thirties" in Saskatchewan, 1914–1937

CURTIS R. McMANUS

UNIVERSITY OF
CALGARY
PRESS

THE WEST SERIES
ISSN 1922-6519 (Print) ISSN 1925-587X (Online)

University of Calgary Press
2500 University Drive NW
Calgary, Alberta
Canada T2N 1N4
www.uofcpress.com

LIBRARY AND ARCHIVES CANADA CATALOGUING IN PUBLICATION

McManus, Curtis R., 1972-
    Happyland : a history of the "dirty thirties" in Saskatchewan, 1914–1937 / Curtis R. McManus.

(The West series, 1922-6519 ; 5)
Includes bibliographical references and index.
Issued also in electronic formats.
ISBN 978-1-55238-524-1

    1. Saskatchewan—History—1905–1945. 2. Depressions—1929—Saskatchewan. I. Title.
II. Series: West series (Calgary, Alta.)

FC3523.M35 2011   971.24'02   C2011-903089-6

The University of Calgary Press acknowledges the support of the Alberta Foundation for the Arts for our publications. We acknowledge the financial support of the Government of Canada through the Canada Book Fund for our publishing activities. We acknowledge the financial support of the Canada Council for the Arts for our publishing program.

This book has been published with the help of a grant from the Canadian Federation for the Humanities and Social Sciences, through the Aid to Scholarly Publications Program, using funds provided by the Social Sciences and Humanities Research Council of Canada.

Alberta Foundation for the Arts   Canada   Canada Council for the Arts / Conseil des Arts du Canada

Cover design, page design, and typesetting by Melina Cusano

To my mother and father.

Acknowledgments

It is a great pleasure to be able to acknowledge the people who have helped in the process of writing this book. I wish to thank Donna Livingstone, John King, and the staff at the University of Calgary Press for their efficiency in putting the book together. They were a pleasure to work with.

I extend thanks to the two anonymous readers who read the manuscript and who offered suggestions and comments on ways in which it might be improved; their suggestions were of high value and the book is better because of it.

The hard-working administrators at most of the RMs I visited provided open and ready access to their archives. Coffee was provided, lunch breaks were shortened, exceptions were made, additional materials were offered, and questions were answered. Mike Sherven of Mankota and Quentin Jacksteit of Golden Prairie (Big Stick) were especially helpful.

The staff at Lakeland College in Lloydminster, where I teach history, has also been of immense help. Bryan Moon was always willing to discuss the book and offer suggestions; Judy Sarsons allowed me to take the necessary time off to complete it; and Kelly Mutter, who after finding out about the book and the fact that it mentioned Hatton ("My grandparents were born there!"), made arrangements for me to meet with his father Mr. Ralph Mutter to talk about the dry years.

I owe a great spiritual and intellectual debt to the University of Saskatchewan and the men and women of the history department. Dr. Bill Waiser has been a great source of encouragement, support, assistance, help, advice, and guidance. I happily acknowledge my debt to him. I wish also to thank the following history professors: Christopher Kent, Martha Smith-Norris, Gordon Desbrisay, Brett Fairbairn, and Jolanta Pekacz. From these professors, I took inspiration and enthusiasm for the study of history.

Dr. Man Kam-leung taught Asian history and ignited in me a lifelong interest in the subject. (He also taught me the value of using unique and surprising sources in the study of history.)

I would also like to publicly honour and acknowledge a special debt to Dr. Robert C. Grogin (retired). When I think of my education in history, I think of him.

Additionally, the staff at both branches of the Saskatchewan Archives Board were helpful, especially Tim Novak at the Regina office. I thank Dr. David Jones for demonstrating that prairie history need not be dull, drab, and boring. I also acknowledge that Dr. Jones was the first historian to explore the dryland crisis between 1914 and 1923 and that *Happyland* was possible only because of his work in this area.

I thank Scott McMillan of Cameron Street Creative (formerly lead singer for the now-defunct White Boy Blues Project), for his help with the graphics and photographs. I would also like to thank "The Reactionary," "The Driver," "Mr. Culham," and "Prime Time" for tolerating my discussions about farmers planting fifty-acre plots of crested wheat grass.

Table of Contents

SASKATCHEWAN URBAN AND RURAL MUNICIPALITIES (detail)

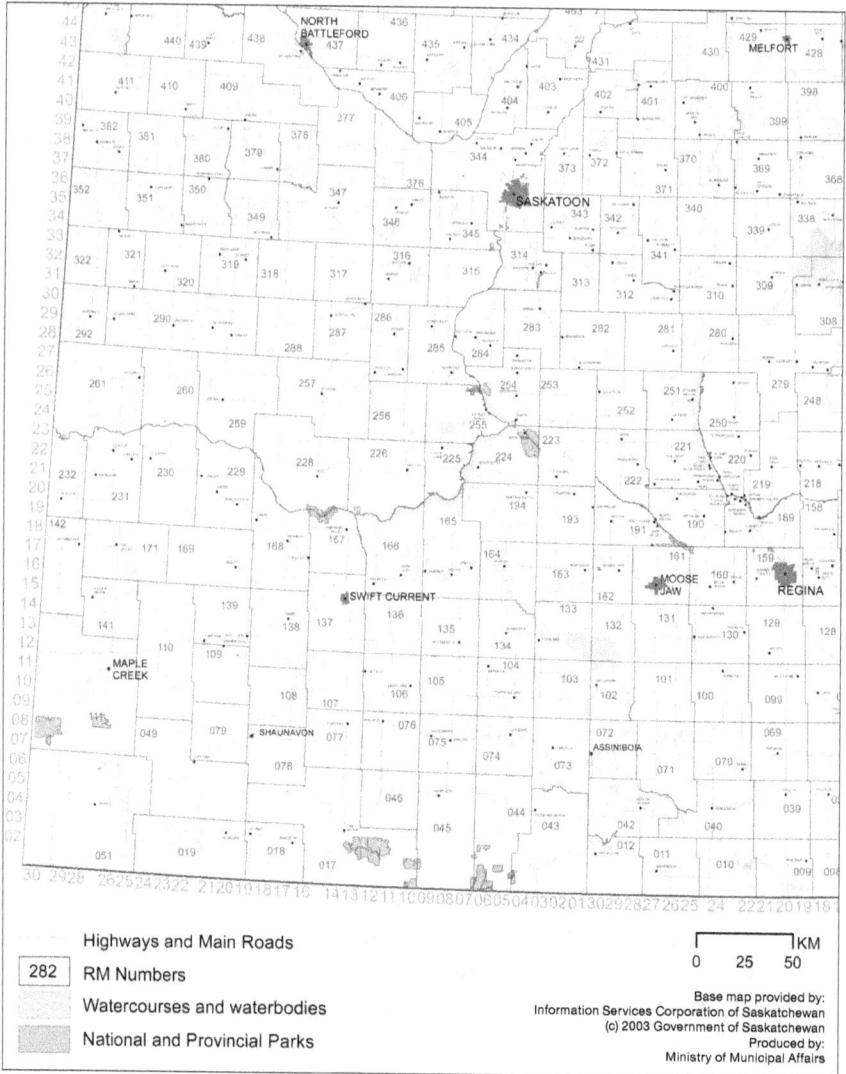

Highways and Main Roads

| 282 | RM Numbers

Watercourses and waterbodies

National and Provincial Parks

KM
0   25   50

Base map provided by:
Information Services Corporation of Saskatchewan
(c) 2003 Government of Saskatchewan
Produced by:
Ministry of Municipal Affairs

Legend to Map

RM 290: RM of Kindersley (location of town of Kindersley)
RM 261: RM of Chesterfield (location of village of Mantario)
RM 232: RM of Deer Forks (location of town of Burstall)
RM 231: RM of Happyland
RM 230: RM of Clinworth
RM 141: RM of Big Stick (location of town of Golden Prairie)
RM 137: RM of Swift Current (location of city of Swift Current)

RM 134: RM of Shamrock
RM 111: RM of Maple Creek
　　　(location of town of Maple Creek, location of Hatton)
RM 49: RM of White Valley (location of town of Eastend)
RM 45: RM of Mankota (location of village of Mankota)
RM 11: RM of Hart Butte (location of town of Coronach)

Introduction: Oblivion

> *Oblivion*: (noun) the state of being unaware of what is happening around one; the state of being forgotten; destruction or extinction. From the Latin *oblivisci*, 'to forget.' – *Oxford English Dictionary*

On a hot, dry day during the blistering, drought-shot summer of 1921, a fire rampaged through the town of Hatton, Saskatchewan, located about fifty kilometres west-north-west of Maple Creek. The conflagration was devastating: thirty-five homes and businesses were destroyed including the regal, two-storey, forty-two-room Forres Hotel. In addition to destroying half of the physical portion of Hatton, the fire completely destroyed something that no one could see and so during that hot, sad summer afternoon no one immediately noticed its quiet incineration in the flames. Along with half the town, the fire consumed that intangible 'thing' that made the settlement of rural Saskatchewan possible – the spirit of the community. It is interesting to note what *did not* happen after the fire: residents of the town did not pledge to rebuild, they did not promise to start anew, nor did they start again from the ashes. Hatton residents gave up. According to a local historian, the fire represented "the beginning of the gradual death of the town."[1] And so after the flames had died and the embers cooled, the forlorn little village of Hatton, on a smoky, sultry summer evening in 1921, began a slow but persistent downward spiral into oblivion.

The death of Hatton was a long drawn-out affair that dragged on slowly but implacably for another thirteen years after the fire. The councillors of this unhappy little village resisted dissolution as best they could, but it was a fight they could not win and in the end they could no longer rationalize their gallant defence. By 1934, there was practically no one left in the town and their determination to save the community could no longer be justified to themselves or others. On a desolate March evening when there was neither charming snow on the ground nor life-affirming leaves on the trees, just cold wind, the village men finally agreed to ask the province to officially dissolve the village. Thus it was that Hatton voted itself out of existence. It had existed for just twenty years.

That Hatton was once a spirited and energetic community-on-the-move is plainly obvious judging from the records of the town council. These records detail the benign and pleasing minutiae of daily life in a recently settled frontier town. Even though Hatton had two police officers – Dan Hanton and Hugh MacLeod – the community often policed itself or rather relied upon the good nature of its citizenry to obey the town fathers when they made a proclamation. There was a certain Mr. Rayton, for example, who was fond of ostentatiously driving his slick, new motor-car through town at excessive speeds. Council twice sent Mr. Rayton a letter "calling his attention to the speed limit" once in May and, evidently because he didn't listen, again in June.[2]

Like most other prairie towns, Hatton had its own pool hall. The local pool hall was an institution in rural Saskatchewan that played a major role in the social life of young lads and old timers right up until the 1980s when pool halls sadly fell out of fashion. Hatton's pool hall even conformed to the stereotype of the degenerate pool room because the town's council received numerous complaints about "the manner in which [owner Mr. Fred Meier's] pool room is conducted."[3] Perhaps rumours had sped about town that hinted at liquor, gambling, and wantonness. Historian William Wardill has remarked that pool halls in those early days were places where "a man could always find a poker game as well as the opportunity to drink himself into truculence or insensibility."[4] Whatever the reason and whatever the vice, the town councilmen gently urged Mr. Meier towards a proper and more gentlemanly form of conduct.

Pool-room ownership was actually a step down on the Hatton social ladder and Fred Meier's ownership of it, to say nothing of the circumstance under which it was purchased, evidently caused some good-natured embarrassment to his family. It seems that Mr. Meier had bought the

Hatton pool-room on a bit of a lark: "while he was in Hatton" according to his family biography, "someone talked him into buying [the] pool room, much to the disappointment of the rest of his family"[5]

When they weren't shooting pool (or, presumably, gophers) the school children engaged in mischief as a way to occupy their days. Young Hatton lads were often seen, much to the sensitive displeasure of the town fathers, "loitering at the school swings during late evenings" and there were numerous reports of "disorderly conduct" in addition to "disturbances around the homes of citizens."[6] Thus the councilmen pleaded with the local school teacher to keep a most watchful eye on her prairie-wild charges.

There were actually two schools in the community that the youngsters attended: one for the German-speaking children, and one for those who spoke English. This circumstance raises interesting questions because one does not need a too-vivid imagination to wonder at the inter-ethnic animosity and conflict that occurred between the Germans and the Anglos since Hatton was settled just prior to the outbreak of the First World War. This question of English-German conflict is not an idle one: one of Hatton's closest neighbours was the town of Leader which, up to 1917, was unfortunately called Prussia, a name guaranteed to offend any Englishman within a thousand miles. Councilmen in the little town of Prussia evidently had trouble shedding their affection for the gnarled institutions of the Old Country – not only did Prussia have streets named 'Wilhelm' and 'Kaiser,' but also, members of the Army and Navy Veterans Association from Regina made an emergency trip to the little community in 1917 to encourage the Germans to reconsider their plan to name a boulevard after RMS *Lusitania*, a liner sunk by the German navy killing hundreds of civilians and prompting the entry of the United States into World War I. The visit was "most successful" in view of the fact that Prussia's council not only refrained from celebrating the loss of the *Lusitania*, they also agreed, in a demonstration of nervous devotion to their new country, to change the name of the town to the much less antagonistic 'Leader,' the name of the Regina daily newspaper.[7] The German kids in Hatton, though, were perhaps better behaved than their English counterparts: the German school was operated by the "Reverend Mr. Krug," whose very name seems to suggest that he did not have a problem with discipline.

And social services in Hatton, such as they were back then, were delivered by the municipality itself, a derivative of that very English custom in which helping the poor was deemed a purely local concern. In 1925, for example, Councillor Stephens agreed to give a Mrs. Dewey fifteen dollars for one month because it seems her "invalid boy" had been taking up all her time and the relief was meant to "provide her with the time required to get a job and earn her own living."[8] This statement suggests that there was the opportunity to find work in Hatton even if only on a nearby farm. Hatton, it should be noted, was the largest grain distribution point in western Canada in 1915–16.[9]

Even as late as 1929, the death of Hatton was still not an entirely foregone conclusion. Councillor Mr. Gottleib Pfaff (a terrifyingly stern-looking Bessarabian immigrant whose own farm would burn to the ground in 1930) successfully argued for money to be spent on two "Welcome!" signs to be posted on the highway at both ends of the village. Council also agreed to give Mr. Yee Lung seventy-five dollars to help rebuild his fire-damaged Chinese restaurant. Chinese restaurants were one of the few avenues of employment open to Chinese immigrants fleeing from the creaking and debauched Qing Dynasty at the turn of the century. The local Chinese restaurant became an institution in rural Saskatchewan and played a major role in its social life.[10] Still does.

In addition to Yee Lung's restaurant and Fred Maier's troubled pool-room, Hatton at its peak featured a downtown core with two banks, four stores, three restaurants, a hardware store, livery barns, laundries, and a theatre to complement the estimated eight hundred people who resided in and around the small community.[11] Allie Auger ran the general store and one of the lumber yards, William "Bill" Watson was the postmaster, Norm Robson was the proprietor of the hotel, and Happy Nicholas had a majority stake in the local blacksmith shop. Hatton was even located on a rail line that hauled both grain and passengers, though Mr. George Murray of nearby Golden Prairie recalls that the CP passenger train service through Hatton wasn't very reliable even then because "in order to board the train, it had to be flagged down."[12]

Life in Hatton, then, had all the appearance of life in other frontier communities. There was a thriving business sector, recreation for the residents, and the nine grain elevators strung out along the main line were a proud testament to the wisdom of settling that region. Hans and Bertha Mattson arrived in the region from Denmark in 1912 and she fondly recalls Hatton and the fact that the little community "was the focal point for all the homesteaders in the area."[13]

But the damage had been done. The wounds inflicted by the summer fire of 1921 soon began to putrefy. By 1929, on the eve of that greatest of prairie disasters, the Dirty Thirties, so many people had fled the community and its surrounding area that town council came to the sad realization that it could no longer levy and collect property taxes because there were "[too many] houses being removed from the village and there [was] too much dead real estate."[14]

Losing houses meant losing people and thus ratepayers and as a consequence council had no way to finance infrastructure improvements. Broke and dying but still fighting the good fight council persisted, as rural councils still do today, in pursuing infrastructure improvements. Lacking any other sources of funds to pay for the improvements, council agreed to "get some man who owes the village money" to repair the sidewalks on Main Street. The councilmen justified this prairie variant of indentured servitude by arguing that a man's debt should, if no other means were available, be paid back with his labour.[15] Servitude of this type was a very common feature of life on the south plains in the early settlement years even though it was a morally messy arrangement with a high probability that the man who decreed another's servitude could be and quite often likely was either a friend, employer, neighbour, or acquaintance.

In 1932, Hatton began seeking a buyer for the town's fire hall, which had been built in 1923, just two years after the Big Fire of 1921. (Mr. M. Gnammbe was paid sixty-five cents per hour to do the work and Mr. Leonard Jahnke was paid forty-five cents an hour as his helper.) Council asked the nearby rural municipality of Big Stick if it was interested in purchasing the fire-hall ("it's a good fire-hall") presumably because so many houses had been burned down or moved out of the town that there were no longer any houses to protect.[16] Indeed, the removal of buildings had created safety problems because of the open cellars and basements left behind. Mr. Gottlieb Anhorn (a man about whom we shall later have occasion to hear more) was ordered to fill in the cellar on the municipal property he owned because council had "declared [it] a nuisance."

The end for Hatton advanced but council fought for as long as they could. They declared that they were "capable and able and willing to continue to administer the public business cheaper and better" than the Department of Municipal Affairs.[17] But time had simply run out. With no people left to speed down the streets, no kids left to "loiter" in the school grounds or cause "disturbances" around the homes of the citizens (indeed with no more homes around which to cause those "disturbances"), with no pool hall left in which to congregate or in which to drink or play poker, no Chinese restaurant in which to socialize, and no hotel bar to which tired and overworked settlers could repair, village councillors held their last meeting in March 1934 stating the obvious: "there does not appear to be any reason to expect a revival of business and development in Hatton." Council transacted its final business (the settling of some $200 in unpaid accounts) and then walked into the fog of history.

Today, nothing remains of the town. It is not even allowed the grim dignity of being called a ghost-town because there is nothing there: it is precisely as though it never existed. There is nothing at all to suggest that a town and the immediate area that surrounds it sat astride grid 635 and was home to as many as eight hundred people at its peak. The "Welcome!" signs were torn down many years ago, likely after being shot full of holes with .22 rifles as is the common fate of road signs in rural Saskatchewan. The land that surrounds the site of the dead community has been turned back to prairie. Nearby "Bitter Lake" vanishes during dry years. And still, the intriguing question lingers: why did the townsfolk choose not to rebuild their community? Hatton, after all, had been one the largest grain distribution points in western Canada, and in addition to stores and services located in a burgeoning downtown core, it also had a railway line for both grain and passengers. The answer to the question "why?" envelops us in one of the great tragedies of western settlement and indeed all of Canadian history.

Up to the summer fire of 1921, Hatton had been, or rather nervously pretended to be, just like any other community in the burgeoning rural province of Saskatchewan. But it wasn't like any other community. Not really. Hatton had the geographic misfortune of being located near the centre, the core, the arid and barren heart of Palliser's Triangle that great swath of land between Regina and Calgary dismissed by the heroic gentleman-adventurer Captain John Palliser as "unfit for human habitation." Indeed, Hatton is not too very far away from the Great Sand Hills, a region characterized by cacti, coyotes, petrified wood, and sand dunes. By even the loosest definition, that area is a desert and recent studies support this idea. Just two hundred years ago, at the opening of the nineteenth century, "a large swath" of southern Saskatchewan was an active desert that featured sand dunes and other features we usually associate with Death Valley or the Sahara.[18] Local historian Mr. J.R. "Bud" Thompson from the Alsask district a couple hours north of Hatton picks up on this desert theme. Describing west Saskatchewan in a drought, Mr. Thompson explains that "the earth becomes drier and drier until very little vegetation will grow. Water holes, sloughs and shallow wells will begin to dry up until they are completely empty."[19]

This region of Saskatchewan, the south-central, south-west and west-central area, was the epicentre in 1908 of one of the largest mass movements of humanity the world had ever seen when thousands upon thousands of immigrants came to Saskatchewan and Alberta during the last great land rush of modern times: it was billed in the promotional literature as The Last Best West. But it was just a few short years later between 1914 and 1937 that Hatton and the millions of acres of land that surround it would be the grim, joyless epicentre of the largest wholesale land abandonment disaster in all of Canadian history.

Tens of thousands of people fled the area between 1914 and 1937, dragging behind themselves ruined lives. In all of Canadian history there is no other period quite like this one: it is unique in our country's history and the tragic arc of Hatton's existence parallels this twenty-five year period of land abandonment. The fire in Hatton occurred in 1921 almost exactly midway through the virtually unknown land abandonment crisis of the 1920s. Prefiguring the Dirty Thirties by a decade, the period between 1917 and 1924, saw an estimated 30,000 men, women, and children flee the south and west plains of Saskatchewan because of drought, crop failure, starvation and destitution.[20] While the fire gutted the town of Hatton, drought gutted the countryside and so in this context it becomes easier to understand why Hatton residents gave up: their town and the country that surrounded it were being emptied of human life. Residents of Hatton packed up what they saved from the fire and fled two steps ahead of drought, crop failure, relief aid, and indentured servitude. The twenties roared; just not in Hatton.

Hatton was officially dissolved in 1934, again almost exactly mid-way through the crisis of the Dirty Thirties during which an estimated 40,000 people fled this same region. All those who hadn't fled in the first round of drought in the 1920s did so in the second round of the 1930s presumably because the prospect of enduring a third seemed unappealing.

And Hatton was incorporated in 1913, just one year before the Dominion government, the provincial government, and thousands of settlers experienced the full-on fury of the legendary and devastating drought of 1914. Fully $8 million in relief aid was funnelled into the south plains of Saskatchewan over the course of that year; today, that drought is widely recognized as one of the worst south plains droughts of the twentieth century.[21] 1914 was also the year in which the basic pattern of life for settlers on the south and west plains of Saskatchewan was established for the next twenty-five years down to 1937 and beyond: drought and crop-failure would be followed by starvation, relief-aid, indentured servitude, labour-gangs, land-abandonment, perdition.

It is a common enough belief that nothing much of consequence occurred on the south plains prior to the Dirty Thirties. It has been suggested that there is often a tendency to emphasize the healthy nature of the years prior to 1929 in order to make the crisis of the 1930s appear that much more dramatic and compelling. This reluctance or failure to explore the nature of the years prior to the 1930s has resulted in a historical vacuum in which a great deal of the history of that period has either never been told or indeed has been lost altogether.

The "Dirty Thirties" proper, that period between 1929 and 1937, is actually only one element of a much larger story. The Dirty Thirties did not begin in 1929, coincident with the crash of the stock market, nor were the Dirty Thirties a singular event without precedent. The "Dirty Thirties" as we understand the term to mean agricultural devastation, drought and misery, starvation and land abandonment began in 1914, was strictly limited to the south and west plains, and with a few exceptions, lasted all the way down to 1937 when the fever, as it were, finally broke.

Between 1914 and 1937, there were three different and distinct stages of drought, crop failure, and land abandonment. Each stage was worse than the one before and these stages ultimately culminated in the calamitous dust storms, starvation, and catastrophic land abandonment of the 1930s. The "Dirty Thirties" was not a sudden cataclysmic event that caught surprised settlers unaware, heartlessly tearing them from prosperity and contentment. What happened in the Dirty Thirties was a simple and basic fact of life on the plains of southern Saskatchewan for decades and which occurred *only* on the south and west plains: dust storms ("black blizzards" as they were called) did not happen anywhere else in Canada. By focusing only on the 1930s, only half the story has been told and the other half has either been remaindered or forgotten.

In addition, then, to re-calibrating the years in which the "Dirty Thirties" occurred, this work attempts to untie another equally difficult conceptual knot. Often times, the Dirty Thirties and the Great Depression are thought to be the same event, that they were somehow necessarily intertwined. In public discourse, one frequently hears both phrases used interchangeably when in fact they denote different periods entirely – our day-to-day language reflects the common assumption that the two events are the same. They are not. Even though both events occurred at roughly the same time, the Great Depression in a number of important ways actually had very little to do with the Dirty Thirties. Most obviously, the Depression was a global economic crisis while the Dirty Thirties was an agricultural-environmental crisis that struck at a defined and particular region. The Depression mattered only insofar as it made a bad situation punitively worse. At thirty cents per bushel, what little wheat was grown on the south plains during the Dirty Thirties was virtually worthless because of the global commodity price failure. But, as we will see, for literally years on end, absolutely nothing or the next best thing to absolutely nothing was grown on the south plains. If one is not growing anything, the price of what one is not growing does not really matter. Nothing of nothing is still nothing.

Academics have been strangely silent on the Dirty Thirties, strange because it is, after all, the seminal event in Saskatchewan and indeed western Canadian history. The silence on the pre-history of the thirties is thunderous. While there are some precious few studies of the 1930s, there are none on the subject of the pre-history of those years. Even local community histories are largely silent on it. There is an enormous historical vacuum in Saskatchewan historiography.[22] The existence of this vacuum was explicitly recognized by one of the rural councillors who fed starving settlers during the crisis of the 1920s. Former Big Stick councillor Mr. R.L. Carefoot wrote proudly of the role he and his fellow councilmen played in saving settlers from starvation during the 1920s: "we had to get hay, oats, and relief for the people," he recalls, "[but] I don't suppose anyone remembers those days anymore."[23] He's right. They don't.

There have been no detailed single-volume works on the history of the Dirty Thirties since writer and historian James Gray published his justifiably famous *Men against the Desert* more than forty years ago. In that work, though, Gray gives the reader only a proxy history of the 1914 to 1937 period. The focus of his work is on explaining how and why the Prairie Farm Rehabilitation Administration (PFRA) developed; thus, he does not explore the nature and detail of the crises that struck at the south plains between 1914 and 1937. Gray's book is a fine and exceptional work well-deserving of the respect it receives, but it is one to which virtually nothing has been added in the decades since he wrote it. Additionally, historian Dr. David Jones wrote a book about the land abandonment crisis of the 1920s, but this work, for the most part, explores the nature of the Alberta experience – not Saskatchewan.[24] This emphasis on Alberta is not a fault: Dr. Jones is an Alberta historian and he explored this interprovincial crisis with an eye on the drylands in that province.

In Saskatchewan, though, there has only been silence on this period in our history. There have been no works that examine the terrible drought of 1914 and its implications; there has been no work on the land abandonment crisis in south Saskatchewan between 1917 and 1924; there are very few studies of the Dirty Thirties, none of which have examined the 1914–37 period from the perspective of the small rural municipalities that were scarred by the crisis. The social problems that arose from the droughts – the suicides, the drunkenness, the ubiquity of sex (both illicit and pre-marital), the temporary suspension and corrosion of moral codes and personal values – have likewise never been explored. The present work attempts to address those deficiencies.

The disaster of the dry years between 1914 and 1937 was as much a man-made crisis as it was an act of God. It was an ecological disaster created by naturally occurring forces (the drought) and brutally primitive farming techniques (summer-fallowing) that stripped and pulverized the soil to the point where it became in many cases quite literally sand, and when the soil turned to sand people fled. Responsible estimations place the number of people who abandoned only the south and west Saskatchewan plains between 1914 and 1937 at 70,000 men, women, and children. They fled in the hundreds from towns like Hatton and from forlorn and forgotten communities like Senate, Ravenscrag, Estuary, Scotsguard, Vidora, Robsart, and Aneroid. And by the tens of thousands they fled from rural municipalities like Shamrock, Mankota, Pinto Creek, Big Stick, Deer Forks, Hart Butte, and Happyland, leaving their land behind to blow into sand.

The greater tragedy is that the events that occurred in Hatton and the rural areas of the wider south and west Saskatchewan plains also occurred with dulling and tragic monotony in every American state directly south of Saskatchewan all the way down into the Texas Panhandle: Palliser's Triangle is, after all, the northern tip of what is called the Great American Desert.

There is no other region in Canada quite like the south and west plains of Saskatchewan and the south and east plains of Alberta. It is not just the geography of this region that is unique (there is very little water; trees are viewed with alarm) but its history too. The social and moral dislocations that occurred in the dry years, to say nothing of the population haemorrhages, are completely without parallel in Canadian history. Likewise, there is no other period in our country's history that features such abundant helpings of the ridiculous and the absurd, for that, in the end, was what the dry years became. In fact, the line between tragedy and absurdity is crossed so often and with such enthusiasm by so many people between 1914 and 1937 that it becomes nearly impossible to untangle the absolutely sad from the utterly ridiculous.

The "Dirty Thirties" is a singular historical event with its own causes, courses, and consequences; it has its own history, nature, and trajectory quite separate and distinct from the Great Depression. Of course, the separation of the two events is not absolute: that was not the case at the time nor shall it ever be. But the Dirty Thirties did not need the Great Depression in order to happen; the economic collapse did not cause the agricultural catastrophe nor did it give to the droughts their dark and desperate dynamics. The two events happened at the same time, true, but that was only ever only a coincidence. The Dirty Thirties would have happened even if the sun had been shining, the birds had been singing, and all remained right in the world.

The Descent

Tragedy: (noun) an event causing great suffering, destruction and distress. From the Greek *Tragoidia*.

Folly: (noun) foolishness; a foolish act or idea. From the Old French *folie*, 'madness.'

Mad[*ness*]: (noun) mentally ill; extremely foolish or ill-advised; showing impulsiveness, confusion or frenzy. From Old English. – *Oxford English Dictionary*.

Between 1914 and 1937, an estimated 70,000 men, women, and children abandoned their farms, homesteads, and communities and fled from the southern and western plains of Saskatchewan. They took trains up north, they loaded their wagons and headed east, and, if they had a car, they hitched it to their horses (thus creating a "Bennett buggy") and began the long trek into the green valleys of British Columbia where, just as often, they were "sent back to the dried out areas" as happened in the 1930s. Occasionally, the settlers simply "walked out," leaving behind whatever they couldn't carry on their backs – this happened repeatedly in the Mantario district east of Kindersley during the 1920s.

Hundreds of millions of dollars were spent on food, clothing, and relief aid during these years. Tens of thousands of men were sent to work on hard labour road gangs. Millions of acres of land were left to rot and blow into sand. One-room school houses were temporarily shut down and then, in disbelieving exasperation, torn down because there were no more children left. Homes were abandoned. Towns like Hatton first burned and then atrophied. Lives were put on hold; lives were ruined.

In the early years of the crisis, the Saskatchewan government insisted that there was not a problem and even if there was a problem then helping the settlers get out of the south country was certainly not the answer. This was especially true during the 1920s: while Alberta evacuated every south plains settler it could possibly get its hands on in one of the largest government-directed evacuation programs in Canadian history, long-standing and influential members of the Saskatchewan government preferred to chastise settlers for creating their own problems and thus refused to help, hence the observation of one settler in 1923 that he had seen many settlers "walking out" of the drylands.

Such is the raw material of the history of the south and west plains during the dry years.

The single most prominent theme in this "unholy mess," as historian James Gray termed it, is the capitulation of hope. Ultimately, hope is what the dry years are about. If there was hope in those years, even a thin and slender variant of hope, the people of Hatton, to say nothing of the tens of thousands of others who fled, would have stayed. If there was any reason at all to think that they could make a go of it, they would have remained. If there was hope, then 70,000 people would not have abandoned their home and friends and family and communities between 1914 and 1937. But they didn't stay because there was no hope. It is not economics, it is not politics, and it is not obscure impersonal historical forces: it is "hope" and its degenerative twin "hopelessness" that are the chief engines of the history of the south and west Saskatchewan plains between 1914 and 1937. Between these years, drought struck at the south plains with punctuated though repeated ferocity. In between the droughts, a fire would ravage a community to keep things moving along.

Drought is qualitatively different from fire in a number of ways, and it is instructive to compare the two. Generally speaking, the wounds that drought inflicts are affective or spiritual, whereas the wounds inflicted by fire are usually and predominantly physical. And while fire destroys in minutes, drought lingers and it suffocates, and only gradually over time, over years, does it extract its due. When thoughtfully considered, land abandonment is the physical manifestation of the wounds that drought inflicts on the human spirit.

Fire can achieve in an hour what it would take drought years to achieve. Fire destroys instantly and thus forces people to make immediate choices. During a drought, though, these choices can be deferred. In a drought, there is always the hope that the next year will be better; there is always the hope that it can't possibly get worse. This is the great deception of drought. Fire does not contain deception. Many Hatton residents did not stick around to rebuild the town after the fire in 1921. They fled. In the four years between 1917 and 1921, corrosive drought had eaten away at hope; the fire merely incinerated the little that remained.

Both fire and drought leave behind physical wreckage, too. Fire leaves ugly scars and burned-out buildings. Drought, by contrast, leaves forlorn detritus of a less obvious, less brutal nature. Much of the land south of Mankota, for example, has been turned back to prairie, but on that prairie one can still see rock piles sitting silently, overgrown with weeds. These are not just rock piles, though, but museums of a sort. They are monuments: to futility it is true, but monuments nonetheless. These rock piles represent the efforts of a settler who had diligently cleared his land of stones in order to farm it. Oftentimes in those early pioneer days the settler did this with little more than a pickaxe and a crowbar. When the rocks were cleared, the settler then set about farming his land until all attempts at doing so proved futile. Futility and hopelessness on the south and west plains of Saskatchewan were achieved after five years, or quite often ten. In some cases, it took many men fifteen or even twenty years to arrive at the end point. This astonishing persistence was predicated on the relentless hope that it could not possibly get worse. But it always did. When the settler recognized the futility of his situation, he took his family and fled, and he did so entirely unaware that the rock pile he left behind was a monument, a lasting and permanent testament to one of the grossest policy miscalculations in Canadian history.

The man responsible for that gross and ultimately inhuman policy error was Mr. Frank Oliver, the Minister of Interior from 1905 to 1911. If there is anything at all to the Great Man Theory of History (and "Great Man" here does not necessarily mean "good man") and the idea that history can be driven forward through the exertions of one individual, then Mr. Oliver provides us with a fine example. It was his 1908 amendment to the Dominion Lands Act that repudiated almost forty years of land use policy for the south plains of Saskatchewan, resulted in the settlement of the drylands, and set the stage for the most agonizing and frustrating period of the lives of thousands upon thousands of men, women, and children.

From the 1870s until 1908, the south plains were administered largely as a cattle-ranching preserve. Swift Current, Maple Creek, and, further east, Moose Jaw served as the dryland's three principal communities in 1908. The rest of the area from the American border up to an east-west line at North Battleford, and from the Alberta border east to Moose Jaw remained, for the most part, empty. Prior to opening the region for settlement, it was observed that outside these communities, Maple Creek and Swift Current especially, the infrastructure of the entire region consisted of "a railway and two roads."[1]

This ghastly emptiness was not an accident but was instead the calculated result of the Dominion government's land use policy. Oliver's predecessor in the Department of Interior, Mr. Clifford Sifton, and before him men like lands manager Mr. William Pearce, ensured that the cattle rancher would be favoured with profitable and agreeable grazing leases at the expense of settlement because the region was deemed unfit for agriculture.[2] The simple but well-founded belief that the area was excessively dry formed the basis for assumptions around which land use policy for the drylands was structured from the mid-1870s to 1908: the rancher was in and the settler was out. Over the longer term, it was thought that settlers would eventually be allowed in, but this settlement would occur slowly and gradually and only after better agricultural practices had developed and advances like irrigation introduced.[3]

This gradualist approach can be seen in the Conservative government's late-nineteenth-century legislation concerning ranch land on the south plains. In 1886, for example, the "no-settlement" clause was dropped from all newly issued grazing leases and this allowed for small-scale settlement on small patches of land here and there.[4] In 1892, in a further move that had the potential to allow for limited settlement, the Conservatives announced that all the old "closed" grazing leases would be cancelled in four years, though ranchers were given the option of purchasing these leases for $1.25 per acre to keep them closed to settlers.[5] These policies reflect a drive toward a comfortable middle ground in which the government protected the lands used for cattle, while at the same time conceding to demands for land by allowing for and gently encouraging small-scale experimental settlements in the area. This gradualist approach, however, did not mean that the region was open for settlement. For all practical purposes, the south-country remained closed and this was the Dominion government's policy regarding the south plains all the way down to 1908. There was never any doubt that the land was best left to the rancher.[6] Frank Oliver, though, had other ideas.

Mr. Oliver was the very antithesis of his predecessor, Clifford Sifton. Oliver became Interior Minister upon Mr. Sifton's resignation in 1905 and Oliver had zero-tolerance for the latter's practice of courting and mollycoddling the cattle rancher. Historian Pierre Berton has crafted a revealing portrait of the two men: Sifton was "an Ottawa sophisticate," where Oliver was "cadaverous [and] rough-hewn." Sifton was a "pillar of the Ottawa Hunt," while Oliver, by bland and colourless contrast, was the "President of the Edmonton Bicycle Club." Sifton was emotionally conservative where Oliver was "explosive."[7] But Oliver also possessed a unique distinction that Sifton did not have: according to the editors of the always-abrasive Calgary *Herald*, Oliver's newspaper, the Edmonton *Bulletin*, was "the meanest paper published by the meanest man in Canada."[8] It was the meanest man in Canada to whom was given responsibility over the Dominion government's land use policy in western Canada. Fitting, then, that the results should have been so tragic.

Oliver had long believed in settler's rights. "Unrestricted settlement" was one of the messages that blared forth from the pages of the Edmonton *Bulletin*. But underneath that sentiment lay a rattlesnake's nest of thoughts and assumptions about farmers, ranchers, and cattlemen, and it was out of this turgid intellectual swamp that the 1908 amendment to the Dominion Lands Act developed.

Simply put, Mr. Oliver did not like cattlemen. This dislike (though perhaps distaste is a better word) was mostly political not personal. The way Oliver saw it, ranchers were "a landed and reactionary establishment" with too-strong ties to the Conservative party and in many ways Oliver's ideas were actually more in step with the mood of the country at that time.[9] Settlers had long been viewed as "the emblem of democracy and progress" – they were the underdog battling the wealthy cattle baron.[10] These halcyon ideas conform nicely to the even-broader body of thought current in North America at that time that cleaved to the idea that the Yeoman Farmer somehow embodied man's essential goodness. This highly unsound body of ideas about the intrinsic dignity and goodness of the farmer specifically and of agriculture generally (remnants of which are still apparent in public discourse today) was a creature of eighteenth- and nineteenth-century Jeffersonian America.[11] And in Canada, Oliver adopted, or rather co-opted, these dreamy ideals for his own purposes.

Oliver supported settler's rights for political reasons, but he justified and rationalized that support using this mystique that was attached to the farmer, that noble and honest tiller of the soil. In Oliver's hands, these ideals were a political expedient that he wielded in large part because of his political antipathy toward cattlemen. Oliver's delicate, lifelong liberal sensibilities were no doubt offended by the close, amicable ties shared between the ranchers and the Conservative party.[12] Historian Lewis G. Thomas explains that it was not the ranchers but the settlers who "appealed to a morality that was much more in step with the buoyant enthusiasm of nation building."[13] Oliver entered the Dominion Lands office in 1905 soaked through with this intellectual baggage.

When Oliver arrived at his new office in Ottawa, he faced the prospect that very soon, there would be very little land left to settle, and the fear was that prospective immigrants would settle elsewhere if new lands were not made available ("elsewhere" should be read as "the United States").[14] Lands boss Clifford Sifton had succeeded beyond all expectations in settling those parts of Saskatchewan that it was deemed appropriate to settle between 1896 and 1905. Thousands of immigrants had responded to the Dominion government's efforts to attract people. These were the years of Mr. Sifton's famous "settlers in sheepskin coats." But Oliver had neither the temperament nor the inclination to be upstaged or to quietly exit the pages of history, and so he began seeking out new lands for development in addition to his yet unspoken plots and schemes to settle the south plains.

The more sensible of these extra-curricular efforts at finding more land came in 1907, when Oliver dispatched adventurer Frank Crean to the north country of Saskatchewan and Alberta. Crean, a terrible alcoholic, was sent to scout for additional agricultural land north of the North Saskatchewan River. While his efforts ultimately were successful, and indeed many luckless burned-out settlers would flee to these lands in the 1930s, Crean's ventures in the north were remarkable for another reason unrelated to south plains settlement: he was the last man in a long and distinguished line of agricultural explorers who had cleaved, grunted, hacked, and sweated their way through the wild and unsettled parts of Canada (British North America as it was called back then). Crean can be readily and easily included amongst those legendary figures of the Canadian west – men like the dashing Captain John Palliser and the adventurer Henry Youle Hind.

Despite the good sense shown by scouting for agriculture lands further north, it should not come as a surprise that a man like Oliver had less sensible ideas about where he could find more land. In 1907, he began taking back reserve lands granted to Indians. Oliver bought or removed from Indian reserves thousands of acres of land, making already small reservations smaller and their people less inclined to pursue an agricultural existence.[15] These land surrenders were not insignificant. The Cowessess and Kahkewistahaw bands in Saskatchewan, for example, gave up 53,985 acres of land under the land surrender policy of Oliver who, unfortunately one imagines, was also the superintendent of Indian Affairs.[16] This particular land surrender amounted to 337 quarter sections of land. Reserve lands, he argued, retarded settlement because Indians "make no practical use" of the land and thus it should be taken away, settled, and farmed.[17] Fittingly, Oliver even flirted with the idea of settling the lands without the consent of the reserve population.[18]

Despite these efforts to locate new arable lands and take back lands already committed to Indians, Oliver's monomaniac mind remained focused on the vast expanses of the south plains. For Oliver it was frustratingly obvious: the land was flat, barren, and clean and according to the logic of the day *therefore* suitable for agriculture. He ignored the reasons why it had remained empty for so long and instead concentrated his mind on the second great phase of Canadian settlement.

It is often said that one man's tragedy can be another man's blessing. This is exactly what happened during the winter of 1906–07 – a tragedy for the cattlemen turned into opportunity for Mr. Oliver. Of course later, that opportunity would morph into an even greater tragedy than that which had given birth to the opportunity in the first place: fate on the south and west plains operates, much like the weather, in unforgivingly cruel and ironic cycles.

The brutal winter of 1906/07 wiped out south plains cattle herds almost down to the last cow. The winter and its death toll are legendary in Saskatchewan. Historian Barry Potyondi suggests that there were some 40,000–50,000 head of cattle in the south-west that died over the course of that winter.[19] Ferocious blizzards and terrible snowfalls lasted long into March of that year. When the weather finally cleared, historian Bill Waiser notes, "the dead were everywhere, bloated and rotting in small groups."[20] Famed Saskatchewan-raised novelist Wallace Stegner, who grew up in the Cypress Hills, writes that the winter was nothing but "unrelieved hardship, failure, death, and gloom."[21]

In southeast Alberta, the winter decimated herds with equal facility. Mr. Gene Johnson recalls one rancher who started the winter with 200 head and entered the spring with seven. The P.K. Ranch started the winter with 3,500, and ended with 300. There were ranchers who survived but they were very few. Mr. Johnson tells the story of H.G. "Happy Jack" Jackson.[22] "Happy Jack" was born in Georgia, wandered Kansas, rode through Oklahoma, and sweated out Texas before finally settling down in Mexico where he shot snakes with his .45 calibre pistol and brought down majestic hawks with his shotgun: "his stories were legion about his part in the Texas sheep-cattle wars."

Happy Jack came up to the Alberta drylands in 1903, but when the devastating winter hit, Mr. Johnson records, Happy Jack "had the skills to get nearly all their cattle through [that] fierce and cruel" winter. The tag "Happy Jack" by the way was a bit of an ironic misnomer because apparently Happy Jack rarely laughed.

For all of that winter's misery, the practical result was that it cleared the drylands of the cattle rancher in a way that legislation could never do. Thousands upon thousands of cows froze and starved to death ("a liquidation," as Waiser calls it) and that had one single and important effect: it emptied the south plains of the cattlemen. Many of these ranchers sold their leases and some lit out for the hard-scrabble dirt of south Texas, leaving the plains behind for some other luckless soul.

The killing winter of 1906–07 shares many important similarities with the legendary drought of 1937, which we shall cover in due course. Both events are conceptually important because of their parallel similarities: in the same way that the winter decimated cattle herds and thus emptied a great deal of southern Saskatchewan of both people and cattle, the drought of 1937 decimated the crops of Saskatchewan and also resulted in the emptying of a good portion of the south plains (1937 featured the highest levels of land abandonment in the dry years).

In addition, each disaster acts as a bookend for the catastrophic years of drought and land abandonment: settlement started in the year following the devastating winter, while the Dirty Thirties ended in the year following one of the worst droughts on record up to that point. But in 1908, the future was, as the future always is, gently bursting with hope and promise. The settler was eagerly awaiting his chance to farm, Oliver was eagerly awaiting the opportunity to give the settler his chance, and the south and west plains were eager for the chance to teach the settler something about unrelieved hardship, failure, and gloom.

In 1908, Mr. Oliver amended the Dominion Lands Act and thus opened to settlement the entire tract of land between Moose Jaw and Calgary south of North Battleford. This legislation enabled settlers to file on 160 acres of land after paying a small ten-dollar fee. After satisfying the settlement obligations, which included residence on the land for six months in each of six years, settlers could then "pre-empt" or have first-right-of-purchase on an adjoining or nearby quarter-section to be sold for three dollars per acre: this was the famous "free homestead." Settlers were also obliged to construct a house of not less than $300 assessed value. Thus in one fell swoop, what Oliver called "the retardation" of Canada was ended, all lands would be filled, and a source of money would be created that would provide the funds necessary to construct a railway to port at Hudson Bay.[23] Oliver solved a lot of problems with the amendment. He created just as many.

Oliver was not insensible to the potential problems that settlers faced in farming the drylands of the south plains, but he quite reasonably claimed that his amendment took account of those dangers. Through the pre-emption provision, the amendment essentially expanded the usual size of homesteads from 160 acres to 320 acres. Oliver offered the fatuous explanation that "if a man can only farm one half of his land each year (the other half laying fallow, 'collecting moisture' as the argument went) then he must have twice as much land."[24] In 1920, though, just twelve years after Oliver made these statements, Saskatchewan's Better Farming Commission pointed out that repeated crop failures proved beyond doubt that a half-section farm in the arid districts was a useless, hopeless, ridiculous proposition. Indeed, long before Oliver amended the act, settlers in Nebraska had already discovered the pitfalls of half-section farms. Owing to gross homestead failure rates, the Kincaid Act of 1904 enlarged homesteads to 640 acres of land.[25]

Oliver justified his optimism (which, it should be pointed out, wasn't in fact 'optimism' but instead more of a blind, ill-informed belief) in the strength of the 320-acre farm by pointing to the famed dry land farming scientists. According to these experts, "inflated like blimps with their own self-importance" as historian David Jones gently observes, the science of farming would render dryness irrelevant.[26] Such faith was quite misguided and, quips Dr. Jones, "somewhere deep in the Universe, the blaring of these blowhards of the settlement era still reverberate[s]."[27] Chief amongst these "false prophets" of the new faith was Angus MacKay, the superintendent of the Dominion's first western experimental farm at Indian Head.

MacKay explained, reasonably enough, that the purpose of summer-fallow was "to store up moisture against a possible dry season."[28] Settlers were encouraged to plough deep and conduct mid-season surface tillage. This method, according to MacKay's contemporary W.R. Motherwell, would "put the necessary non-conducting soil mulch on the top to … prevent loss of soil moisture by evaporation."[29] If this approach was diligently followed, Motherwell explained, the growth of "at least two successive crops is secured even though drought should occur." He did not mention what would happen if ten years of drought should occur, or twenty years of drought spread out over twenty-five years.

Motherwell later amplified his point. During the height of the drought in 1921 he argued (whilst "in a snit" as Dr. Jones notes), that agricultural success "is chiefly, if not entirely, due to straight good or bad farming."[30] This observation was wildly wrong on so many different levels that it boggles the mind, but the settlers would have to survive the terrific beatings administered by decades of drought before the wrongness of it could be demonstrably proven so in the 1930s.

Both Motherwell and MacKay and many others at that time sincerely believed that the science of farming could overcome drought. These beliefs even trickled down and poisoned and befogged the minds of the staff of Saskatchewan's Department of Agriculture. Saskatchewan's Deputy Agriculture Minister A.F. Mantle, for example, could scarcely contain himself in 1912 when he extolled the virtues of summer-fallow: "the result is a guarantee for the next season against everything but hail and frost. What progress it reveals!"[31]

In the spirit of fairness, though, it must be noted that both McKay and Motherwell did in fact recognize that summer-fallow created problems of its own. Summer-fallow, MacKay noted, had two distinct disadvantages: it contributed to soil drift and it caused the "partial exhaustion" of the soil.[32] Motherwell too admitted that summer-fallow "restores nothing to the soil."[33] While these not insubstantial side-effects were duly noted, both men went on to vaguely suggest that somehow these deficiencies could be easily overcome. MacKay suggested that when soil drifting is corrected (and he did not say how this would be achieved), soil exhaustion "will disappear."[34] This unfortunate and pronounced tendency toward wishful thinking was a unique characteristic of that era in Saskatchewan and it even affected our province's first premier. Mr. Walter Scott believed that "honest labor could overcome even poor soil and weather conditions."[35]

Backstopped, then, by either an unrealistic optimism or misplaced faith in science, anxious to end the political power of the ranchers and unable or unwilling to admit that there was no good land left to settle, Oliver amended the Dominion Lands Act and threw the drylands open to settlement on 1 September 1908.[36] That Oliver may have been overstepping his bounds by single-handedly orchestrating the amendment to the Dominion Lands Act was not lost on other members of the House of Commons. Running as an undercurrent beneath the debates on the amendment itself was a secondary antagonism over the concentration of land-policy power in

Oliver's hands. Qu'Appelle Member of Parliament R.S. Lake called Oliver an "absentee landlord [with] practically despotic powers" who had more power than any constitutional monarch.[37] Future Interior Minister W.J. Roche agreed. Roche called it "dangerous" to vest in one portfolio power over immigration policy and blanket administration of public lands that included swamp lands, timber rights, grazing rights, pre-emption prices, and mineral control.[38]

Oliver, however, remained quiet during this energetic discussion and rarely spoke to the charges of despotic power though he no doubt gritted his teeth as he endured the final onslaught launched by excitable North York M.P. George Foster. Foster called Oliver a "despot" and argued that Oliver's power contained within it the seeds for "infinite deviltry." He drew what in 1908 was the fairly accurate conclusion that Oliver was "the boss of all of us."[39] Flattering though Foster's assertion may have been to Mr. Oliver's no doubt substantial ego, this frontal assault on his power did little to move the man who had long believed in "unrestricted settlement." He ended debate on the amendment by boldly declaring that "we are not closing anything to settlement."[40] And so it was.

Fittingly, just as the ink on the amendment was drying in September, drought was laying waste to the crop of 1908 in the south and west plains. It seems that the small number of farmers who had settled the region had tried but failed to grow a crop that year. A provincial spokesman observed that the south and west areas of the province showed significantly smaller yields than the eastern and central regions: settlers in the Kindersley area grew ten bushels per acre, while settlers down Swift Current way grew an average of nine.[41] The provincial average approached twenty bushels per acre. "Doubtless" the official suggested with beneficent tolerance, "there was not stored in the soil sufficient moisture to withstand the hot winds."[42] He added that "proper cultivation methods" would have no doubt increased yields.[43] In Alberta, of seventeen crop districts, only the Medicine Hat region in the south-east fell below fifteen bushels per acre. The Dominion government spent just under $1 million providing seed relief to the newly arrived settlers.[44]

The otherwise reasonable and sensible Interior Deputy Minister W.W. Cory displayed an uncharacteristic streak of irrationalism when he claimed that the failure was "momentary" and that the $800,000 worth of seed aid distributed by the department that year would prove the exception not the rule. Like so many others after him, Mr. Cory succumbed to the easy temptations of blind optimism and wishful thinking when he claimed that the crop failure "demonstrated beyond doubt that if the expectations of one season are not realized, those of the next year may be safely relied upon."[45] Logic, too, suffers rigorous abuse during the dry years.

Despite the ominous start to a plan that undid almost forty years of land policy, the effects of the amendment were immediate and actually quite breathtaking. In some regions, like the Alsask district, as Mr. J.R. "Bud" Thompson observes, "virtually every quarter or half section was taken up and homestead shacks sprouted like grain on the prairies."[46] Thousands of people converged on the region between Moose Jaw and Calgary to try their luck in the Last Great Land Rush of Modern Times. These were people who, according to the provinces chief statistician, had heretofore been only able to "look with longing eyes" at the opportunity passing them by in this soft gentle Eden of the south plains.[47] This poetic ejaculation was delivered by transplanted Prince Edward Islander Francis Hedley Auld, a logician who got his start in the Department of Agriculture's statistics branch. Mr. Auld would later become Deputy Minister of Agriculture and his thoughts and policy direction between 1914 and 1937 run like a terrible jagged scar across the entire period.

The Dominion Lands offices were not prepared for the massive onrush of humanity that accompanied the amendment. The Department of Interior had only one land office in the south at Moose Jaw with which to handle the thousands of homestead applications that poured in during the second half of 1908. The harried and overworked James Rutherford claimed that 1908 was "the most successful ever experienced" for homestead applications and he added that the "greatest stampede for land" showed no signs of slowing.[48] Of the 21,154 homestead entries filed in Saskatchewan in 1908, Rutherford processed 8,710. By comparison, the next busiest land office at North Battleford processed just 3,385. The remainder were scattered throughout the province.

In all of Alberta, only 13,771 homestead applications were filed in 1908, though the Medicine Hat land office was conspicuously busy. Land agent J. W. Martin noted that in the month of September alone, "more quarter sections were disposed of than in any month since the land throughout the west became available for settlement," which, in other words, meant since the nineteenth century.[49]

American farmers made up the largest single group of settlers homesteading in the drylands in the early years after 1908.[50] It seems, unlike Europeans who likely didn't have a clue what to make of a country with no trees or hills or water or lakes, Americans preferred (or had long since adjusted themselves to accepting) the vast, empty stretches of open prairie.[51] During 1909, 41,568 people filed a homestead claim in the pre-emption area.[52] Of this number, 13,566 were American, mostly from the states that bordered or were near to the international boundary itself. They came from the Dakotas, Minnesota, and Nebraska. The tiny southern community of Mankota in southern Saskatchewan, whose story will feature in this work quite heavily, received many of its settlers from Manitoba and the Dakotas, hence Mankota. There were even six people from Alabama who made the trek to the drylands as did one lonely and adventurous self-flagellating puritan soul from Delaware.[53]

The high rate of American emigration was rooted, in part, by the vast and strange differences between the west's of Canada and the United States. Alongside the fact that lands in the American west had all been settled, it seems many thousands of Americans in the middle-western states existed in a state of apparently permanent tenant farming and were unable to own their own land.[54] Land had been purchased by companies and combines and no room had been left for the individual farmer. But whatever the circumstances, Interior Deputy Minister W.W. Cory was enthusiastic with the on-rush of Yankees who, he felt, were a "highly desirable class of people [that] require no instruction."[55]

The stream of Americans into the drylands continued at a vigorous pace in those early years and Saskatchewan played host to most. Of the 39,000 settlers who filed a homestead claim in 1911, 10,978 were from America (though none came from Alabama or Delaware that year).[56] And of those 39,000, 20,484 were absorbed into Saskatchewan compared to 15,184 for Alberta.[57] Saskatchewan, not Alberta, was once the destination of choice for those coming to the western plains. The young province absorbed the majority of the new arrivals in each year: 17,556 in 1912 and 14,504 in 1913, compared to Alberta's 12,942 and 12,208 in the same years respectively.[58]

Mr. Carl Anderson was one of those Americans who came up to the drylands of Alberta in 1910. The government-issue literature encouraging settlement had "persuaded him to come and see what it was all about" and so he settled in the Alderson district south of Medicine Hat. Perhaps he should have stayed in Minnesota. Paraphrasing an already indelicate observation, Mr. Anderson noted that by 1940, all the original settlers in the district had fled or were dead.

At any rate, Mr. Anderson filed on his claim in Medicine Hat and he recalls the heady, exuberant excitement of those years: "there were people from all walks of life and from almost every country in Europe clamoring to get free homesteads."[59] It was amidst this astonishing level of growth telescoped into a few years that Deputy Cory had the pleasure to report by 1912 that all across the south and west plains, "contentment, optimism and progress prevail."[60]

The very geography of Saskatchewan changed upon being swamped by these incoming thousands. Prior to the introduction of the amendment to the Dominion Lands Act in 1907, there were only 1,677 farms in south-west and west-central Saskatchewan and just 106,900 acres of land were under cultivation.[61] In 1908, the number of farms exploded to 5,294 with 516,577 acres under cultivation.[62] The year after that saw 5,860 farms and 503,172 acres under cultivation.[63] The success of the amendment was immediately, deceptively clear.

Mr. Tom Simpson came out west from Ontario in 1910 and he was one of the first arrivals in the Aneroid district in the southwest and he must have felt that he had landed on the far side of the moon. Mr. Simpson was one of thousands of people who came out west from back east because Saskatchewan, unlike Ontario, was one of the few places in the country that had plenty of available land. Mr. Simpson was in fact one of the first men on the ground in the south. He distinctly recalls that "only about three shacks could be seen for many miles in any direction and not ten acres of land had been broken."[64]

By most measures, Aneroid even today is still pretty isolated, far removed from the rest of the province. The isolation faced by Mr. Simpson, then, was of another magnitude altogether, one that is difficult to fathom. Isolation and loneliness were the constant companions of the early settlers and this spiritual challenge is one that is easy to forget because it is affective or emotional rather than physical – but it was everywhere and it was real. It was "especially true" of the early pioneers, suggests historian Fred Wilkes, that homesickness was common and that a heavy sense of loneliness "harassed" settlers in the early years.[65] Thus it was that work became the prairie cure-all for affective disorders and spiritual distempers.

While each settler wrestled in his or her own way with the intense isolation and loneliness that necessarily came with breaking new land in a remote area of a barren, treeless country, they gallantly held those feelings at bay with work and this included the necessary business of building a home. "Bud" Thompson has been around Alsask for decades and he recalls talking with the old timers about the early settlement years. Mr. Thompson recalls the tale of one man who arrived in the Alsask district from Ontario shortly after 1908 and found, like Mr. Simpson did, "a few tents" and not much else.

The man arrived in early spring and so felt reasonably safe enough to sleep under his wagon – only to wake up shivering in six inches of fresh snow.[66] The patriarch of the Mutter clan experienced something similar. Arriving in Winnipeg from Odessa, Ukraine, in 1905 (and on the west plains shortly thereafter), Gustav Mutter, whose family had owned a substantial brickworks factory in addition to land in the old country, settled down for the pioneer life near Hatton. His grandson, Mr. Ralph Mutter, recalls his grandfather "sleeping out in the pasture to be on the land" to demonstrate that the land was rightfully his.[67] Housing, then, was usually quite high on the priority list. The fabled 'sod-house' of prairie legend was the first choice for many pioneers because it was free, all the materials were right at hand, and by all accounts they were very warm and accommodating.

Mr. Leonard Gackle remembers that there were certain tricks, subtleties and nuances to building a Soddy as they were known not without affection. The Gackles were Germans who had fled Russia in 1911. Andrew's second oldest son David had served, as the law required, in the army of Czar Nicolas II for three years. This was an "unbelievably bad" experience. Mr. Gackle "wish[ed] to spare his third son the anguish of such an experience" and so the family fled to Canada and freedom and they quickly became expert at making something out of nothing.

Leonard recalls that if the sod "wasn't right" it would soon crumble and so one had to take care to choose sod that was "well-rooted."[68] This well-rooted sod would be then "cut about three to four inches thick in depth" and then "built up like bricks." It would then be patched with mud, windows carved out, and a doorway put in. They were, Mr. Gackle recalls, "fantastically warm."[69]

Sod was the material of choice but there were other related materials at hand. Mr. Charles Geller's parents, Martin and Kristina, came from "Bocowina," a region in the Northwest Carpathians, which at that time belonged to the Austro-Hungarian Empire but these days is jointly controlled by Ukraine and Romania. The Gellers arrived to freedom in 1908 and Charles well remembers the house: "[It was] a mud house with a sod roof. In our mud house we just had a mud floor and every Saturday, Mother would coat it with new mud."[70] Martin the patriarch was also something of a neighbourhood barber and would occasionally cut hair in the mud house and this, Charles ruefully recalls, "did not do much for Mother's clean mud floor."

The Holbrooks of England opted for a hybrid soddy-wood shack. Howard and Ada arrived in 1909 and built their first home out of wood and sod and they lived in this house for ten years.[71] One must assume that their spirits grew tired of living in wood-earthen structures because they moved to a new location in 1919 "and the house there was built from cement." Soddies were usually only temporary accommodation, though temporary could often mean between five and ten years. The Gackles, for example, lived in theirs for several years, at which time they got rid of it without ceremony by "dragg[ing] it into a hole in the field." It was replaced by a "wooden structure" that had been cannibalized from the vanishing community of Hatton.

After the business of building a home was done, the even harder work of making a living became the primary concern. One blanches at the awesome challenges faced and incredible fortitude shown by some of the early pioneers. Their days, it seems, were made up of a scarcely credible routine of hard labour followed by work. Mr. Henry Marks, for example, had no money and no equipment when he arrived from Germany, but he had to clear his land somehow, and so he chose the only option which was available: he dug stones and cleared his land with a pickaxe and a crowbar. He did this until he could afford to buy oxen and a plough and when he finally got that plough, he ploughed in the morning, picked stones in the afternoon, and then ploughed again in the evening.[72]

The lives lived by the pioneers can sometimes strain the limits of what many people today think is possible of one individual. Mr. Hans Mattson left his home and family in Denmark, travelled half way around the world and settled in the Richmound district near Hatton. He built and lived in a sod house for years, cleared rocks, ploughed land, worked two off-farm jobs so he could buy horses and machinery, enlisted in the Army in 1916 and was wounded twice in the Great War before being honourably discharged. In 1918, he lay down his sword, returned the Richmound district and once again picked up his plough and carried on with farming. He was just in time for almost two unbroken decades of drought.[73] It was a hard life, lived by men and women whose capacity seems to have always been stretched to the breaking point or somewhere very close to it. When Mr. Henry Mark's wife passed away, for example, her family tenderly wrote that "she finally got the long rest for which she so ardently prayed."[74]

But it would be a mistake to paint things as merely grim for those who arrived on the south plains in the early years. Annie Pain and Alf Corbin's father George Corbin arrived with his children in 1905 and they all remember good times in those early years. The school house (also built of sod) was the site of literary societies, debates, spelling bees, match-box socials, music and singing: Alf recalls that "people came from miles around to attend these functions."[75]

The number of bachelors and single men who attended these events was likely quite high because, in those early days, there was a frustrating absence of women on the frontier. One night, a newly arrived settler and his family saw fifteen buggies frantically wheeling into their yard, all driven by grimy, sod-busting men lonely and desperate for female company and eager for a date with the settler's daughter. The father was aghast, the mother bemused, the daughter likely hidden in the cellar. All bottled-up and lacking any and all outlets for their natural and urgent desires for female company, it is not surprising then that the story of fifteen hard-working ham-fisted settlers seeking the companionship of one woman does not have a sweet and happy ending: the old-timer recalling this story remembers that "there were broken harnesses, broken wheels, and black eyes."[76]

Single sod-busting men, by the way, were at a distinct disadvantage where matters of sex were concerned when compared to their urban counterparts. Men of the cities in the early settlement years had pleasing and convenient access to the copious brothels that had sprung up all across the prairies: houses of ill-repute fairly lined the streets in Regina, Saskatoon, Calgary, and Edmonton. Even little Drumheller had a bawdy house.[77]

In many cases, the men who peopled the early western Canadian cities were young men and these young men were, by and large, labourers who dug ditches, built railroads, constructed buildings, paved streets, and worked with stone: "Here in short," writes James Gray, "was a male population in the prime of life, glowing with the virility of youth and in the superb physical condition which a steady diet of hard work produced."[78] And at the end of a day, when they put their tools down, they would clean up and head straight for Regina's River Street to "sample the delights awaiting them in their favorite bordellos." This was a diversion unavailable to the young men of Aneroid. Perhaps the absence of opportunity for sexual release on the frontier accounts, at least in part, for the jaw-dropping ubiquity of sex in rural Saskatchewan during the Dirty Thirties. But before that development occurred, the frontier substitute for sex was broken harnesses, broken wheels, and black eyes.

Mr. Edward Keck's family came from Russia in 1910 and lived in a wood shack just west of the Sand Hills, and he relishes the memory of the early years: "we skated – minus skates – on Herringer's slough." There were Christmas concerts on plank stages with white bed sheets for curtains, there were pine trees with "real candles" and Sports Days in the summer.[79]

Mr. Harry Holbrook fondly remembers the trips to Scobey Montana for supplies, the winter sleigh-rides for groceries and the itinerant peddlers who naturally followed the settlement of western Canada and who brought with them materials for dresses, combs, caps, overalls, and sewing kits.[80] Mr. Harry Keeble's daughter Ethel recalls her favourite pony "Nigger" and the three days it took to go to town ("one to go, one to shop, and one to return"). Mrs. Gladys Hollopeter was six years old in 1910 when she came up the Big Stick Trail to Richmound. She recalls a Saskatchewan most of us have never experienced, a wild Saskatchewan that can no longer be accessed, which is forever gone. She recalls the absence of people, the barrenness, the tame prairie chickens, the bumpy and rickety buffalo trails, the bleached and dried buffalo bones, the enormous herds of wild antelope that were everywhere.[81] Mr. Ralph Mutter recalls his grandmother reminiscing about this very thing. She said that there was "still the odd buffalo around, and natives coming by for food and water in the early years."[82] Thus it was that the Mutters, Germans from Odessa, Ukraine, arrived on the dry western plains just in time to witness the final death throes of a Saskatchewan that was lost forever after settlement.

Those were also the days of wild prairie fires that swept across the plains with alarming frequency. Mr. Simpson from Ontario was at first alarmed by these fires but then grew to accept them as a normal part of life just as settlers would learn to adjust in the 1930s to the violent, preternatural dust storms that were a constant companion to life on the south and west plains. Indeed, it seems that life in the drylands seemed to have been largely a matter of constantly adjusting oneself to a bewildering variety of natural disasters (drought, prairie fires, locust invasions, "black blizzards", dried cod fish). At any rate, Mr. Simpson not only adjusted himself to prairie fires but also to the odd and curious sight of singed, partially burned rabbits running past his farm. These smoky, unhappy little rodents were indicators that a fire was nearby and, remembers Mr. Simpson, "it was considered the duty of everyone to go to a prairie fire."[83]

Thus it was that Saskatchewan and western Canada was settled. People trickled in on wagon, on rail, on foot, or on horseback. They came from all corners of the globe, though principally they came from the United States, Canada, and Europe. But wherever they came from they all shared a common bond: the long, hard at times desperate process of fashioning a life from little more than dirt.

The rush of life onto the drylands created a not-insignificant amount of revenue for the Department of Interior. A total of $530,589 was generated by homestead and pre-emption fees in 1908, which helped push total revenues to $3,200,000, well above the department's previous record of $2,700,000 in 1906–07. "The net revenue," gushed Interior Deputy Cory, "is the largest in the history of the Department."[84] It is illuminating, though, to put that figure in the perspective of later events: $3 million would be spent between 1929 and 1937 sustaining life in the two south central rural municipalities of Mankota and Pinto Creek.

The drylands, however, demonstrated its Janus nature with the crop of 1909. As if to prove William Cory's wishful estimate that "the next year can be safely relied upon," Saskatchewan's arid regions posted the highest yields in the province that year. At twenty-nine bushels per acre, the south-west and west-central areas outperformed Saskatchewan's eight other crop districts, which averaged twenty-two bushels per acre of spring wheat.[85] Deputy Agriculture Minister A.F. Mantle approved of the "splendid showing" of the dry regions when he noted that "when sufficient moisture is available ... this land can grow crops unsurpassed."[86]

The glowing circumstance of 1909 was similar just a few miles across the border in south-east Alberta, where spring wheat yields reached twenty-three bushels per acre.[87] Echoing Mantle's and Auld's estimation of the wonders of summer-fallow, Alberta Agriculture Minister George Harcourt, in a delusional fit of over-excited optimism, suggested that since the principles of dry land farming "are so sound and so applicable to all districts ... a strong and persistent effort is being made to change the name."[88] Indeed.

The rate of settlement onto the south plains rose and fell in proportion to what actually happened on the ground. Of 19,139 homestead applications filed in Saskatchewan's nine Dominion Land's offices in 1909, 9,573 were filed at the Moose Jaw office.[89] So in two years almost 20,000 homestead entries had been recorded in the drylands. This continued rush of the "Mossback" or "Sodbuster" into the dry lands continued to upset and anger the region's dwindling but dogged cattle ranchers.[90] Deputy Minister Mantle noted in his annual report for the year that there were a high number of complaints being registered with the department from the ignored but far-seeing ranchers who felt that "a long tried industry" was being forsaken and destroyed "for the sake of a precarious one."[91] 1910 reinforced the cattlemen's point.

In 1910, four Frenchmen arrived in Saskatchewan to take up farming in the Val Marie area. Jean Marie Trotter was from Lac Pelletier and he acted as a guide as he took the four of them over the dried out barren south plains. Mr. Denniel was amongst the group of four Frenchmen and he found this region in that year "something of a desert." With charming continental irony, he recalls that the monotony of the land was broken up every now and then "by a gopher standing up on its hind legs."[92]

As the four Frenchmen arrived in 1910, the first exodus from the south plains began, though caution must be used in calling it an exodus because those who were leaving had not stayed long enough to establish themselves in any meaningful way. This movement out was perhaps formed in large part by those adventurers and "world-rovers" who flitted in and out of the prairie west's of both Canada and the United States who would try their hand at farming, throw some seed at the ground, grow a crop or two, make a few bucks, and then move on ("suit-case farmers" as they were called in the American West). But they were still justified in their departure: in 1910, not much of anything was grown on the south and west plains.

Crop district number six, the west-central region, was hardest hit in the failure of 1910. The average yield was seven bushels per acre, while district three in the southwest posted yields of just ten. To provide an idea of the scale of the failure, both federal and provincial levels of government at the end of the 1930s settled on using the five bushel per acre benchmark to determine whether or not a region was a disaster area requiring relief aid. That year the provincial spring wheat average was a respectable twenty bushels per acre.[93] But for the south plains, the news was grim: there was an almost inconceivable drop in the amount of actual grain produced in district three from 3,400,000 bushels in 1909 to 170,644 in 1910.[94]

Southeast Alberta suffered a similar fate. Crop district six in that province registered yields on spring wheat of just seven bushels per acre.[95] And, as in Saskatchewan, there was a quick effort to denounce the poor showing as the result of bad farming. Minister George Harcourt believed the crop failure was caused by "a lack of intelligent methods."[96] Mr. Harcourt, in a comic twist on his efforts at removing the word "dry" from "dry land farming" also resisted using the word "drought" opting instead for the much less judgmental "droughty." Alberta dispatched its publicity commissioner on a damage control tour that year. The excitable and enthusiastic Mr. Charles Hotchkiss arrived in Portal, North Dakota, on a hot summer afternoon because of an apparent "returning exodus" of American settlers.[97] All who listened to his street-corner bombast were informed that any rumours of drought and failure were just that, rumours, which were "exaggerated and untruthful."[98]

The perception problems of the Departments of Agriculture in both Alberta and Saskatchewan were shared by Dominion land agents. E.B.R.

Pragnell was the agent at the newly opened land office in Swift Current. Pragnell, too, was unable to correctly see the nature and magnitude of the problem with which the south-west and west-central areas were faced. In words which would have made George "Droughty" Harcourt proud, Pragnell dismissed the 1910 failure as due to "momentary … excessive dryness." He also added the hopelessly obvious observation that "if conditions tend to favor the farmer this year, the crop should be abundant."[99] Moose Jaw land agent James Rutherford was in step with Pragnell's estimation of the nature of the problem though he noted that business transacted in 1910 was quite light compared to that first harried year of the rush.[100] But despite the wishful thinking of all levels of government and their agencies, the numbers of people cancelling their homesteads is really the most reliable indicator of how successful south plains settlement was in those early years.

Starting in 1911, the year after the second crop failure in four years, the numbers of settlers in the south plains declined dramatically, in some instances by as much as half and this was complemented by highly worrying levels of homestead cancellations. Moose Jaw land agent G.K. Smith noted that between 1909 and 1910 the number of settlers filing on land in south-west Saskatchewan dropped from 10,921 to 5,503, skidding to 4,087 in 1911. He explained this by saying that "land suitable for farming is fast becoming scarce."[101] Fair enough. But that only tells half the story.

In 1908/09, homestead cancellations at Moose Jaw were at an agreeable figure of roughly 30 per cent, a figure shared by most other land offices.[102] That figure, however, climbed to 60 per cent in 1910 and lodged itself at 80 per cent between 1911 and 1913, again this was a figure *not* shared by other land offices. Of 4,087 homestead applications at Moose Jaw in 1911, for example, 3,419 people registered cancellations. Smith failed to give the cancellation numbers for 1912 but 1913 saw just 2,000 homestead entries next to 1,749 cancellations, or a cancellation rate approaching 90 per cent.[103] Cancellations demonstrate one vital theme in dry land settlement: the number of settlers pouring into this region was almost always equal to the number of people leaving shortly thereafter.

The Swift Current land office opened for business in 1910. The office did not include any cancellation rates until Frank Forster took control in 1913 when the rate was recorded at almost 80 per cent. Of the 2,039 applications filed that year, 1,468 people filed cancellations.[104] Forster noticed that, despite the seeming bounty of the crop that year, an unusually high number of people left the region. He vaguely explained the exodus as the first "process of elimination" that saw "many undesirables, as well as many desirables

... migrating again." He minimized the problem when he explained that the cancellations really represented nothing more than settlers "restlessly moving, as they always will," though he hinted at what was actually happening when he said he respected those who "pulled through."[105]

The situation was similar in the Maple Creek land office, which did not open until 1912. The 2,771 homestead applications received that year were counter-balanced by the 1,696 cancellations filed at the office, which is roughly a cancellation rate of 80 per cent.[106] By comparison, the land office at Humboldt in east-central Saskatchewan saw a cancellation rate of between 25 to 35 per cent in 1910 and 1911. There were 1,762 entries in 1910 alongside just 481 cancellations, and in 1911, of 1,739 entries, just 656 people cancelled their homesteads.[107]

The early years after the amendment to the Dominion Lands Act were deceptive, deception of course being one of the characteristics of the south plains. A sturdy and healthy crop might be grown as in 1909, but then there was an inevitable fall back into mediocrity and this was just as frequently followed by a stumble straight into drought and absolute failure: this is exactly what happened in 1914.

1914 was a return to the rule not the exception. Deputy Agriculture Minister A.F. Mantle was forced to concede total crop failure "in those districts that have recently been settled."[108] In a year that Mantle characterized as "slow and backward," crops in south and west Saskatchewan averaged between absolute failure of two bushels per acre and the only slightly less worrying partial failure of ten bushels per acre. The other seven crop districts in the province averaged sixteen bushels per acre and above.[109] Of the seventy-four million bushels of wheat harvested that year, just seven million came from the west and south plains, and of that only 857,000 from district three, the area surrounding Swift Current-Maple Creek.[110] Mantle reported that "the land in the south-west district was said to be drier than it had been within the memory of the oldest settler." Crops were ploughed under, creeks in the district dried up. As evidence of the lifeless nature of the region, it was remarked on by many settlers that they didn't hear birds singing in 1914. There were no birds in the drylands that year – they were all dead.[111]

Chief Statistician F.H. Auld held firm to his faith in the practice of summer-fallowing. He noted that 1914 was "a trying one for many new settlers whose land had not been properly brought under cultivation."[112] But future Big Stick rural municipality councillor Mr. R.L. Carefoot recalls it somewhat differently. He notes that the crops that year started out beautifully, but because there was no rainfall that year until September "the crop just disappeared."[113] Jake Bassendowski also remembers the disappearing crop of 1914. Mr. Bassendowski recalls that the wheat crop that year was so short the binder could not make bundles out of it. So, with typical prairie ingenuity, the Bassendowski's, who were German-speaking Russians like many in their district, removed the bundle carriers, replaced the carrier with a box and when the box was full they would empty it onto the ground. They would later rake the smaller piles into one big pile. It was thus that the Bassendowski's harvested 800 bushels of wheat on 160 acres or about five bushels per acre.[114] Mr. George Murray arrived in the area in 1908 and he recalls "[being] told by the people of the area that the land was no good for farming."[115] 1914 would seem to have supported that argument.

There was some nervous posturing as the drought slowly revealed itself. In the Kindersley district, for example, the local newspaper chose to highlight not the drought but the apparently splendid crop grown by a Mr. J.R. Froom, which, the paper explained in late June of 1914, has "not been bothered by any elements detrimental to the progress of grain."[116] And while there was a "good soaking" of rain in July, it simply wasn't enough. The crop was an utter failure.

The same situation was evident across the border in south-east Alberta. During the course of the summer, the manager of Ogilvie Milling, Mr. W.A. Black, toured the region and according to the scribes at the Medicine Hat *News*, he "did not consider the situation as encouraging at all."[117] But despite the fact that the heat and dry weather had brought ruin and little else, the scribes insisted that Mr. Black and the company he represented have "faith" in the grain-producing power of the district. For all the salutary and healing effects that faith can have on the spirit, it can't feed the body, and so in 1914 the provincial governments in both provinces had to take steps to alleviate the problems that faith could not.

In 1914 the province orchestrated various relief programs, a development that would become a mainstay of policy, in fact would *become* policy for the south and west plains until the end of the 1930s. The first line of defence was to dispatch settlers whose crops had failed to road-gangs or threshing crews around the province. The government and the CPR (in an always rare show of generosity) approved a program in which settlers would pay a rate of one cent and they would then be shipped around the province to get to work on these crews.[118]

It was one of the more shameful elements of the 1914 failure that men lied about their status as failed farmers to get relief work on these crews.

The province realized that there were some men who "misrepresented themselves," apparently claiming destitution because of the crop failure in order to get work on road gangs. Once this bit of skullduggery was sniffed out, the government withheld the cheques from men "not really in need" and gave the money to a failed settler who had been "unjustly deprived of it."[119] And when the full extent of the crop failure became clear after weeding through faulty relief applications, the province decided to increase the amount it had earlier budgeted to spend on "road construction" from $500,000 to $750,000. In total, there were one hundred and fifty hard labour road crews of about twenty-five men each working throughout the southwest and west-central areas of the province pre-figuring the thousands of men sent to work on the road gangs in the 1920s and the tens of thousands of men who would follow in the 1930s.

The Alberta government was doing much the same thing as Saskatchewan. After a spring and summer of news in which hope was splashed on the front pages of the Medicine Hat *News* in the form of positive weather reports ("Heavy rain fell all around the city"; "conditions reported good – summer following [*sic*] will increase yields"[120]), the realities of drought soon became apparent. Prefacing its intention to use burned-out settlers as harvest help, the provincial government indicated that it "did not think it would be necessary to import any labor from the eastern provinces this year" and thus went about dispatching its settlers to regions of the west where there was no drought.[121]

Settlers in Alberta received the same kind of reduced fares as those in Saskatchewan. In early August, the Medicine Hat *News* recorded the departure of between sixty and seventy men in a single day.[122] In addition to the harvest work, there were also plans, as one might expect, for road work. The Public Works Minister and the local MLA took a tour of the city "with the object of undertaking as much work as possible on the roads for the homesteaders."[123]

It was always a case in the early years of getting something in return for aid, even if it was only the promise or hope that settlers would be able to do their own heavy lifting in the future. The impulse toward blind and unquestioned charity ("subsidies" as they are called today) was always a little more blunted and stumpy on the south plains in the early years and this reflects a general set of cultural ideas that favoured a man pulling himself up by his boot straps.

The editors at the Hat *News* felt that the best way to help settlers was to give them a one-time gift of steers and dairy cows. They argued that this was a "better arrangement" because it neatly avoided "giving them [the settlers] money or buying provisions for charity."[124] The editors also made the not entirely unreasonable suggestion that allocating cows to settlers would afford them a plentiful supply of fertilizer. The Hat *News* editors did not know, indeed could not know, that when drought became decadal instead of seasonal, as it did in the 1920s and 1930s, both cattle and man starved and that settler would finally turn his herds loose into the withered and stumpy fields because there was neither feed nor money to maintain their herds. The crops failed and what little crop was grown was fed to the cows and this reflects a basic recognition of the grim truth that man has the mental and emotional resources to endure starvation while animals do not. But that was some years in the future. Amidst the optimism and cacophonous boom of the early settlement years, the editors cannot be expected to have known all of the bestial dynamics associated with starvation farming on the south plains; the editors could not have known that the surface water around the Hatton area was poisoned and that, as Mr. Ralph Mutter observes, "the cattle would not drink the water because of the sour gas" seeping up through the ground and ruining the water.[125] In 1914, a cow for every man seemed a perfectly rational and logical solution.

If a man couldn't have cows, then he should at least have the proper seed-grain and Marquis Wheat held substantial promise. Although it was developed by Mr. Charles Saunders in the 1890s, Marquis Wheat, the saviour of west plains agriculture, was not commercially available until 1911. And where there were no authorized seed dealers, then the local priest seems to have done the trick.

The Reverend Walker, for example, came to south plains in the early years. His son Edward recalls that his father "chose to go into areas where there was no Ministry" like the jungles of Africa. The Reverend Walker settled on Aneroid, a tiny little frontier settlement in the south-west whose strange name recalls a lost barometer and not anti-inflammatory ointments. The Reverend Walker arrived in Aneroid in 1913 and, according to his son, "his main mission in life was to bring the gospel message."[126] His second mission was to sell Marquis Wheat. Farmers heard of this and came from miles around to buy the reverend's seed. Given the propensity for naïve and wishful thinking in those years, one cannot avoid drawing the conclusion that some pioneers felt that seed sold by a Man of God must be special seed indeed. It wasn't though.

Debt mediation made its entrance in 1914 and would remain a staple policy for both Saskatchewan and Alberta governments fighting drought-induced crop failure. Debt mediation (discussions between debtor and creditor to resolve a debt) was only ever one step away from debt moratorium (in which the collection of a debt would be temporarily stayed). In 1914, the province began a two and a half decade long debate with itself over whether to choose mediation or moratorium because of crop failures in the drylands.

According to the Department of Agriculture, "unbridled credit at high rates of interest" had placed many debtors in a very difficult position, a position in which they were threatened with "financial extinction."[127] The drought brought that extinction very close to reality. Debt mediation was handled for the province by the fast-rising logician Mr. Francis Hedley (F.H.) Auld, who could scarcely contain his contempt for the average settlers' near complete lack of knowledge about sound accounting principles. In just three months in 1914, Mr. Auld handled 7,000 requests for mediation.

After some investigation, Mr. Auld found "in quite a few instances, a deplorable lack of the application of business principles to their affairs."[128] Auld warmed to his theme: "Every farmer," he grumbled, "should have at least some knowledge of bookkeeping" and he added that "many farmers lack a real grasp of the business end of their operations."

It helps to remember that, in many instances, the settlers Mr. Auld was endeavouring to assist had poor English or none; perhaps they had little education or none; they had little familiarity with English poor laws, or none; little conception of property law or none; little knowledge of finance, accounting, mortgages, or how real property law worked or none. It was with a noticeable tinge of affection that Mr. Auld spoke of the "highly efficient collection agencies."

Understanding that thousands of settlers could not pay their bills because of the crop failure, Saskatchewan Premier Walter Scott attempted to secure a lid on the fast-boiling pot in an open letter published in dryland community newspapers. He explained to the settlers what the government was doing in addition to mediating between debtor and creditor. The province pledged to get settlers to work on road-building and threshing crews and also announced that lower feed rates for cattle would be introduced.[129] Premier Scott also tried to allay the fears and encourage resiliency. Scott understood that the bright hopes of spring had been "replaced by a condition bordering on total failure" but despite that he admonished burned-out settlers to "accept the buffetings of fortune in the spirit of true pioneers."[130] The editors at the Maple Creek *News* agreed with Scott and issued their own guilt-tinged entreaty: "The men and women who settle new countries are called pioneers and we have always been led to believe that pioneers are plucky, energetic, resourceful people. This is a year that calls for those traits of character and the people of Maple Creek district will rise to the occasion."[131] The plucky Oscar Anhorn of Golden Prairie, about thirty miles north of the Creek, accepted the buffetings of fortune (which, for the settler, generally meant starvation) by hunting rabbits. He remembers that "things were awfully poor [in 1914]. I can remember going out rabbit hunting so we could have meat to eat."[132]

The premier, though, likely stunned his readership when he highlighted those things that were good about the crop failure. Mr. Scott believed that "a gratifying feature" of the 1914 crop failure is that "good returns can be obtained from properly summer fallowed land."[133] How he arrived at this conclusion he does not say. Instead, he rambles further and further afield, rambunctiously turning logic and common sense on its head when he attempts to argue the point that "our faith in the excellence of our soil ... is only strengthened by the experience of this year."

One is inclined to understand that Scott was merely trying to bolster the sagging shoulders of the settlers by trying to find the good in the bad. (As a life-long manic depressive, Mr. Scott likely had experience with this). He simply went about it the wrong way. The editors of the Maple Creek *News* exercised a more carefully articulated brand of hope when they tried to find the good in the bad. Noting that "90%" of crops between Maple Creek and MacLeod are "burnt up," they decreed it good news "if in the end it drives home to the farmers the necessity of good tillage."[134]

Mr. Scott, like many men in those days, was a bit of a dreamer. Unlike the Mr. Oliver, though, Premier Scott had deep and genuinely held philosophical ideas about what it meant to farm and to be a farmer. For as poor as his logic appears at times, Mr. Scott sincerely believed in all of those Jeffersonian ideals surrounding agriculture which, for Mr. Oliver, were merely a cynical expedient. The premier commonly referred to agriculture as "the foundation of civilization" and he additionally argued that without farmers the country would be useless because agricultural commodities were the real basis of all business and commerce.[135] Given these feelings and beliefs, it is not surprising, then, that Mr. Scott steered away from accentuating the problems of the crisis or addressing the uncomfortable questions it raised. After all, for Scott, "the dignity of agriculture" could surmount any difficulty.[136]

Premier Scott believed that the fate of the province of Saskatchewan was intertwined with wheat-based agriculture. This was an idea developed and ceaselessly perpetuated by the collective mind of the Scott government.[137] For Scott, the crop failure of 1914 was a threat to that intertwined fate. He clearly understood that land abandonment would be the logical implication of crop failure. Mr. Scott's appreciation of the implications of the crisis of 1914 was shared by his successors, most notably Premier Charles Dunning, and those views would create similar intellectual roadblocks during the droughts of the 1920s and persist well into the 1930s.

So, while the Scott government busied itself extolling the excellent philosophical virtues of crop failure, the federal government got busy applying a tourniquet to a very bad, deep, and bloody wound. Correctly fearing an exodus, the Borden administration instantly moved to prohibit the cancellation of any homestead applications until after seeding in 1915.[138] Settlers were made aware of this restriction via newspaper ads. Land office boss G.G. Blackstock informed Kindersley area settlers that "no application for cancellation [of] existing entries are to be accepted until further notice."[139]

The Dominion government established relief depots at Swift Current, Maple Creek, Medicine Hat, and Lethbridge, which were (and are) the principal cites of the drylands. These depots provided fodder, flour, and coal so that "there will be no hardship or suffering and no sacrificing of stock and implements necessary for work on next year's crop."[140] The Dominion government also shared in the cost of reducing ticket rates to transport the stricken settlers to threshing crews. This was one of the last times these two levels of government would operate with shared purpose regarding the drylands. The land abandonment crisis of the 1920s would see the development of opposing and very antagonistic views over what should be done with the settlers of the south plains. But in 1914, there was a unity of purpose. The total cost of the Dominion government's one year relief aid package for the south plains came in at a mind-boggling $8,892,517, which is almost exactly half of the estimated $18 million that the Saskatchewan Relief Commission would spend in the first three years of the droughts of the 1930s.[141] And the Dominion government contributed this mammoth sum because "it recognized its responsibility" in settling this region.[142]

All of these measures, the feed, the fodder, the relief depots, the labour gangs, and the penny train tickets were designed to do one thing and one thing only: prevent the settler from abandoning his land. The Conservative government's press agency emphasized what it was doing to help and reminded people that the aid program was "*in keeping with the avowed policy of the government to protect and assist its new settlers.*"[143] Leaving no stone unturned, the Dominion government also pledged that all of the horses required for the Royal North West Mounted Police would be purchased only from stock breeders in the drought-stricken area.[144]

Despite the fact that millions of dollars were spent in relief aid, settlers still got the short end of the stick. In 1914, seven hundred men from the Maple Creek area signed up for road-work. The editors of the town's newspaper had agitated for road work on behalf of the men, although one wonders if the labourers were as pleased with the efforts of the newspaper as the editors seemed to be. The editors argued that the government often employed out-of-province men (usually from Ontario) to do road work. But the failure of 1914 offered a perfect opportunity to change that. And as an inducement for the government to change its hiring practices, the Maple Creek *News* argued that "the work could be done cheaper now than … when normal conditions prevail."[145] So, with thousands of acres of land lying in ruins, the editors obliquely encouraged the province to pay settlers less than that which was normally paid for the work in order to complete the work. It is not recorded whether or not the province seized on the idea of getting bargain basement labour costs at the expense of desperate, hungry men but one is inclined to give the province the benefit of the doubt, at least on this. As it was, a married settler/road-worker would be allowed to work until he had been paid $115; single men were given work until they had made $75. These men were "forwarded" around the province because, given the total crop failure of that year, there was apparently "plans for a lot of road work."[146]

For as much as the thought of being under-paid would have soured and curdled the enthusiasm of the men who came to Saskatchewan to farm but who were instead put to work on heavy labour details after their crop failed, both Borden and Scott appreciated that they had met the crisis squarely and won. There was no exodus. Mostly this was because the federal government had made it illegal for people to cancel their homestead applications: but still, it worked. The Borden administration played up its success: "this prompt and effective action by the government has successfully met a serious situation which threatened the depopulation of a large area in the west and has protected settlers in that area from financial ruin and great hardship."[147] Despite all the grim and ominous portents of that year, the editors of the Maple Creek *News* blithely suggested to a very willing and responsive readership that 1914 was "an exceptional year and its like may never be experienced again."[148] This statement was just plain wrong; they could not have been more wrong even if they had tried.

The crop disaster of 1914 would have been an opportune time to re-evaluate the wisdom of settlement in the dry regions and that re-evaluation almost happened, but to the dismay of history it did not. *The Ranching and Grazing Investigation Commission* (the Pope Commission, as it was known) was established in 1912 at the request of Mr. W.J. Roche, the Conservative member who replaced Frank Oliver as head of the Department of Interior after Oliver, and the Liberals were finally thrown out of office in the famed Reciprocity Election of 1911. The commission consisted of three men led by George Pope, after whom the commission was named. Their purpose was simple: under orders from the Department of Interior, they were to re-evaluate settlement on the south plains and arrive at some conclusions regarding further agricultural settlement in the region. They were also under orders to try and find some ways of improving the lot of the region's long-suffering cattle industry.

The commission travelled throughout the south plains in late 1912 and held a dozen meetings at key locations in Swift Current, Maple Creek, and Medicine Hat. Like the brief and summary 1908 amendment to the Dominion Lands Act, the slender 1913–14 Pope Commission report represents far more than might be suggested by looking at its meagre physical contents. It recommended, for the second time in six years, a near-complete reversal of land use policy for the drylands.

As of 1914, only six years had elapsed since Oliver had allowed the first settlers to homestead on the south plains, and it took only that long for the pattern of crop-failure and relief aid to establish itself. Mr. Roche and the members of the Pope Commission were not insensible to what had been allowed to happen and they understood the enormous folly of settlement in the south and west plains, but their hands were tied because the amendment, much to the delight of Mr. Oliver, had been wildly successful. The region had been settled, municipal institutions had been established, and crazed rail-line construction had begun (the fight over retaining all those main lines, branch lines and sidings is a fight that continues down to today and is led by the Saskatchewan Association of Rural Municipalities).

The very act of establishing the Pope Commission meant that the Department of Interior was flirting perilously close to asking the unappetizing question: "How can we undo settlement?" That question would be asked again and again in the 1920s and in the 1930s, but it was an impossible question, a question to which there was no answer, or rather the only answer was land clearances and that was not feasible, at least in Saskatchewan it wasn't. By the time the 1920s rolled around, the Alberta government began evacuating every settler it could find and essentially emptied the region of almost all human life. And where it could not buy the settlers out with a train ticket, the government forced the settlers off the land, as happened in Byngville and Brutus, two dryland communities that were appropriated by the federal government (with little or no resistance from the Alberta government) and handed over, lock, stock and barrel, to the British Army as a training ground.[149] But, like the 1906/07 winter and the drought of 1937, nature would ultimately achieve what legislators in Saskatchewan would not.

Commission chair George Pope did not mince words: "there are considerable areas of land … which are altogether unfit for settlement" in the south and western plains.[150] Pope added that the public meetings he and the other members had attended produced the "emphatic and unanimous" opinion that an estimated four million acres of land should be withdrawn from settlement because it was "a matter of common knowledge" that these lands could not successfully be farmed over the long term.[151] The entire region that had been opened to settlement was about twenty-eight million acres, roughly half of which lay in Saskatchewan, and so the Pope Commission urged the immediate abandonment or closure to settlement of almost 40 per cent of that land. It was not simply the lack of moisture that made agriculture in this region difficult, it was that wide swaths of land had soil "altogether unfit for homesteading" and these regions, the committee warned, must be closed off to prevent "disastrous consequences."[152]

The commission was actually attempting to steer land use policy back to what it had been in the years before Frank Oliver. In an effort to atone for Mr. Oliver's gross policy error, the commission endorsed recommendations that nurtured and developed the cattle industry, which had been knocked stupid from the sudden and all-consuming rush of settlers onto the drylands, to say nothing of the devastating winter of 1906–07. The commission recommended enlarged grazing leases where available land made that possible and they asked for extended grazing leases on lands currently used for such purposes.[153]

It's not that the recommendations were overtly antagonistic to the settler but they certainly favoured the cattlemen, and in spirit the recommendations very closely resembled the land use policy of the 1880s. Indeed, in these recommendations, one can see the seeds of the ideas that would guide the actions of the Prairie Farm Rehabilitation Administration (PFRA) in the 1930s when that organization would actually remove sub-marginal land from production and dump the settlers somewhere up north.

Time, circumstances, and the logic of the day, however, ensured that the primary recommendation would be ignored: the four-million-acre tract of land in south-west and west-central Saskatchewan would remain open to settlement and it was from precisely this region that settlers would flee by their thousands in the 1920s and, for those who remained, later in the 1930s.

Settlers played a not-insignificant role in keeping the region open. They were unnerved by the suggestion to clear off and shut down millions of acres of land to settlement. Such a move threatened to isolate and then strangle the life out of the budding agricultural industry in the area. Like the legislators of that era, the settlers clung to their own beliefs and faiths and had their own reasons for persisting in their beliefs about farming an area that no one thought should have ever been settled. And so settlers petitioned the Department of Interior and the province to reject the land-closure option of the Pope Commission.[154] The province, buoyed by the spirit of optimism and supported by a third year of consistent agricultural mediocrity in the dry lands, supported the effort to keep the region open.

Just after the outbreak in August 1914 of that pointless, gruesome, and bloody industrial slaughter which is known to history as "The Great War," agricultural production in Europe was devastated and the Dominion government encouraged a wheat-production program whose like had never been seen before in Canada. Between 1914 and 1918, 12,000,000 acres of land was put to the plough and this included millions of acres in the south plains.[155] Any sense of caution that might have developed during the 1914 crop failure was easily brushed aside at the prospect of vast markets desperate for wheat. Had someone but stepped in and urged caution in expanding agriculture on the south plains, had someone more forcefully advocated that the government adopt the recommendations of the Pope Commission, had there simply been less of an impulse to 'go all in', the extent of the disasters to follow in the 1920s and 1930s might have been mitigated in some way. But everyone involved at that time was in it up to their necks and the only direction possible was forward on a gamble and with blind faith that the land would produce.

The failure of 1914 was deemed momentary. It was a blip, an exception, something out of the ordinary whose like would never be seen again. And in a world where it was sincerely believed with little or no irony that hard labour and sweat was enough to overcome anything, there were no cautious backward glances. On a quiet February day in 1914, ignoring forty years of land policy and the recommendations of a federal commission, the federal government passed an Order-in-Council that approved the recommendations of the Pope Commission as it related to the redevelopment of the cattle industry. But the federal government did not support the recommendation, which argued for the closure of the dry lands to settlement. The Order-in-Council was passed just six months before the first total crop failure hit the drylands.

"In the Thrill Zone of the Onrushing Calamity"

Futile: (adjective) producing no useful results; pointless. From the Latin *futilis* 'leaky.'

Barren: (adjective) [of land] too poor to produce vegetation; bleak and lifeless; without. From the Old French *barhaine*.

Desert: (noun) a waterless, desolate area of land with little or no vegetation; a situation or area considered dull or uninteresting. From the Latin *desertum* 'something left waste' and *deserere* 'leave, forsake.' – *Oxford English Dictionary*.

As the dry regions descended from mediocrity into failure and from thence into relief-addled destitution and land abandonment, there was a brief detour through the lush, green, and pleasing valleys of 1915 and 1916. In a strange and fitting inversion (an inversion that would be repeated in 1928 just before the roof caved in in 1929), the dry regions in these two years outproduced every other crop district in the province. Newly minted Deputy Agriculture Minister Francis Auld was ecstatic: "nature produced with marvelous prodigality and her greatest generosity was shown towards the farmers in districts where the crop in 1914 was practically a failure"[1] (why he felt it necessary to deploy the adverb "practically" instead of "completely" is a mystery known only to Auld). He even went so far as to produce a list of the twenty-six highest producing farmers in the province (all from the south and west plains) in a carnival-like show-demonstration of the vitality of the region's soil. Peter Hackenlieb from Leader (formerly Prussia) produced fifty bushels per acre of spring wheat. J.P. Firnquist of the now non-existent Stone district somehow managed to squeeze 3,800 bushels of wheat out of seventy-six acres of land.[2] In total that year, the drylands averaged thirty-one bushels per acre while the province itself averaged twenty-five. The total production for 1916 was an astonishing 173,723,775 bushels of wheat. These amazing yields were exactly what Saskatchewan's founding fathers had in mind when they envisioned the future of Saskatchewan: year after year, dizzy with success, wallowing in the bounty of glorious wheat production.

The shine started to rub off in 1917. Yields plummeted to twelve bushels per acre that year, seed relief aid re-appeared in 1918 as the yields bottomed out to catastrophic proportions of four bushels per acre and the Municipalities Relief Act was passed in 1919, expanding the aid responsibilities of the rural municipalities from not only seed, but also flour, fodder, and coal.[3] The Frenchman, Mr. Denniel who had come through to the Val Marie district and commented that it looked like a desert in 1910, took a walk up the local creek one day and found that not much had changed. He walked for four miles along the Frenchman River and "found only one small watering hole."[4] The river had dried up.

The turnaround from orgy of 1916 was quick and sudden. Debt mediation re-appeared in 1920 "owing to the failure of crops in the southwest and western parts of the province."[5] In just a few months of that year, 500 cases of bad debt were mediated. These cases related mostly to items such as lumber, machinery, and real estate mortgages.

1920 and the three years preceding it starkly demonstrated the dangers associated with dryland farming and these failures should have brought the experience of 1914 into proper context. Should have, but they didn't. While low yields were indeed suffered by many crop districts in Saskatchewan that year, it was only on the south and west plains where failures were absolute, it was only on the south and west plains where relief aid depots were established, it was only ever in the drylands that starvation threatened whole districts and it was only on the south and west plains where the droughts and crop failures were so bad that a Royal Commission of Inquiry had to be called.

The Royal Commission, known to history as the Better Farming Conference, was called in direct response to the escalating crisis in dryland agriculture. The utter futility of dryland farming was nicely captured in, of all things, a weather report filed by staff of Alberta's Department of Agriculture. The south-east area of that province had undergone successive crop failures of a similar scale during the period after 1917 and the following report filed by staff of the weather bureau reads like an S.O.S. from a sinking ship: "crops very poor; farmers going north; many fields are being ploughed under; wheat is a failure."[6]

The Better Farming Conference was set up in Swift Current during July 1920. According to one commentator, "it was evident that only senior levels of government could provide the leadership to develop a system of agriculture" suited to the south plains.[7] This is a very odd (though very Saskatchewan) observation to make for two reasons. First, in a strange Hegelian way, this statement seems to glorify the state by making the implicit suggestion that it knew more about farming than the settlers. This silly little conceit, no doubt held with sincerity by a number of men in Ottawa, certainly Mr. Oliver, had been proven incorrect a number of times by 1920. In fact, it had been proven incorrect repeatedly and with astonishing regularity. Second, "senior levels of government" were responsible for getting settlers into this mess in the first place.

At any rate, settlers were relieved to see that something was being done to try and figure a way out of this impasse. Tompkins area settler J.H. Veitch noted that "such a conference would have been considered mad" in 1915–16, but it was not such a bad idea in 1920.[8] Veitch, the secretary treasurer of the Vidora chapter of the Saskatchewan Grain Growers Association, wrote to Saskatchewan Agriculture Minister Charles Hamilton to explain that it had become "painfully evident" that even the best summer-fallow "falls pitifully short of solving the problem [of crop failure]."[9] Farmer Lewis Harvey added that most Vidora area settlers were "groping, as it were, in the dark for the proper methods." Mr. Harvey warned that "conditions are fast approaching acute and in a short time distress will be general."[10]

The Better Farming Commission set up its operations in Swift Current amidst the suffocating drought of 1920. As a first order of business, the commission conducted a road tour through the hard-scrabble south plains in order to gain a ground-level appreciation of what had occurred. The entire area of Vidora-Consul-Senate region and north up toward Maple Creek was written off as "very bad." Belatedly proving the point, forty-six farmers from Senate along with their families (approximating some 120 people) were evacuated from that region and moved en masse to Tisdale in east-central Saskatchewan in 1923.[11]

From Maple Creek north to what would prove to be the appropriately named RM of Big Stick, conditions were much the same. The committee noted that there were many instances of soil drift in this region which was naturally accompanied by the ubiquitous presence of funereal misery in whose grip dusty settlers struggled. Indeed, according to the report from the road tour, the settlers were "simply hanging on in the hope that something will turn up to better their conditions."[12]

At Big Stick, just past the western edge of the Great Sand Hills, the committee's brief tour of the drylands ended. But this arbitrary end to the tour was a conceptual mistake because the areas devastated by drought and crop failure, and also one of the areas which would suffer worst from land abandonment, stretched north from Big Stick all the way up to Kindersley-Alsask, an area that would lose the majority of its settlers in the 1920s.

The conclusions of the sub-committee merely restated the obvious: "rainfall is not sufficient." The half-section farmer, despite what Frank Oliver argued in the 1908 Dominion Lands Act, "is very handicapped [and] cannot hope to make a success," and cattle or mixed farming is "absolutely essential" for any enterprise to be a success.[13] These conclusions were long known and considered common knowledge, even the point about mixed farming but, as settler Mr. Veitch had pointed out to Premier Charles Dunning in early 1920 "the cry 'go into cattle' or 'go into mixed farming' … placed many a man in a more embarrassing position than he might have otherwise suffered."[14] This is to say that many men, already stretched financially thin from four years of drought, went bankrupt trying to diversify.

The information from the sub-committee's road tour formed the basic conceptual outline for the much more formal and intensive 'Better Farming Conference' in Swift Current. The commission agreed at the start that one recommendation above all others must be pursued: "to find ways and means [of evacuating settlers] to more suitable land."[15] Two-and-a-half more years would pass before the province would finally relent to this resolution and even then it did so reluctantly, by half-measures and under very great pressure to do something rather than nothing.

The Royal Commission's report dealt a blow to a number of assumptions that had guided the effort to settle the south plains. Chairman George Spence, for example, was forced to concede that the summer-fallow method was not as safe and efficient as had been previously imagined. Spence and the commission argued that summer-fallow was "forced on us by necessity" before anyone realized that "it removes from the soil, ingredients necessary to produce a crop."[16] Spence, on behalf of the Commission, declared, "we are looking for a new system" for farming in the drylands and thus recommended the establishment of an experimental farm at Swift Current.[17] Previous to 1920, the only experimental farm in the drylands was located at Lethbridge, which was established in 1908.

In addition to a formal recognition that summer fallow could not "guarantee results" every year as A.F. Mantle argued it could in 1912, there was also an assessment of the climate. Meteorologist Sir Frederic Stuart explained that the south plains were simply prone to cycles of drought "although variations do occur" such as they did in 1915 and 1916. But he concluded that he "could not imagine any portion of the world where there was less chance of [climatic] change" than in the south.[18] Drought was the rule and not the exception.

Aside from the establishment of an experimental farm at Swift Current, the core recommendation of the committee was the evacuation of settlers. The idea of evacuation was the first resolution passed by the conference in 1920 and its presence as an idea in the final report is unmistakable. Commission Chair George Spence concluded that "to abandon such lands would be the first step towards finding a way to use them."[19] And while he would not admit that settling the region was a mistake ("I am not prepared to take that ground at the present time"), he did recommend that the Dominion Lands Act be suitably amended to allow homesteaders to leave the region and file on a second homestead elsewhere.[20]

Conspicuously absent from the Better Farming Commission's report was any detailed explanation of how settlers might actually farm better. True, the Commission made three recommendations: substitute crops like forage which arrest soil erosion (here it must be noted that soil erosion was a problem that began long before the thirties), community pastures (which was obliquely suggested by the Pope Commission in 1914) and water supplies (dugouts, which became a common feature on the south plains in the 1930s and was the PFRA's chief and early claim to fame).[21] But these things did not address how farmers might make a go of it in a dry land with the resources they had at hand.

Arriving at a determination as to what constituted the best methods for agricultural production in the drylands seemed at times to be a bottomless question with no real answer short of the simple one: rain, and since that could not be legislated actual answers to questions about proper farming went unanswered, dangling. This absence of thought on dryland farming was not a mistake, though, but rather an indication that by 1920, the first cracks had begun to appear in the ludicrous notion that summer-fallow was a guarantee against everything except hail and frost, which meant that, in 1920, neither the province nor the experts knew where or how to proceed.

The uncertainty over agricultural practices was felt by those even at the forefront of agricultural science. University of Saskatchewan agronomist John Bracken published a book in 1921 in which he found himself having to explain the horribly obvious point that "[summer-fallow's] most intelligent practice does not make crops grow in the absence of rain."[22] He further noted that even those on the cutting edge of agriculture did not have any idea of how to successfully farm in the drylands. Bracken threw up his hands on the dangers of summer-fallow when he said (and the tone of frustration here is obvious): "if the fallow dissipates organic matter and nitrogen – and it does to a serious degree – then we shall have to dissipate organic matter and nitrogen until we find a better way because we must have water in the soil and the fallow is the best way to get it there."[23] Bracken knew that the practice of summer-fallow did more harm than good, but there were no other options at the time. Indeed, seed drills and direct seeding (a process by which seed is 'injected' into the ground thus reducing or eliminating the necessity of tillage), the saviours of south plains agriculture, would not be commercially available for another sixty years.

Bracken's matter-of-fact statements about the possibilities and limitations of summer-fallow were substantiated by his colleagues in the United States whose experience in the drylands had taught the same hard lessons. United States Department of Agriculture agronomist E.C. Chilcott took aim at men like Motherwell, Mantle, and MacKay and their unreasonable single-minded belief in the possibilities of dryland farming when he noted that the claims of what summer-fallow could actually achieve were "undoubtedly responsible for more false reasoning about dryland agriculture than any other thing."[24] Both Chilcott and Bracken offered the painful observation that summer-fallow is fine, but only if it rains regularly.

The lack of knowledge about proper farming was not limited to the experts. Settlers, too, still had no clear idea of the best methods and practices that should be employed. Thinking that the province might know something he did not, Prelate Secretary Treasurer J.J. Keelor implored the Department of Agriculture to do something to educate settlers because "the message [was] not getting through."[25] Mr. Keelor observed in 1921 that settlers' knowledge of proper agricultural techniques remained limited. In fact, their knowledge had not progressed much beyond the common practice of simply throwing seed into the ground and hoping something might come of it. "I am afraid" Keelor told Auld, "that some of the farmers have not gotten away from that idea."[26] Settler Mr. Carl Albrecht was a chucker. He seeded his land by taking handfuls of wheat and throwing it around the field. A family member recalls that "he was very good at it." He always had the ability to throw it "where he thought it was needed."[27]

Mr. Keelor reasonably thought that the province ought to be able to do something to remedy this lack of knowledge, "to spread good information." He also fully understood the implications of inaction: unbound by cancellation restrictions and government aid, Keelor observed that "a number of our farmers left last spring [for the United States] and I believe this fall or next spring will find quite a number more pulling out."[28]

It was not a case of Mr. Keelor throwing up his hands. He and the men in his district desperately wanted to stay and he emphasized this point to Deputy Auld. "This particular part of Saskatchewan," Mr. Keelor explained, "has been too well developed and there has been too much money put into the district to have it go back [to prairie] without at least trying to do what we can to help out."[29] But Keelor's request for educational forums was denied by Deputy Auld. The deputy said meetings "will [only] be considered" because he was "simply not sure at the present moment just how definitely any person can speak to the farmers in your district" on proper farming methods.[30] Fair enough. But Deputy Auld also took the time to disabuse Keelor of the notion that the problem of the lack of rain was limited to the south plains when he (Auld) said that "sentiment" was true "everywhere."[31] The Dirty Thirties would finally, and at long last, force Auld to admit that there was a certain area of Saskatchewan prone to drought, but in 1921, he had not got there yet.

One is inclined to give the deputy the benefit of the doubt because he is essentially correct in his position that the province could not hold forums because it did not know any more about farming than the settlers did. But it is instructive to consider what Alberta's UFA government was doing during the same period when Keelor was asking for more information and not getting it. Knowledge or not, Alberta routinely sent out its representatives into the drought-stricken south-lands. James Murray was the Department of Agriculture's representative in the Medicine Hat region. In just six months, between July and December of 1921, he conducted or attended thirty-five meetings and published two circulars distributed to area farmers, all of which dealt with growing fodder crops, for example, which apparently reduced the danger of soil exhaustion.[32] Murray felt that it was desirable to "get first-hand knowledge of [farmer's] conditions and their problems." And Murray's knowledge likely came from the Lethbridge experimental farm, a dryland experimental, something which, at that time, Saskatchewan did not have.

This "first-hand knowledge" was exactly what a Bickleigh area farm group dared the province to get. Angry over the implicit and, in some quarters of the Department of Agriculture, explicit insistence that success or failure was due to good or bad farming, the Bickleigh branch of the Grain Growers Association (Bickleigh sits on the north east edge of Palliser's Triangle) fired off an angry letter that asked the province to send out an expert to take soil samples. After hail destruction in 1916, drought in 1917, and "drought, wind, frost and hail" in 1918, 1919 had them scratching their heads. The group wrote that they had "followed the best known methods [and] have lost heavily."[33]

The Saskatchewan government, by contrast, went one step further in the wrong direction. The Better Farming Train was cancelled in 1923. This train had been operating since 1914 and its creation was a direct response to the crop failure in the drylands that year. The train stopped at various communities explaining the latest agricultural practices and seed advancements.[34] Agriculture Minister Charles Hamilton noted that "they [the trains] were expensive to equip and operate." In 1920, the cost of the train was $6,817.73, which included fifty-eight stops throughout the province attended by some 35,000 people;[35] in 1922 that cost had escalated to $12,876.59.[36] Hamilton insisted that "this is, we believe, one of things we can get along without."[37] The practical effect of this move was to stop the circulation of what little information had been circulating.

So, bereft of information and technique on how to farm properly, rural municipalities thought, not unreasonably, that drought problems might be legislated away. Guided by the principle that doing something is always better than doing nothing, the RM of Big Stick near Hatton demanded the province help with the ever-present problem of Russian, Sow, and Canada thistle by "enact[ing] such drastic legislation as will compel all weed growers to keep their weeds on their own land."[38] It seemed that settlers, when cultivating their land, would allow their weeds to congeal in rows and these rows of weeds were then carried hither and thither on the wind spreading the weed infestation into neighbouring fields. The proper cultivation and weed control techniques seem obvious today; but in Big Stick, in 1922, it was not.

The RM of Maple Creek threw up its hands on the matter of soil drifting. A certain settler, Mr. A. Bernard, complained to his local council about soil drifting and demanded something be done about it. But the councilmen, conduits for the expression of those noble and heady egalitarian ideals that characterized the intellectual world of the North American west, lamely fell back on the idea that "every man has the right to plow his lands as he sees fit." It wasn't that they were insensible to the problem but rather they simply did not know how to deal with it. It was definitely an irritated council that tersely informed Bernard that "up to present we do not know of any way to prevent soil drifting and if you do we would be pleased to hear it."[39] The tension and growing frustration in their words is palpable partly because soil-drift was such a serious problem. Essentially, soil drifting "spread" drought into adjacent fields so that when one settler abandoned his land and allowed the soil to drift, the soil would also drift onto his neighbour's field thereby making it impossible for that settler to grow a crop. Call it 'drought-creep.' It must be noted also that soil-drift is commonly thought to have been a creature of the Thirties. That is not correct.

Abandoned land also resulted in huge swaths of prairie becoming incubation beds for grasshoppers, another problem that plagued settlers on the south plains. In desperate response to this growing problem, the RM of Clinworth embarked on an enforced grasshopper killing campaign. Clinworth paid for the poison to kill the hoppers and salvage at least some of the 1921 crop from the one-two punch of hoppers and drought. Clinworth council, though, overrode the plough-as-you-see-fit Rights-of-Man sentiment in the RM of Maple Creek, and forcefully compelled all settlers to purchase and use the poison; the RM would then recover costs for the campaign in that time-honoured fashion of placing liens against the lands of the settlers.[40]

Progressive-thinking Clinworth even went so far as to take the step of writing to the Department of Interior asking for an investigation into the possibility of irrigating the enormous tract of land from Sceptre west to the Alberta border.[41] Council argued that recent years "have demonstrated that it is with difficulty that farming operations can be successfully prosecuted" in the drylands and that irrigation remained the only way to "bring water to the land."[42]

Technically speaking though, there was another way. With the Better Farming Train about to be cancelled, the Department of Agriculture resistant to the idea of educational tours on how to farm better, and the toll from crop failure mounting, Prelate Scretary Treasurer J.J. Keelor took the further step of asking the province to see about attracting ace rainmaker Charles Hatfield "regardless of what people think."[43] Mr. Keelor was not alone in his desperation. It seems other communities, risking no mild derision, enlisted the help of the famed American rainmaker. He seemed to have actually worked success in the Medicine Hat region. Indeed, when he arrived in that city in 1921, he was "accompanied by a light drizzle."[44] The logician Auld, however, would have none of it.

Deputy Auld, though, displayed a very uncharacteristic streak of naïve credulity when he approached the American Department of Agriculture's weather bureau in Washington, D.C., and asked for its opinion on Mr. Hatfield. The critique of a rainmaker by a man of science was predictable: "The most elementary consideration of physics, chemistry and simple calculations" reasoned bureau chief C.F. Martin, "[are] sufficient to convince scientists that these schemes are wholly impracticable." Furthermore, "no reputable scientist acquainted with the laws and phenomenon of evaporation and condensation [can believe in the possibility of rainmaking]."[45] The appearance of Mr. Hatfield in historical records was an expression of the desperation felt by settlers and their willingness to try anything which, again, was based on the principle that doing something is better than doing nothing.

Hatfield's claims to generate rain were not exceptional for this period in history, at least where logic and rational thinking is concerned. We have noted that wishful thinking, and dreamy desire were common intellectual habits of the day and the early twentieth century, proved to be fertile ground for a number of absurd and exotic intellectual curiosities. Mr. Hatfield's claims to be able to make rain travelled in the same warm and pleasing intellectual currents as the "rain-follows-the-plough" idea, another one of credulity's bastard step-children, which developed in nineteenth century America. As the trans-Mississippi region was settled after the Civil War, the slow and steady settlement of the Missouri region was accompanied by an increase in rainfall. This freak and chance occurrence soon morphed into a matter of science.[46] "Rain-follows-the-plough" became accepted dogma at the University of Nebraska, where Natural Sciences Professor Samuel Aughey taught the idea. According to Dr. Aughey (who, in this quote, is taking a highly ill-advised shot at rainmakers), it was "not by any magic or enchantment, not by incantations or offerings, but instead in the sweat of his face toiling with his hands [by laying rail steel across the plains], that man can persuade the heavens to yield their treasures of dew and rain upon the land."[47] Silly American curiosities, perhaps. But, in Canada, such ideas became an accepted part of the Dominion government's efforts to settle the west. When construction was being done on the CPR mainline through the south plains in the latter third of the nineteenth century, concern was raised about the legendary dryness of the area. This worry was overcome by the strange belief that "with settlement rains will come."[48] According to experts, the steel of the track will "disrupt" electrical currents "thereby" causing rain.[49] It is the "thereby" that one finds deeply depressing.

Mr. Hatfield, by the way, didn't make it rain, at least not for the men trapped in the dusty, hothouse furnace of the Schuler district south of Happyland and just inside the Alberta border. The men there agreed to give the rainmaker more money, "providing of course that he leaves the country."[50] The men and women of the once burgeoning now-dead community of Estuary were just as cynical as the settlers of Schuler. Hatfield charged $1,000 for five inches ($7,500 for 12 inches) but, as Historian William Wardill notes, "nobody from Estuary offered him so much as a nickel," although this statement tends to suggest that they did at least discuss it.[51]

Against this backdrop of absurdity, life for the settlers in the drylands got worse and worse. RM of Mantario Secretary Treasurer C. Evans Sargeant explained to Deputy Auld in 1921 that "this municipality is faced with the most complete crop failure that has been known since it was settled."[52] There was no rain, no crop, and no hay and Sargeant added that "unless something can be done, some 1,500 people … are faced with the prospect of starvation this winter."[53] While there is no record of starvation, or of relief provided in response to this specific crisis, 345 farmers abandoned the RM of Mantario #262 between 1917 and 1924: assuming that each man had a wife and child, just over one thousand people fled.

While the threat of starvation may or may not have been accurate, there is some level of corroboration from the local Member of the Legislative Assembly W.H. Harvey. Wheat yields in 1921, Harvey confirmed, ranged from the abysmal figure of zero to the only slightly less abysmal ten bushels per acre, which was a charitable way of saying the failure was absolute in some areas and partial in others. He added that "there are practically no oats" (and here one is reminded of Dr. Samuel Johnson's famous quip that in England oats are fed to horses, but in Scotland oats are fed to people).[54] Again to ward off the apparent threat of starvation, a concerned Harvey recommended settlers be put to work on road gangs to ameliorate the effects of the disaster.[55] He explained that settlers "are becoming discouraged with conditions and many of them are broke."[56]

The condition in which these settlers found themselves led to the establishment of local relief charities in the drylands. Thirty miles east of Mantario in Kindersley, for example, the local Grain Growers Association and the local chapter of the Imperial Order Daughters of the Empire (IODE) both set up deposit locations for food and clothing and, as winter approached, locations for coal and mittens. The IODE asked "those more favorably situated" to contribute because many settlers in the areas have had "no crops, or only a little, for some years now."[57] In one instance, the RM of Clinworth appealed to the Regina Red Cross for aid. It seems a settler in the Clinworth district asked council for "boots and shoes for her children to go to school." But the RM at that time was on an enforced austerity campaign and so was compelled to ask the Red Cross in Regina for help.[58] The Red Cross actually conducted a health survey on school kids in Alberta's half of the dust bowl in September of 1921, the fifth continuous year of crop failure. Health officials found that of the 638 schoolchildren they examined in the Bow Island district, nearly two thirds suffered from malnutrition.[59]

Despite all of this, the province remained resistant to enact the Better Farming Conference's recommendation to evacuate the area. Auld explained to dryland farmer Pete Harder a full year after the evacuation recommendation was made that the chance to be removed from the drylands and of obtaining a second homestead was "a rather remote possibility."[60] Instead, Auld urged the Clinworth district settler to "review very carefully the chances of success [where you are]" and additionally advised Harder that winter rye has been grown to some advantage in his region and that perhaps he should try that.[61]

Auld's admonition to grow rye was not an isolated suggestion but an alternative that had gripped the minds of a number of policy and opinion makers in the drylands, and that with great fever. The editors of the Medicine Hat News fairly flung themselves at the rye option. After making the observation that "a different method of farming must be adopted," they claimed that if settlement on the south plains was to be successful then surely rye must be part of that change. The editors felt confident enough in the rye option that they drew firm conclusions without blinking: "rye is the grain that will solve the farming problem in this part of the country."[62] Precisely what this frantic optimism was based on is not clear but one rather suspects that the editors learned over coffee one morning that rye is more resistant to drought and has a shorter growing season and "therefore" it would solve the drought problem. It was a frantic hope at which they flung themselves with all the desperation they could muster. There was even a rye growing conference in Medicine Hat, which was attended not only by farmers but also by members of the Rotary Club, the Chamber of Commerce, and city councilmen. This conference is interesting for another reason: it points toward the idea that what was essentially a rural problem, drought, did in fact have significant implications in urban centres as well. The urban and rural areas in the early years were joined at the hip – as went rural, so went urban. The unique physical, cultural, and spiritual gulf that separates rural and urban areas today was much less acute in the 1920s and 1930s.

In the absence of a formal government-sanctioned evacuation plan of the type operating in Alberta, settlers became involved with Colonization Companies and even there the government set up road-blocks. A group of thirty German settlers from Leader (formerly Prussia), for example, enlisted the help of Western Colonizers Limited in 1926 so they might get help abandoning the drylands. W.C.L. spokesman J.P. Murphy informed Agriculture Minister Charles Hamilton that "these people … have not had any crop for ten years [and] had no resources to sustain them through the coming year."[63] The group had apparently marshalled together its meagre resources to purchase a block of land "owned by a syndicate" in the Davidson district south of Saskatoon. The province, however, refused Murphy's request to help the settlers because it feared the "very grave difficulties" that might arise out this sort of commercial movement of settlers.

The threat of "very grave difficulties" was the same reason the province refused assistance to settlers represented by Theodore Herzu. Herzu, a representative of the CPR-owned Canada Colonization Association, asked the province to assist with the removal of an unspecified number of "Baptist families" from the south plains. Herzu urged the province to seriously consider his aid request in view of the fact that the CCA was not making any special deals for services rendered to stricken settlers. But again, Hamilton refused. He insisted that the drylands "will support a population though necessarily less thickly settled than where there is abundant rainfall."[64] Reflecting the province's concern with the de-population, Hamilton noted that his refusal was rooted in the concern he had for those "[who] are anxious to maintain their municipal institutions."[65] And this sentiment of Hamilton's is the key to the whole story: evacuation meant the eventual rot and death of rural Saskatchewan in the south and western plains. The drylands were on life-support and the Saskatchewan government refused to pull the plug unlike their counterparts in Alberta, which not only pulled the plug but virtually emptied the southeast and east central plains of all human life in the 1920s.

Ultimately, it was the human element that makes the prevarications of the Saskatchewan government appear coarse and unfeeling. Settlers whose government was assuring them of the ultimately wondrous possibilities in the drylands could, and did, opt instead for what amounts to little more than indentured servitude.

A large German-speaking Russian family representing a number of people entered into an agreement in 1923 with Cluny-based Western Stock Ranches. President H. Honens asked the province to assist the Konschuhs with the cost of moving their goods. Honens explained that his company would provide the settlers with food, clothing, and shelter. In return, the refugees were to work the company lands at Cluny, Alberta, paying off the debt with the proceeds from their crop.[66] The historical record on this particular element is thin but common sense suggests that if this happened once, then it happened twice. One does not often hear of such things occurring on the Canadian plains. Indentured servitude, paying off desperation debts with labour, strikes us as something straight out of Old Europe and quite out of place on the egalitarian western plains, but there it is.

Honens used the word "destitute" to describe the Konschuh clan but even that seemed an understatement. The hardened and leathery sixty-one-year-old Phillip Konschuh along with his sixty-year-old wife and other members of the family had all fled Russia just ahead of the "pitchfork and machine gun reforms of the Bolsheviks."[67] After seven years of farming in the Fox Valley region, however, Konschuh had amassed over $1,500 in liens against his land and as of 1922 had not produced more than three bushels per acre in the six years preceding his departure. The year he moved he managed to grow nothing.[68] Mr. Konschuh was one of the few lucky ones – the province consented to pay for the removal of the members of the Konschuh clan.

The Konschuhs had arrived in Canada in 1902 from Saratov, Russia. Phillip was a shoemaker by trade. And although they came from Russia they were Germans, part of the thousands of Germans who had been encouraged to settle in Russia first by the idiosyncratic, westward-looking Europhile Peter the Great, and later by rulers like Catherine the Great. The political and social instability of the dying Russian Empire helped to prompt the Konschuhs to leave and they arrived in Calgary in 1902. Later they migrated to Fox Valley in 1913 just in time for the crop failure of 1914.[69]

Those years of drought and failure were not easy for the Konschuh clan. In later years, after they had left the south plains behind, Phillip would tell stories "of the many severe storms ... and of evenings spent reading the bible."[70] Phillip's son Jacob ("Jake") used his time profitably: he not only homesteaded but also "studied steam engineering."[71]

Neither faith nor science could overcome the drought, though, and the Konschuh clan left Fox Valley en masse. Opal Konschuh, the later wife of David, the youngest of the Konschuhs, and the only member of that branch born in Canada (he was born in Calgary in 1902), wrote that "poor soil combined with drought conditions and the urging of friends who had preceded [the Konschuh's] prompted the move to Cluny."[72] Ida Konschuh was six years old in 1923. She distinctly recalls "the train pulling up to the station at Maple Creek and watching them load cattle, horses and all our earthly belongings."[73] Despite the desperate circumstances under which they left and the saddening prospect of entering into a kind of indentured servitude, Ida favourably recalls Mr. Honens. He was a good man, "a well known land lord in the community" who "helped people to buy farms and build homes."[74]

While the Konschuhs may have been pleased to leave the drylands, their horses certainly weren't. A number of their horses escaped from the new home at Cluny and guided by some strange instinct for home no matter how poor, sandy, and desperate it was, tried to make their way back to the drylands. Some were captured near Medicine Hat heading west but most were never found.

For those who had neither access nor money to enlist land or colonization companies to act on their behalf, or for those to whom indentured servitude was just too much, the local priest seemed to have served the role as intermediary. The Reverend H.J. Schmidt of the Maple Creek district wrote the province on behalf of "forty-four Baptist families" who could no longer afford to farm in the drylands and asked the province to help in getting them out. No response was recorded.[75]

The Mutter clan from Odessa, Ukraine, relied on the local schoolteacher to help get them out. Ms. Clara Crouse had been teaching at the English school in Hatton for a few years. Her family had settled in southeast Saskatchewan after having come up from a fenced compound in North Dakota (it was fenced because of the Indian Wars). They arrived in the Dakotas from Boston. Prior to Boston, they lived in Nova Scotia, where they had arrived from Germany in 1780 after having received a forty-acre timber land grant from the British crown.[76] As such, the Crouse family likely formed part of that movement to settle the Maritimes in the aftermath of the sad, tragic and wholly unnecessary expulsion of the Acadians between 1755 and 1763.

Gust Mutter, the son of Gustav the original settler, was born in Hatton and recalled that "Clara's accounts of better conditions in the Macoun area convinced Dad and a couple of our neighbours to look for greener pastures."[77] In 1926, they took the barn apart board by board, straightened out the nails for reuse, and shipped the barn, the nails, and the women to the south-east by train; the men followed in an old Model-T Ford, a journey that took three days.

The above snapshots of mass removal and evacuation between 1921 and 1926 demonstrate a crucial point. Auld and the department could not claim ignorance. They clearly knew what was occurring in the drylands. This is not the question. The problem was that it seems as though the province, guided and influenced by the painfully abstract and highly influential F.H. Auld, was using the lives of the settlers to prop up and sustain rural development in an area that many at the time felt should not have been settled in the first place. As indicated before, there was only one way in which settlement could be "undone" and that was land abandonment. The Dominion government was less opposed to undoing settlement than was the province. But the province called the shots on the south plains and within the province, those shots were called, or at least directed by F.H. Auld: a forty-year veteran of the department, Auld outlasted half a dozen premiers, and a dozen agriculture ministers and almost to the very end persisted in seeing these events as non-exceptional.

Using impeccable logic, for example, Auld (who was raised on Prince Edward Island and so we can legitimately question the level of his understanding about his adopted province) explained to Swift Current area settler Thomas Lannan that merchants do not come begging for assistance when they fail and therefore settlers and farmers should not come begging for assistance either. Indeed, Auld was "unable to see why there should be any distinction raised between various classes in the community."[78] Although Auld admitted that the federal government "probably [has] a moral obligation" to help burned-out settlers, he stated that the province did not. Auld told Lannan to go and work on a harvest crew or a road-building gang "for a year or two."[79] One doesn't know whether to laugh or cry.

Deploying his fearsome logic-chopping abilities, Auld raised an interesting and today still compelling argument. Why *should* farmers come begging for help when no one else does; why should distinctions be drawn between the various classes in the community? Today the matter is more complex but in the 1920s it was still fairly simple. Settlers formed the vanguard of that class of people who would build, develop, and sustain the province of Saskatchewan. Premier Walter Scott and Prime Minister Wilfrid Laurier did not peg their hopes on merchants, cattlemen, industry, or real estate in the development of the west: both governments explicitly stated that *agriculture* would be the basic building block of the province. Settlers would grow and export natural resources and commodities such as wheat; eastern industry would have captive markets. This is the basic theme of Canadian history: the west was the colony of a colony and the settlers were that one single crucial component in nation-building that allowed this province to develop and expand. For their part, the settlers saw agriculture as an opportunity to be free men, freed from their lives as tenant farmers, servants, and stevedores, and in some instances freed from slavery in the United States. Farming offered men freedom; that was true then and it is true today.

The relationship, then, between settler and government was mutually agreeable. Saskatchewan was not built by merchants or speculators or industry: it was built by agricultural pioneers. The province explicitly recognized this. And it is here in this special, nation-building relationship between government and agriculture out of which develops the moral obligation to help and this is precisely why distinctions between the various classes in the community *should* have been made by Auld and the government in the 1920s. But Auld, being from Prince Edward Island, never understood this. Instead of helping with evacuations (the recommendations of two commissions), Auld and the province put the men to work on road gangs to make sure they stayed put. During the crop failure year of 1919, for example, 1,213 men were put to work on road-building gangs on the south plains.[80]

For all of Auld's hair-splitting, reasoning, and prevarication, the province finally did manage to piece together some kind of plan to get the settlers out of the south plains (this was the plan under which the Konschuhs were moved). And it seems as though it was an American settler who helped, at least in part, by drawing attention to conditions about which the province was likely unaware. In 1922, the sixth year of continuous crop failure in the drylands, Anton Huelskamp, his wife Nettie, and their two daughters Katherine and Polly were all living (perhaps a better word is existing) in the starvation-threatened RM of Mantario. In the dry summer of 1921 (the same year in which half of Hatton and all of its hope would burn to the ground), and giving credence to the suggestion that the people were starving for want of oats, the Huelskamp's were obliged to feed upon "porcupine stew." But even in starvation there can be humour. With a lightness of heart, little Polly recalled years later that one evening in the dry years, a John Deere collection agent appeared at their home. A visitation by a collection agent is never a good thing but the Huelskamp's offered him a seat at their dinner table and fed him a bowl of this stew on which he apparently gagged.[81]

In 1922, Huelskamp penned a four-page letter of distress to Premier Charles Dunning outlining his predicament and that of his neighbours and his RM. "We have been six years without a crop," he wrote, "and near as long without rain" and he raised the compelling philosophical query "is it fair or is it right" that the province should not aid its settlers in relocating to better lands under these circumstances.[82]

Huelskamp estimated that "hundreds" of settlers had already fled the region by 1922, and those with no money left were seen simply "walking out." According to his estimation, loan companies owned two-thirds of the homesteads and pre-emptions in the district. The four-quarter farm he had built up had been advertised for sale for some time in both Canadian and American newspapers but he could not sell it. Huelskamp stated the simple and obvious truth: "I could rent any number of good safe farms if I could get my stock and machinery out of here."[83] But he was unable to do that, and that was the problem.

Premier Dunning's blithe response to Huelskamp was characteristic of so much of what occurred during the dryland crisis. Dunning, apparently taking his cue from Auld, was "pleased to be able to state" that the conditions Huelskamp described affected "only a small area."[84] Dunning pointed out that the province was already providing aid to stricken settlers, a statement which was not, strictly speaking, very accurate. As per their responsibility, the RMs were obliged to borrow money for relief aid for the settlers who would then pay back the relief loan with the proceeds from the following year's crop. Since they couldn't grow anything, they couldn't repay the loans to say nothing of paying taxes. It was the RMs who borrowed money for relief from the banks and the RMs that took land as security, and the RMs that were responsible for debt collection, though the province acted as a guarantor. Huelskamp was pleading for evacuation and that only the province could arrange.

Dunning answered Huelskamp's philosophical query of the rightness and fairness of the province's actions by saying that it was not the province's problem: "we have not been able to see our way clear to assume a responsibility which, properly speaking, belongs to the federal government in connection with opening up unsuitable lands for settlement."[85] Dunning, however, agreed to send out an investigator from the province's field crops division to establish the veracity of Huelskamp's claims. Apart from the breezy road tour of the sub-committee of the Better Farming Commission, the late summer of 1922 appears to have been one of the first times that the province undertook a ground-level investigation of any district in the western area of the drybelt.

The speedy and efficient J.M. Smith arrived on the scene later that summer. He spent three days with the Huelskamps, toured the RM, asked questions, probed, investigated, and tried to determine the extent of the devastation. His report was essentially a recapitulation of Huelskamp's letter to the premier. Smith agreed Huelskamp was in trouble: "his land is a tough proposition."[86] The RM, Smith noted, was overrun with Russian thistle and the average wheat yield in the past six years was between five and eight bushels per acre, though, in an appropriate absurdity, Smith noted "[this district] probably gets more rain than other RMs" in the area.

Smith went on at length about the district and its suitability for farming. The land itself was excessively sandy, with too many rocks and too much alkali.[87] "Community effort," like hope down Hatton way, "[was] not very apparent." He finished by saying the Municipality overall "is a poor one." As for hope, that precious and mysterious commodity that underpinned the migrations of most people into the Last Best West, there was none left in the Huelskamp household, and Smith duly noted "[Anton's] wife, by the way, is the more emphatic of the two on this point."[88]

During the course of his fact-finding mission, though, Smith was cornered by a number of farmers in the district who asked him an awkward question. It seemed that it was not just Huelskamp but many others in the region who had heard that Alberta was evacuating its settlers out of its drylands. Huelskamp's neighbours wanted to know what Saskatchewan was doing in this regard. The very question betrayed the fact that settlers were not aware that evacuation and second homesteads were the essential recommendations of the 1920 Better Farming Conference. All that Smith could tell them was that he "knew [of] no such assistance" and characteristically added "the dominion government had control of such matters."[89] Smith wrapped up his investigation shortly after.

Time passed and Huelskamp heard nothing more from the province. On a chill, late October day, he borrowed money from a neighbour, packed what he could into a horse-drawn cart and abandoned Masonville, leaving behind most of the machinery, the land, the house, and six years labour.[90] Huelskamp later explained to Dunning in 1923 that "there was no feed to keep the stock through the winter" so they were compelled to leave because arrangements had at last been made in Brock, where he would rent land located about a hundred miles east of where they had homesteaded.[91] He asked the province to reimburse him for the move in the hope that he could be pay back his neighbour. But he also wrote for a more important reason: he had heard that many of his old neighbours had "secur[ed] transportation out" at provincial expense.

It seems that in the six months between the departure of Smith and Huleskamp's departure for Brock the province had finally agreed to sign onto an existing removal plan developed by the Alberta government in 1922. Other farmers who had left the Alsask district had also requested to be reimbursed. But Auld refused Huelskamp. If Huelskamp was given aid, Auld carefully reasoned, then everyone who left prior to the agreement would be entitled, and Auld felt "it was better not to establish a precedent of this kind."[92] This mass rejection of aid helps explain, in part, how it came to be that the Department of Agriculture could claim that the land abandonment was only ever a minor problem at best. According to the department's own statistics, just 187 people received evacuation aid in 1923.[93]

Huelskamp received his letter of refusal in late spring 1923. Upon reading the contents of the letter, he turned the paper over and scrawled on the reverse side a brief message pregnant with meaning and promptly mailed it back to the provincial Department of Agriculture: "this letter might be marked as, 'One of the principal reasons why so many of our settlers are going south.'"[94] The man who seemed to have played a role in prompting the province to accept at least some of the responsibilities recommended by the Royal Commission of Inquiry into Farming Conditions was himself denied aid.

Developing a removal plan was not an easy task, particularly for a government that quailed and backed away from anything that even resembled responsibility. This reluctance was exacerbated by the other pressing question of what to do with the evacuated settlers. Where do they go? It was one thing to evacuate people, still another to find a place for them to settle so that they might become productive once again.

Alongside the idea that depopulation interfered with the fate of Saskatchewan as an agricultural powerhouse, the second largest difficulty with which the provincial administration struggled was that of responsibility: solving the crisis was not their problem. The Department of Interior explained to Saskatchewan's Department of Agriculture that in order to effect the evacuation, Saskatchewan would necessarily be responsible for the details of the plan. This included investigating and adjudicating claims for either a simple evacuation or a request for evacuation and a second homestead. These responsibilities included the typically more mundane aspects of removal, which included partial costs, organization, and staff. But an internal Department of Agriculture memo demonstrates precisely how far away the province was from accepting these propositions. The unsigned memo indicates that the province had no staff, no investigative capacities, and "should not be required to incur the expense of providing for such a staff."[95] The unidentified writer of the memo argues that the Interior Department's position unfairly placed on the Saskatchewan government "the onus for rectifying mistakes for which the province had no responsibility."[96] Burned-out and bankrupt settlers were "brought here by the federal government" and any provincial involvement in righting that particular wrong "seems as unreasonable as it is unwarranted."[97]

Clearly, the province was not overly disposed to participate in any plan for evacuating the settlers. But, for as much as it resisted satisfying the portion of its responsibilities contained in the Royal Commission, Saskatchewan was eventually compelled due to either sheer weight of pressure or the nagging sense that they were not entirely without responsibility to at least make an attempt at solving what in 1923 was a problem entering its seventh year. The worst of the Dirty Thirties, we must recall, lasted between eight and nine years.

The Alberta government had already laid the groundwork for evacuations in early 1922 when it developed and organized a plan for settler removal.[98] Essentially, the participating province, the Department of Interior, and either the CNR or CPR would each pay a third of the costs associated with transporting the belongings of the settlers out of the dry areas to a maximum of two freight cars per family. The families would place all their belongings into these cars, including cattle and machinery. Phrased rather indelicately by the highly abstract CPR freight agent G.H. Smith, settlers were evacuated by a plan "similar to that under which feed oats were moved" in 1922.[99]

A first level of difficulty developed, however, when it became apparent that the rail companies would contribute their third only if the settlers did not change rail service. Neither the CNR nor the CPR would participate in the plan if it turned out that they would be required to move a settler to an area in which the other company was operating. Auld, showing an uncharacteristic streak of softness, requested that "some arrangement" might be developed whereby the settlers would "not be penalized for changing railway allegiances."[100] But he received a quick and terse reply in a letter whose only words were: "we do not reduce our rates on settler's effects moving them from a point on the CP line to a point on the CN line."[101] Auld had also asked about free transportation for settlers and was rebuffed here too when A.E. Hatley replied that "no consideration has been given to transportation of settlers at reduced rates."[102] Curiously, a year later, in 1924, the Alberta government negotiated the free removal of not just the settler's belongings but the settlers themselves.[103]

The plan for allowing drought-stricken settlers to file on a second homestead was also not simple. And while the province and Ottawa eventually did come to an agreement on this, like the recommendation to move settlers out, it was accepted by the government of Saskatchewan only grudgingly and after a continuous back-and-forth of letters and imprecation.

By the early 1920s, William Cory, the Deputy Minister of the Interior was a man bent on putting things back the way they were before 1908. Mr. Cory, we will recall, was optimistic in those early years about the possibilities of the south plains, but, by the 1920s, he wasn't. By this time, "he'd had his fill of tearful tillers from the area."[104] Instead, the dryland farmer in the words of one department underling became "a liability" and added that "the sooner it is realized he is a failure and cannot continue, the better the country will be."[105] So, in a roundabout and backhanded way, the Department of Interior was on the side of the settler but only because it had grown weary and tired of hearing how bad things were in the drylands thus being reminded of how wrong their decision had been to open the south and west plains with little or no consideration of practical realities.

Deputy Cory, then, adopted the role of fiscal libertine. Mr. Cory argued that, since he could not understand "what can possibly be gained by paying part of the removal expenses of the settlers and give them fresh grants of land if they are making their fresh start under a load of debt," he euphemistically urged the province to encourage its settlers to "wind up their affairs."[106] Deputy Auld did not like this. The Deputy didn't like this at all. His feelings on the matter were not unusual, though, considering that in 1914 the Deputy had grumbled about the lack of sound accounting principles employed by settlers. The "class of people" he steamed, who would use bankruptcy to apply for a second homestead were "of no particular value as settlers" and he would not countenance the idea to encourage settlers to declare bankruptcy.[107]

The province feared that the use of bankruptcy to "wipe the slate clean" would result in "an exodus of people from large areas," which Auld argued would be "not a little embarrassing."[108] The erudite Agriculture Minister Charles Hamilton agreed when he said that "a whole lot" of settlers could apply for a second homestead using the bankruptcy claim and therefore the whole of the south lands could be emptied.

Despite the parochial bleatings of the province, the Department of Interior remained wedded to the bankruptcy notion and even went one step further when it also supported the relaxation of settlement duties and the reduction of the pre-emption fees for the second homestead.[109] There was enough libertinage in this suggestion to make Auld's hair stand on end. But Auld and even Hamilton would have none of it: "I am of the opinion," the latter wrote, "that it is not desirable that settlement duties should be made too easy." Mr. Hamilton informed the Department of Interior that the province would not encourage bankruptcy, it would not support a relaxation of settlement duties, and it would not agree to lower the pre-emption fee and all for the same reason: the province feared a massive out-migration.[110]

The Department of Interior, though, was obliquely supported in its profligate approach to the problem by its brother-department, the Ministry of Immigration and Colonization. Deputy Minister R. Black suggested that, while up to this point his department had not been targeted for blame by settlers who "became unfortunately located," he insisted that "the time has come when something definite must be done."[111] After much wrestling with the issue and exploring its many sides and possibilities, the province and Ottawa agreed to shut down the south plains to further settlement and allowed settlers to file on a second homestead.[112]

By 1923, three full years after the recommendations of the Royal Commission, the province and the Department of Interior finally had in place the rules governing all elements of the drybelt evacuation, though to call it an evacuation is a bit of a stretch. The province certainly approached the problem with tepid enthusiasm: "The prolonged drought of the last five years," intoned the Department's annual report, "raised doubts in the minds of many farmers as to whether their districts are suitable for successful agriculture." These measured and carefully used words suggest the government still thought that the settlers were wrong and this helps to account for the fact that in 1922, just sixty-two farmers and their families were removed, and just 127 applications were received for second homesteads.[113] The province simply never believed there was a real problem.

In 1924, Interior Minister Charles Stewart defined the evacuation area as the region south of township 31 (just north of Alsask) and extending in a south-east line from that point toward the American border and including the present-day Grasslands National Park.[114] The Interior Department, perhaps at the request of Saskatchewan, also restricted second homesteads to those who had lost a patented or "proved up" homestead.[115]

Lands boss Charles Stewart was wholly supportive of the second homestead plan because he recognized both the utility and importance of such a plan. "The granting of a fresh homestead entry," he argued, "is the only thing that will keep these farmers in Canada."[116] And echoing his deputy's sentiments, Stewart once again tried to interest the province in lighter homestead requirements because "it strikes me that it would be good business sense" to lower the pre-emption fee or reduce interest rates on settlement fees.[117] Premier Dunning this time did not respond to Stewart's suggestions. Instead Deputy Auld took a month working himself into a lather before responding that those who have lost their lands "are the least competent of our settlers [and] are not entitled to further assistance."[118] For Auld, the issue wasn't about a natural disaster, it was about competence. While he tempered these comments with the observation that many settlers are bankrupt due to "circumstances beyond their control," Auld would simply not go that extra mile for the settlers.

Certainly nature did nothing to ease the burden. The average yields for the drylands in the mid- to late 1920s are similar, very nearly the same, to the worst of the years between 1917 and 1937: five bushels per acre was grown in some districts in 1924, nine in 1925 and between eight and twelve in 1926.[119] Despite the removal plans and the possibility of second homesteads, the settlers remained hopelessly stuck between the hammer and the anvil. Even though the second homestead option existed and there was a half-hearted removal plan of sorts, and even though "hundreds of settlers would take advantage of this," many more thousands did not.[120] The Konschuhs were one of the lucky families and they got a ticket out. The Huelskamps were one of the unlucky families, one of the hundreds in his district who simply "walked out." Officially, the province assisted with the removal of 200 farmers between 1917 and 1924. Between 1917 and 1924, however, the west and south plains lost 10,469 farmers and if we not unreasonably assume that each farmer had a wife and child (the Konschuhs were over a dozen in number, the Huelskamps four; thus, two farmers represents sixteen people), then we arrive at a figure well over 30,000 people.

It is one of the stranger occurrences of the crisis of the 1920s that the land abandonment disaster that was occurring did not really register in official public government documents of the time. We can see how the province toyed with the reality of the situation when we reconsider the Huelskamp example. Anxious, you will recall, not to "set a precedent of this kind," the province refused to assist in the evacuation of untold dozens, likely hundreds of settlers in the Mantario region. They simply and quietly "walked out," as Huelskamp put it, and there are precious few sources that highlight and explore this loss. There are no newspapers from the region that survive to tell the story, no pictures, no editorials.

This failure of the crisis to register in the public mind was not by accident but rather by design. Debt mediation was reintroduced in 1920 and was explicitly designed to deal with the crop failures in the south and western parts of the province; debt mediation was actually a bit of a sop, a concession, because there had been calls for a debt moratorium. Historian David Jones explains that the Saskatchewan government went to great lengths to keep quiet about all the talk of a moratorium on debt and of the growing crisis on the south and west plains. The province made a deliberate point of keeping meetings about the issue out of the press.[121] As Dr. Jones observes, "the collapse of the dry country made such liars out of so many of them that reports of it were hardly appreciated," and, as a consequence, there are very few references to this story in the press. Stories frequently bubble up in local community histories (the Huelskamps and the Konschuhs, for example) and the crisis scars virtually every page of municipal minutes from those years. But in the press, and so in the public mind, there is only silence. The long-time editor of *The Farm and Ranch Review*, C.W. Peterson, observed in 1921 that "a fight is being waged in some of these dry areas in Alberta and Saskatchewan that the general public knows little about."[122] Little was known about the crisis at the time and so it becomes easier to understand how it was dumped into the dustbin of history and forgotten about.

Auld never referred to the larger exodus of which the Huelskamp family was a part, and he minimized the smaller "official" one when he noted that "it would have been remarkable if some of those who took up land had not decided that their choice was unsatisfactory."[123] In 1925, he actually blamed the settlers for the problems they were in when he said that lands were homesteaded "without due consideration of the quality," unwilling to acknowledge that most settlers trusted that the government would not deliberately settle unfit lands, and that the promotional material for the south Saskatchewan region was not a lie, that the area was in fact "a land blessed of the Gods – a land over which bending nature ever smiles and into whose cradle she emptied her golden horn."[124] The settlers sincerely believed that summer-fallow was a guarantee against all elements of nature – recall what the Bickleigh area farmers said about following the best practices and still losing heavily. There was a not-insubstantial amount of implicit trust between the settlers and the governments and that trust was often abused.

Furthermore, Auld denied the existence of an area prone to drought and crop failure when, deploying a kind of pre-'post-modern' reductive logic, he said that "such lands" occur in every province and in Saskatchewan "are not confined to the ... southwest."[125] From start to finish, from 1917 to 1924, Auld and the province retreated from either practical or moral responsibility; they downplayed the crisis and even went so far as to hide the problem from the media and the public as it mushroomed to greater and greater proportions. Auld's refusal to admit to the existence of a dry area would survive all the way down to the 1930s when that belief was finally and with much sweat and tears, bludgeoned out of him.

The province feared depopulation and refused to countenance any suggestion that evacuation would solve the dryland crisis and in fairness one must at least try to understand the province's impulse rooted as it was in the goal of building a grain-growing Eden. The life of a very large area of the province was at stake and the province did not, like Alberta, pull the plug. But the idea that life in these regions must be sustained *at all costs* necessarily resulted in a striking disregard for the existence of the settlers in the drylands (the whole "go work on a road-building gang" sentiment seems preposterous). This disregard is all the more striking when one considers that Alberta had, by 1924, long since committed to removing its settlers from the drylands. But then again, Alberta and Saskatchewan handled the crisis differently.

Unlike Alberta, the fate of Saskatchewan was tied exclusively to wheat production. The belief that wheat farming was the only formula for success in Saskatchewan was a belief that hindered the response of the province to the crisis. That same belief also resulted in deep self-inflicted wounds for the settler who persisted in growing wheat to the exclusion of everything else. Vidora-district farmer David Stonehouse was one of those settlers who suffered in the crisis and he spoke very deep truth when he explained to Auld that "it is not possible to make things what they ought to be unless one sees clearly what they are."[126] Thomas Lannan down Ingebrit way argued that "any man of ordinary intelligence who has been on the job here since 1917 knows what this country is and knows that it will never do for farming."[127] The province simply would not acknowledge this truth.

While the government fiddled and the settlers burned, the province's rural municipalities did not fare much better. Long before the days of handsome, neon-lit federal aid packages, settlers in trouble were expected to go the local RM office for relief. The same was true in Alberta. Carl Anderson settled in the Carlstadt (later Alderson) district in 1910 and he recalls that there was no government assistance, no bonuses or acreage payments, no drought assistance: "if a school was built, it was up to the people living there" to get it done.[128]

In both Alberta and Saskatchewan, there was a steady flow of people into and out of RM offices. It was here that settlers could obtain flour, fodder, coal, seed grains, and other necessities of life. The RM office, then as now, was a crucial and highly important element of life in rural Saskatchewan. RMs were the basic building block of rural Saskatchewan. In the early frontier years, and indeed down to today, all roads led to or through the reeves and councilmen of these tiny political units.

One of Saskatchewan Premier Walter Scott's first tasks was the establishment of "territorial units" (RMs) to be comprised of nine townships (1,298 quarter sections) in rural Saskatchewan.[129] By 1914, 295 RMs were established and functioning as local administrative and political units, a testament to the rapid growth of the province.[130] These local political units were responsible at the ground level for executing Scott's vision for a rural, wheat-growing Eden. The municipalities were responsible for a number of mundane yet vitally important elements in the development of rural Saskatchewan: local road and bridge construction, local telephone service, financing their own existence based on tax collections from settlers, and, sadly as it would prove, "granting aid or relief to a needy person."[131]

The editors of Saskatchewan's first guide to municipal bylaws assured the local administrators and councillors that they were engaged in a noble calling: "The man who gives his time and energy to the work of improving the government and institutions of his home municipality is engaged in one of the noblest employments open to subjects of a free nation."[132] This grand sentiment is echoed by that profound and thoughtful nineteenth-century French historian/thinker/aristocrat Alexis de Tocqueville. He felt that "[municipal government] is the only association so well rooted in nature that wherever men assemble it forms itself."[133] De Tocqueville added that "man creates Kingdoms and Republics but townships [RMs] seem to spring directly from the Hand of God."[134] De Toqueville's famous work *Democracy in America*, from which these quotes are derived, was likely available in rural Saskatchewan in the 1920s in those handsome red faux-leather editions and no doubt the men of the RMs stopped and reflected upon those ennobling words in the 1920s. By the 1930s, the councillors, reeves, administrators (and the local debt collectors) could only stand staring in disbelief, bewildered, and struck dumb by the tempest barrelling down on them like a freight train and whose effects they were required by law to mitigate.

That RMs in 1918 were about to embark on a difficult course of action was not lost on the Department of Municipal Affairs. Deputy Minister J.N. Bayne noted that "under normal conditions, councils are wary of indulging in seed grain distribution owing to the difficulties so often experienced in securing repayment."[135] Bayne girded the RMs for what was to come with a wonderfully Churchillian rhapsody when he said that "while we have seen sunshine and shadow [those RMs] will be stronger and self-sufficient whose fate it was to struggle."[136] And struggle they did.

In 1921, the problem had already gone from bad to worse and from thence into abysmal. The federal government had advanced Saskatchewan farmers over half a million dollars just in relief seed between 1918 and 1920; relief aid amounted to $340,000 in just a couple dozen RMs south of the river during the same time.[137] Thus it is painfully clear that the RMs were simply much too small to handle the crisis on their own. Bayne noted that the drought "has adversely affected the financial standing" of many municipalities and this fate was "especially true of the municipalities ... in the southwest."[138] Bayne sadly observed that banks in 1920 began limiting credit for RMs, as they would do in the 1930s. There was also little and in some instances no money for schools or telephone service. The problem was similar in Alberta. Throughout the 1920s, "feed for both man and beast" was necessary. As in Saskatchewan, debt collection from drought-addled settlers became something of an art, though it was an art to whose peculiar dynamics municipal officials only cryptically refer. Speaking of the collection efforts in Alberta municipalities, one local official offered the slight observation that "active collection of the accounts followed."[139] Local taxes, in both Saskatchewan and Alberta, "took a severe beating"[140]

Under the Municipal Relief Act, councils were empowered to pass bylaws that allowed them to borrow money from lending institutions. Settlers would receive the relief purchased with this money by means of a promissory note "due on demand." As security, statutory liens were placed against the lands and property owned by the borrower of the relief.[141] Tenant farmers, those who rented land, were required to put up some other form of collateral. As for repayment, the example of the RM of White Valley stands for all: "council shall in each year levy on all the assessable property ... such sum as shall be required to meet the interest on the money borrowed" until settlers were able to pay back the principal.[142]

The RMs, in gallant frontier fashion, faced the crisis with a sense of optimism. RM of Clinworth Councilor Thomas Armstrong believed that the 1919 relief debt could "with every prospect, if the crops are normal this year, be entirely paid."[143] That certainly was not the case. By 1920, with relief aid mounting, council passed another by-law, which approved a request for an additional $15,000 for "needy farmers."[144] Admirable, noble Clinworth had assumed a relief-debt load of at least $45,000 in under twenty-four months. During these early years, annual operating budgets could run between $15,000 and $25,000; thus, RMs were advancing in relief aid an amount twice as large as their annual operating budgets.

The province also contributed to relief aid but the level at which this occurred remains fairly obscure due to a dearth of records. Unlike the 1930s when aid became an extension of policy, in fact *became* policy, assessing provincial involvement in aid relief during the 1920s is difficult because the records are incomplete and fragmentary. The province, for example, shipped some $25,450 worth of flour and coal to an unnamed south-west Local Improvement District in 1920.[145] Additionally, government officials attended some two dozen meetings held throughout communities in the drylands (Maple Creek, Mortlach, Leader, and Sceptre), but the ultimate purpose and the outcome of these meetings is lost.

We know that the province asked rural municipalities to submit detailed information on the amount of relief they might need and for how many people and the RM administrators duly submitted this information, sometimes written on borrowed scraps of papers or even table napkins. Municipal official Mr. A.W. Murray, for example, scribbled out a request and informed the province that there were 365 farmers in the RM of Auvergne near Swift Current who cultivated some 56,000 acres of land, and that, all told, the RM would need some $37,500 in relief aid. No record is available that records relief aid payments to this RM.

Despite the vague and oblique involvement of the province in what was turning out to be a much bigger problem than first thought, relief debt quickly spiralled out of control. This shockingly quick slide prompted Clinworth to tighten up its rules governing relief distribution. Mr. W. L. Lawton moved a motion in 1920 that limited relief to "extreme cases" and settlers would receive it "only after being interviewed and questioned before council."[146] This officious approach to granting relief aid was perhaps an automatic response for Councillor Lawton because he had served in the Yukon detachment of the North West Mounted Police for some number of years before marrying the improbably named Bella DeCow and finally settling in Sceptre, Saskatchewan, right on the edge of the Great Sand Hills.[147]

These new regulations produced the expected results in Clinworth. In January 1922, just twenty-five settlers received aid after being "interview and questioned" by council.[148] In large measure, Clinworth enacted these restrictions because mounting relief debt played havoc with the RMs ability to function. Two months after that special aid meeting in January, for example, Clinworth came to the sad realization that the local bank was avoiding the RM because councillors had received no response to their request for an operating loan, despite "repeated protests, interviews, telegrams and phone calls."[149] Clinworth need not have felt bad about being ignored by their banker. South of Hanna, Alberta, the problem had got so bad that the banks stopped lending money for feed or seed.[150] Still, one necessarily appreciates being informed that one's credit has been cancelled.

The experiences of Clinworth were shared by most other dryland RMs. In early 1922, the RM of White Valley was carrying heavy debt made up by a $27,500 operating loan that had been taken out because "in the opinion of council, taxes [owed] cannot be collected this year."[151] The relief debt was similar next door in the troubled RM of Reno. Working under a heavy load of debt, council borrowed an additional $8,380.45 for flour and fodder in 1923.[152] This borrowing continued apace in 1924 and 1925, when some $13,000 was borrowed for flour, coal, and fodder.[153]

In some instances, exact relief amounts are not provided in the records, but we can still gauge the level of relief that was administered by examining the number of instances in which an RM registered a lien against property. In 1920 alone, for example, the RM of Big Stick registered liens against 152 parcels of land.[154]

Relief, unsurprisingly, followed a very basic human pattern: no one wanted to be the first to take it, but once the first settler took relief, the others followed. The RM of White Valley, for example, formulated its first relief loan request for 1920 at its regular meeting in January and at the same time approved aid for just six people totalling $256.90.[155] One month later, ninety-four families applied for aid, totalling $16,490.75 in seed and fodder.[156] And as January made its slow and bitter way into February, council approved another seventy-nine applications for coal, flour, and fodder, totalling $14,265.25.[157] At that same meeting, thirty-three settlers were provided with $7,992.50 in seed.[158] Thus in just two months, the RM of White Valley assumed a relief debt of $38,747. This was another good example of why Clinworth slammed the door on aid because, once one person took it, it seems everyone did. The enormity of the crisis was reflected in the amount of municipal aid distributed across the province during 1920. In this year, just under half a million dollars worth of seed grain was distributed.[159]

Certainly it can be pointed out that these figures of hundreds of thousands of dollars seem small and insignificant next to the tens of millions spent on aid during the 1930s, but that critique, of course, misses the point. The Dirty Thirties were different *only* by degree, not by kind. The essential nature and direction are the same: drought, relief aid, bankruptcy, and either land abandonment or evacuation. The province during the 1930s was simply, and finally, much more willing (willing only because there was, finally, no other choice – pictures of settlers dying of starvation would not look good in the promotional material) to spend money on relief aid up to and including paying for the very limited evacuation and resettlement of settlers. The province could no longer escape its responsibilities because the problem seemed to have grown – in fact, did grow – and was also at that time framed against the back-drop of the greater global crisis of the Great Depression.

The financial quick-sand in which the RMs helplessly floundered was the underlying reason why the province undertook the "Pay Your Taxes" newspaper campaign of 1922. Agriculture and Municipal Affairs Minister Charles Hamilton declared that "local institutions should be the first to be considered when deciding whom to pay."[160] The rather large and handy ad that accompanied the story explained to "financially embarrassed" south and west plains settlers that taxes "provide the lifeblood of your community" and that without taxes "your schools would close, road work would cease [and] all community life would come to a standstill."[161] The ad was accurate on only one of three points: instances of school closure, either temporary or permanent, were characteristic of the crisis. Road work did not cease but instead grew by leaps and bounds. There was never a period in Saskatchewan history when so many roads were built. Saskatchewan between 1914 and 1937 was a road-builders paradise. And instead of a standstill, there was an active movement out of the drylands.

The settlers, however, were not terribly concerned about the financial conditions of the RMs, still less did they care about the message of the "Pay Your Taxes" campaign ("sooner or later all taxes have to be paid, so why not pay yours now").[162] Most settlers were concerned with survival, or, at the very least, mere existence. As such, rules were broken, which further complicated an already desperate problem.

Merchants, like municipalities, were generally low on the priority list when considering who to pay. Business being what it is in a dry land, merchants were often compelled from sheer necessity to accept promissory notes which, more often than not, were not paid in full as the note required.[163] The merchants wanted the ability to register liens against crops and they had fairly legitimate justifications for this. Merchants reasoned that since bankers could apply liens against future crops for things such as twine, or wages, then merchants should be able to as well. The merchants felt that summer food supplies advanced against future crop yields were just as legitimate a charge as any other, but it didn't go their way. When a crop was grown, an Alberta shopkeeper recalls, "the banker, the lumberman or implement man grab[bed] it all up by threatening suits or court action."[164] The merchant finished last.

And while the merchants were generally last in line, they can take comfort from the fact that the RM was never that far behind. Instead of handing over, for example, that portion of their crop against which the RMs (or the banker, or the lumber man, or the implement man, *ad nauseam*) had registered liens for security, settlers often sold their grain to whomever would buy it before anyone else could get at it. This abuse of the relief system prompted the RM of White Valley to issue a proclamation, posted at various points within the district, which "demand[ed] payment [for taxes and relief] and point[ed] out the penalty for disposing of a crop while owing for such."[165]

Settlers like widower Ms. Catherine Slovak provide a fine example of the problems associated with the disposal of a crop while owing for such. She was conditionally given $485 in aid relief from the RM "subject to advice from [her] mortgage company that they are prepared to forestay foreclosure proceedings."[166] The loan company granted its assurance to the RM that it would not foreclose and the RM distributed the aid only to find out later in the year that she had sold her oat stacks to Mr. J.M. MacDonald. These stacks were subsequently seized.[167] Council pursued the matter briefly, but, understanding her position and inclining toward leniency, the case was dropped and the stacks remained with Mr. MacDonald. The Slovak case, though, illustrates the point that settlers looked after themselves first and the RM usually came a distant second. Had Slovak resided in the appropriately named RM of Big Stick, however, her fate might have been different.

Big Stick is a heavily German region not too far distant from Hatton, north and west about forty miles. This particular RM was much more aggressive in temperament than its counterparts in White Valley, Clinworth, or Reno. Big Stick embraced debt collection like no other RM did. Perhaps

Big Stick was the very RM that J.N. Bayne had in mind when he informed the Department of Municipal Affairs that "many councils ... are putting forth special efforts to improve the financial standing of their rural municipalities."[168]

Big Stick first approved a by-law that attempted to pursue tax collection on land that had already been lost or signed over to creditors.[169] Council tried inducements in 1922 during the "Pay Your Taxes" campaign when it pledged to exempt from seizure "not more than 25 percent" of any crop planted with relief seed.[170] With Big Stick carrying heavy relief debt, council passed a motion to the effect that the "[municipal] collector be instructed to seize and sell anything on [a] farm" whose owner owed taxes or relief debt.[171] Council preceded this motion with a warning posted in the district addressed to "all parties who have received seed grain relief" and demanding "settlement within two weeks."[172] But still, Big Stick councillors felt they were working with one hand tied behind their backs and so they challenged a provincial statute that prohibited the seizure of agricultural equipment between April and September: Big Stick wanted to be enabled "to seize [property] at any time."[173]

At the same time as councilmen were wrestling with the debt collection from their neighbours, they were also apparently having difficulty keeping track of the number of people leaving the area. Councillor Begley thus moved a motion to bring some order to the chaos by declaring it "the duty of every councilor to report ... the name of any settler leaving the district."[174] This frenzy of debt collection and settler-tracking in which Big Stick council was helplessly mired was capped off when it turned its gun sights on horses. Council ordered the shooting of two wild horses that were "trespassing" on nearby land and apparently making a "public nuisance" of themselves. For good measure, the high-strung council agreed to "shoot the two horses" owned by the RM as well.[175]

In fairness, Big Stick was not the only RM to show its frustration over a problem with no real solution and which RMs were simply not structurally designed to handle. White Valley, for example, embarked on an aggressive collection campaign as well and agreed to "seize [any] implements or buildings on skids" from farms that looked abandoned.[176] Maple Creek similarly voted to "take any necessary action" to collect tax and relief debt.[177] At the peak of the crisis in 1922, Maple Creek councillor E. Suval argued in favour of exerting "the full force of the law" in debt collection and added "no one shall be exempt."[178]

Alberta dryland municipalities were struck by the same problem between 1917 and 1924. Desperate to collect on the bills incurred by purchasing and distributing "feed, seed, coal and groceries," an unnamed municipal official, with an understated minimalism that would have made Ernest Hemingway proud, remarked that "farm properties were seized for tax arrears and so forth."[179] The RM of Clinworth also undertook aggressive collection because it was broke and councillor Thomas Armstrong pointed out that "this municipality cannot carry them [farmers] any longer."[180]

It was not just RMs but the province itself that could no longer carry settlers struck by drought. Premier Martin held a meeting in 1921 with a select group of organizations (which included the young Saskatchewan Association of Rural Municipalities, SARM) to inform them that the province would not be supporting calls for a moratorium on debt: mediation yes, moratorium no. For Premier Martin, embracing the moratorium would be akin to saying the province is bankrupt.[181] And in 1921, that was not very far off the mark. The Farm Loans Board was "stretched to the snapping point." It received 1,500 applications that it could not fill. By 1922, the board had spent $8.5 million.[182] It was not just the RMs that could not carry farmers any longer; neither could the province.

Unlike Big Stick, however, neither Clinworth nor any of the other RMs sought to challenge the tax statute that limited times of property seizure. Councillors backed away from this approach because, as Clinworth's W.R. Ducie explained, "given the circumstances, this [was] not an opportune time to make seizures" except when it was plainly evident that a farm had been abandoned, or, to use the RMs archaic phrase, when a farmer had "absconded."[183] This reluctance to pursue hyper-aggressive collection measures did not prevent Clinworth, however, from taking "immediate action ... to protect the interests of the municipalities."[184] It was a fine line between the desire for self-preservation and the desire to help.

Such measured and tempered action, admittedly, also appeared in the RM of Big Stick. Unable to browbeat bankrupt settlers into paying tax and relief debt (and limited in the number of horses RM officials could cathartically shoot), Big Stick instead expanded its earlier 25 per cent seed-relief-crop seizure exemption to 50 per cent. This was an exemption that applied to all exhausted settlers "whose land is under application for title by the municipality."[185] Big Stick also, in a touching motion during the dying days of such chivalric ideas, declared that debts on all lands owned and worked by widows like Catherine Slovak were cancelled.[186]

Municipalities were not the only entities seizing land and property. Third party creditors and loan companies were busy taking land on debt. In some instances, land was free of debt but was simply handed back to the Crown as useless: such was likely the case for Anton Huelskamp of Masonville. As a consequence of these varied threads of bankruptcy, Big Stick urged the province to cancel all non-municipal liens against seized land in 1924 because "a great many quarter sections … are becoming the property of the municipality" and could not be sold at the ubiquitous November tax sale until all encumbrances were cleared.[187]

The crisis of the drylands struck at the very heart of municipal life in innumerable ways. White Valley councillors found themselves so "financially embarrassed" that, "owing to present conditions," they voted to eliminate their pay. They opted instead to be paid only transportation costs to and from meetings, which in 1922 were held at different locations throughout the RM each month.[188] Up north at Clinworth, owing to the condition of "things in general," council declined to send anyone to the annual SARM convention.[189] Council also temporarily cancelled all road work because the RM, at that point, was "cut off from any funds at the bank."[190] North of Clinworth, in the RM of Oakdale (which would lose 250 settlers between 1920 and 1927), the manager of the bank at Coleville boarded the windows, locked the door, and left town in 1922, another sure sign that "things in general" were not good.[191]

Apparently the bank's head office felt there was a lack of local business, a reason that the local Grain Growers Association rejected. The GGA, at the same time as it began a search for a new bank, "proteste[ed] against this inefficient system."[192] Likewise the manager of the Union Bank in Lemsford, just south of Clinworth, also fled. Clinworth councillor W.L. Lawton urged council to undertake efforts at attracting another bank because, in a fit of unreasonable optimism, he proclaimed that "municipal accounts alone would make it a success."[193]

The most prevalent and universal way in which municipalities were affected by the crisis, and also a fine barometer of the overall general financial health of the RMs, was the matter of schools. At one time or another during the crisis, RMs were required to close schools either temporarily or permanently, and they also reduce or even suspended teacher salaries. RMs and their school boards also frequently amalgamated school districts because of declining population. These problems occurred in the Alberta portion of the drylands as well.[194]

Financing schools in a region prone to crop failure was a chronic problem. The RM of Reno explains: "the ability of the Municipality to advance the required yearly school payments depend[s] entirely upon its collection of taxes."[195] Schools simply could not operate if the settlers could not pay their taxes and taxes could not be paid if the crop failures and abandonment continued. RM of Reno Secretary Treasurer Lewis Harvey pointed out that it cost roughly $1,000 annually to operate a school and asked how it is possible, given the circumstances, to continue funding local education in this way.[196] Indeed, by 1922, the annual reports of schools in the Alberta drybelt were so saturated with notes regarding the financial failure of this or that school or school district that, as historian David Jones notes, these reports came more to resemble "economic resumes than pedagogical essays."[197]

Reno set out to solve some of the difficulties associated with financing education by various means. School appropriations were reduced in 1920, which lowered the monthly costs from levels that Harvey believed were "excessive," though no details are given.[198] Long-suffering one-room schoolhouse teachers in Reno were next to feel the effects of abandonment and crop failure as their salaries were reduced because "the opinion of council seemed to be that there was the possibility of further savings under this item."[199] Reno also took steps to amalgamate its school districts because the population losses had resulted in the presence of school districts without any children.

The beleaguered town of Hatton experienced the same pressures to alter school district boundaries. Having lost about half its population in the 1921 fire and more since that time, the town fathers in 1924 extended the boundaries of the town's school district further and further into the rural areas, trying to replace the children whose parents had fled with the children of settlers who would eventually leave.[200] Dr. Jones notes that many school districts in Alberta engaged in this practice too "aggressively coveting and invading adjoining territory" to widen their tax base.[201] Sadly for communities like Hatton, which tried this very thing, it only brought "a brief rush of euphoria" because the drought was stronger than the will to stay. The kids left before long.

As they did with relief, most municipalities were obliged to take out lines of credit to keep schools open. Big Stick took out a $16,000 loan so it could get money to the schools "as soon as the funds [were] available" during the parched year of 1921.[202] Securing the loan had actually been the result of an earlier failed effort at collecting overdue taxes in late winter 1921. By 1926, even though abandonment was slowing, Big Stick council demanded that the province "enact legislation as will place responsibility for financing the schools on the province as a whole" because, as council tersely indicated, it was "impossible to keep schools open owing to repeated crop failures."[203]

The RM of Maple Creek was forced temporarily to shut down all of its schools during the crisis. Councillor G.H. Hoffman explained that, since "the borrowing powers [of the RM] are absolutely exhausted" and, furthermore, since council "is at sea as to how to finance [education] until something definite can be ascertained in regards to credit," all schools in the district were shut down in 1922. From November of that year until April 1923, and much to the likely delight of young wheat-chewing gun-toting prairie lads, all schools were shut down.[204]

Maple Creek financed nine schools and this was not an inexpensive proposition. The Haycreek School, for example, cost $1,000 per year, Somerset cost $770 and Aylesford was a little more reasonable at $374.48.[205] But for an RM that had to cancel gopher-hunting bounties, these costs were another fiscal mountain council simply did not have the strength to climb. So the RM furnished the school districts with a list of ratepayers whose taxes were in arrears (and again here we must note the re-appearance of the teacher/councillor/friend-turned-debt-collector dynamic) and urged them to do what they could to collect.[206] Clinworth followed suit in 1924, shutting down all schools in the district from January to March "in view of the adverse conditions and the probable shortage of funds."[207] Maple Creek also turned over collection of school taxes to the teacher and the local school board and this action too was apparently common practice throughout the drylands. Dr. Jones relates the story of the Crocus Plains school board, which wrote a letter reminding one particular resident that the school cannot function without funds. Then the board members laid it on the line: "If [the tax bill] is not paid by [October] your children will be expelled."[208] Such was education in a dry and dusty land.

The hard-hit RM of Clinworth experienced similar challenges as those faced by other dryland RMs, though in one instance, absurdity bounded into the room but to the delight of no one. The Holborn school district petitioned both council and the provincial Department of Education for a new school and council had very real difficulty restraining its impatience with the request which, fittingly, was approved by the Department of Education. Councillors unanimously rejected the idea, noting the proposed school was to be located "on such poor and sandy lands [that there would be] no prospect of ever collecting any taxes."[209] One can hear the stunned incredulity in the voices of the councillors. The councilmen regarded the request merely as "another financial burden when the load should be lightened."

Clinworth also rejected a later request from another school district, which wanted to establish a new school at a new site. Council patiently informed those who had made the request that "the district [was] being depleted of its residents" and they added that "soon there will be no children left."[210] The RM of Reno, whacked stupid by drought, wrote to ask the province "whether it [was] necessary to pay school taxes to a district where no school [was] in operation."[211] In this latter case, settlers had moved on and, once again, there were simply no children left.

The schools crisis was just as bad if not worse across the border in Alberta. The newly elected UFA Premier Herbert Greenfield in 1921 poured money into reopening many of the schools, which, like their counterparts in Saskatchewan, had been closed because the drought had impaired the settlers ability to pay taxes and fund schools.[212] Premier Greenfield also pledged to assist "farmer sufferers" in planting fall rye seed.

Premier Greenfield's valiant and noble effort, though, is what is commonly known as 'throwing good money after bad.' In the first place, educational infrastructure was in terrible shape. The toilets in a Sunnynook school were so stinking and wretched from lack of care that "the children are unable to use them and are using a barn instead."[213] The barn in a nearby school was in worse shape than the Sunnynook toilets. The barn housed fifteen horses five days a week but for eight months they hadn't been cleaned and, as a consequence, the kids left their horses tied up outside "rather than wade into the manure."[214]

In addition to pens and pencils, one dryland teacher in Wardlow, Alberta, also requested a coal pail, a fire shovel, a water pail, a wash basin, a dust pan, a broom, "an axe or an axe handle," three panes of glass, door knobs, a fence, and, of course, repairs to the barn and other buildings.[215]

The crisis in the schools, the too-heavy burden of debt, and the structure of the relief system: all of these elements contributed to a sense of desperation and, finally, near capitulation and surrender. On average, it seems to have taken between three and four years, from 1919 to 1923, for RMs to be pushed to the breaking point and for dissolution to be openly discussed. Big Stick stands as representative of the thought amongst councillors in the drylands when it drafted a 1922 resolution that reads, in part:

> Whereas land in this and other municipalities in south west Saskatchewan is very poor and unsuited to farming;

and whereas occupants of these lands are unable to make an existence on said lands. Therefore be it resolved (that council petition government) to enter into some arrangement with dominion authorities whereby said people be given a chance to locate elsewhere.[216]

Big Stick's resolution was simply restating what the province had been told several times. In 1914, it was the Pope Commission; in 1920, it was the Better Farming Conference; and, in 1921, an internal memo was handed to Premier William Martin that reminded him of the three principal conclusion of the BFC: a soil classification survey, community pastures, and "removal of settlers."[217] These three points, it is worth nothing here, were the basic founding principles of the Prairie Farm Rehabilitation Administration, which was formally set up in the later 1930s.

This resolution from Big Stick was the result of five years of drought, failure, and the pressures created by providing relief. By 1922, in the words of Big Stick council, the failing settlers had in fact become "a burden to the municipality" and, like Clinworth, council decided it could not carry them anymore.[218] Clinworth actually sent Mr. Thomas Armstrong and Mr. F.R. Shortreed to a meeting in Regina in 1921 to see about removing settlers "located on too sandy and rocky lands." Big Stick council said unanimously that they were "strongly opposed to the injustice of the [relief] system."[219] The substance of that resolution would sit undisturbed until 1935, when the always vocal Big Stick would again protest again the relief system, this time under conditions even worse than councillors ever thought possible.

This state of affairs led to calls for dissolution, a move that would have stripped the RMs of all of their responsibilities and autonomy and would have ultimately been the first step toward undoing settlement in the south and west Saskatchewan plains. The town of Hatton, for example, voted itself out of existence when its population dwindled to only a handful in 1934. Big Stick councillors, though, backed away from the idea because they believed "it would not be in the interests of the ratepayers to take a vote against self-government on such short notice."[220]

The RM of Reno provides a similar glimpse of what occurred in the drylands at the height of the crisis. Floundering under heavy debt, angry ratepayers in the RM of Reno converged on a one-room schoolhouse on the heat-ravaged plains of Vidora in mid-summer 1921. The group, whose spokesman was Neils Neilson, passed a motion to the effect that they had "no confidence in the officers of RM 51 [and] call upon the reeve and council of the municipality to resign."[221] This letter was presented to council but was never discussed, at least in an open forum. The RM survived this minor drought-induced revolt long enough to inform the province that council "will not be able to finance applications for relief during the winter" and asked the government to assume the burden.[222] If the intent of Neilson and the others was to force the RM to suspend relief due to fears of bankruptcy and dissolution, thereby compelling the government to assume the burden, then it was a petition that appeared to have been successful.

Support for dissolution grew quite strong in the RM of White Valley. In September 1921, with the RM staggering under relief debt, council agreed to hold a meeting to discuss dissolution because, as they put it, "the expense of self-government can no longer be justified."[223] Since council "cannot be asked to pay bills when funds are not available," it decided that "all applications for relief be denied." Council passed a resolution at that meeting that asked the province "to immediately disorganize this unit as a municipality or in some way arrange that [the debt load] be minimized."[224] While the latter half of this resolution obviously held out the hope that the problem could be remedied, the substance reflects the growing and very real desperation in which the municipalities were mired because they had taken on responsibilities too large for their slender shoulders.

Alberta dryland municipalities shared with Saskatchewan exactly the same pressures for dissolution. One of the hardest hit regions of the drylands, the Lomond area in the Municipal District (MD) of Clifton, is a good example: "conditions were hopeless. People were moving away. Taxes and seed grain and relief liens were not being paid and land forfeited for taxes."[225] After some years of this, it became clearly evident that "special attention to this area was needed" and so finally, in 1937, Clifton was disorganized and put into Special Area Number Four, where it remained until 1951 when a portion of that MD was incorporated into the newly formed County of Vulcan.[226] The very term Special Areas speaks volumes.

Simply cancelling relief aid was obviously the easiest way to solve the problem and Clinworth took steps to that effect in 1921. Earlier in the crisis, in 1920, when it had become clear that the problem did not lessen but in fact grew each year, Clinworth tightened up rules governing aid. Any settler who was approved for aid was granted relief only after being interviewed and questioned by council. By 1921, council moved a motion stopping all relief with the caveat that "only cases of absolute necessity will be considered."[227] Council member John Buck posted notices to this effect throughout communities within the RM. Big Stick was similarly unable to continue providing relief aid. Indeed, of the RMs financing road and bridge building, councillors felt the province ought to "do road work themselves and allow the ratepayers to work on road [gangs] to enable them to pay their taxes."[228]

Closed schools, lost and absconding settlers, debt-collection, failure – all of these elements point toward a worsening crisis, but nothing speaks to the issue of chronic land abandonment in the drylands like tax sale registers. These records do not flinch. Literally thousands of parcels of land were seized by municipalities during the course of the crisis because thousands of settlers owed too much money to the RMs. Most of the liens against the lands were registered by the RMs who sought to recover relief costs and tax debt because of crop failure. Tax sales were one of the essential elements in the dryland crisis. The seized land most often represented either a failed settler or one who has fled. The revenue generated by the sale of the lands represented one small way that the still-young municipalities could keep themselves solvent and functioning. In many instances, abandoned land was sold for a mere fifty dollars in back taxes. In fact, F.H. Auld made the confidential suggestion to a member of the Alberta Survey Board that the crisis had the added benefit of "mak[ing] it easier for those who remain to establish themselves."[229] And, in a way, he was right. Historian Chester Martin noted in 1939 that the size of the average farm in Saskatchewan's pre-emption districts (the drylands) doubled during the 1920s. That growth likely began at the ubiquitous November tax sale.

Bearing in mind that much of the tax sale information is incomplete, the records that do remain provide a tantalizing glimpse of economic life and explain, in the most basic way possible, what was actually occurring in the drylands during the 1920s. The records for the RM of Reno, for example, show that between 1921 and 1925, 419 parcels of land were seized and sold by the municipality.[230] This tax seizure/sale figure means that, conceivably, 210 settlers abandoned their lands during this time period (each settler likely had a minimum of 320 acres). This obscure picture is enhanced and complemented by the incomplete collection files of the Department of Municipal Affairs, which include relief collection cases for the Vidora district, which was located within the RM of Reno.

E.E. Erikson fled to the south-east corner of Saskatchewan, near Kennedy, just about as far away from the drylands as one can get in Saskatchewan and still farm. He rented the land he left behind to a neighbour. Erikson had $1,500 in various liens registered against his land and the province tracked him down, demanded payment, and threatened legal proceedings if the debt was not cleared.[231] Erikson explained to the province that he could not afford to repay relief aid because of crop failure, though he promised to give the Department a payment when he could. The Erikson case demonstrates the nub of the problem. He had suffered "five years in succession without a crop," which was another way of saying he had made no money off the land since he began farming it in 1916.[232] The correspondence stops with an empty and futile promise to pay. In 1926, with the tenant farmer now gone and the land going back to prairie, the file closes with one word: "abandoned."

The list of the province's collection agent goes on and it retains a certain ghostly quality: Paul Thack of Vidora, section 9-3-36-3, "back to the United States"; Wilson James of Govenlock, 21-2-29-3, "abandoned"; section 22-2-39-3, "abandoned"; section 27-2-29-3, "crop failure"; section 1-3-29-3, "no answer to my letter"; section 35-2-29-3, "this man is gone."[233] A widow who hung on scraping a desperate existence off her farm near the non-existent town of Lonesome Butte found her life "very hard" according to the province's oddly sympathetic collection agent. He added, "there will be no payment on this [debt] at all this year; perhaps not at any time."[234]

Hugh MacDonald was likewise chased by the province's collection agents but informed them he could not pay because, like Erikson, he "hasn't received a cent off that land since 1916."[235] The file on section 20-3-26-3 closes out four years later in 1926: "land abandoned; should be forfeited."

Just east of Vidora, in the tiny community of Senate, entire groups of people fled en masse from the dry lands. E.H. Lloyd led the effort to remove forty-six of his fellow Welshman and their families from the Senate region because of drought and failure. They were removed, with government aid, to an area north of Tisdale, where they either rented or purchased land. According to the CNR land agent, "they seem to be well satisfied with the country and the people."[236]

Tax seizures/sales closely followed the arc of drought and crop failure. In the town of Maple Creek, for example, just six lots were sold at the November tax sale in 1915–16, whereas sixty-seven were sold in 1914/15.[237] 1914 was the year the first total crop failure hit the south and west plains. In 1920, the sale figure climbs back up to forty-five. The number of lots sold climbed to fifty-five in 1923, and spiked at 103 in 1924.[238] It is of interest to consider the names of the purchasers of lands at these tax sales. G. Blythman, the owner of the still-extant and flourishing local real estate firm in Maple Creek, was a prominent buyer of these lands, as were some members of the RM council itself. The tax sale records also corroborate the population losses estimated by the Department of Municipal Affairs: between 1920 and 1926, the town of Maple Creek lost 520 people.[239]

In some cases, the tax sale registry is unavailable or non-existent. In this instance it is helpful to consider the number of tax cancellations mentioned in the Minutes of the RM meetings and which, like tax sales, indicate that a property has been abandoned or forfeited in some fashion and thus taxes had been cancelled.

The RM of White Valley cancelled taxes on 140 parcels of land between 1920 and 1924, noting beside some entries that the land had been "abandoned."[240] Big Stick council minutes also reveal what would be found in the tax sale registries if they were available. In one week in 1926, council approved the sale of ten parcels of land seized earlier by the RM. On another arbitrary date, April 1927, nine parcels were sold.[241] Big Stick, like all other dryland RM's, obtained this land through seizure.

The long-dissolved RM of Royal Canadian in the Eatonia district seized and sold 426 parcels of land between 1924 and 1927.[242] In many instances, the land was simply signed over or "purchased" by the municipality. Oftentimes, the land was bought by prominent members of the community. The name of the physician for Eatonia shows up frequently at the RM's tax sales. But it was not always the usual suspects purchasing land. At fifty dollars per quarter section, or about thirty cents per acre, the tax sales were, in their own way, very democratic. Low-wage earners such as Mantario teacher Vera Turner, Eatonia Nurse Miss K. Crimp, and Ferryman William Cleghorn all purchased land at these sales.[243] Mr. Cleghorn worked the ferry at Estuary, a town that nestled the banks of the South Saskatchewan River west of Leader. Between 1920 and 1927, that small community lost 302 people.[244] Today, aside from a few houses and a cement-encased bank vault, nothing of the town remains. In some instances, entire houses were purchased for a pittance at these sales. G. Schneider bought a house in Clinworth for $175 on the quarter located at 4-19-24-3.[245]

For many people, the sales offered a chance to increase land holdings, whatever the cost. Bessarabian immigrant Gottlieb Anhorn (the man whom Hatton council ordered to fill in the cellars in the town properties that he owned because they were a "public nuisance"), had a wife and five children and, being a German from south-Russia, had few places to go when the crisis hit Hatton. So, in true pioneer spirit, Anhorn made the best of a bad situation and "in the year 1925, when neighboring farmers began to move away owing to poor crop conditions, Mr. Anhorn bought and leased additional land."[246]

Using tax sales as a barometer still has limits for it does not take into account all of the land seized. Recall the RM of Big Stick trying to wrest a tax debt out of a parcel of land against which liens had been filed by the Beaver Lumber Company. Clinworth councillors were trying to sell land that had been seized or let back to the Department of Interior. Council wrote to the Department of Interior in 1924 and asked that liens be removed against fourteen parcels of land because the encumbrances were blocking the RMs attempts to sell this land.[247] Unable to resist a parting shot, councillor James Wardell kindly pointed out the Department had an obligation to cancel the liens because "in the first instance [these lands] should have never been settled."[248]

In 1926, Deputy Auld tried to make sense of the crisis that had just passed. Auld had apparently examined the homestead entry records of Montana, records that included the previous occupations of its settlers and, in a radio address delivered that winter, drew parallels with the Saskatchewan experience. In Auld's view, Montana was settled by people who should not have been farming in the first place: along with the doctors, lawyers, and clerks who tried to farm, the previous occupations of settlers also included "two deep sea divers," "one world rover," and "two wrestlers."[249] Making breathtaking leaps of logic, then, Auld concluded that "under these conditions, need we be surprised if there have been some failures [in Saskatchewan]."[250]

But what he failed to consider is that while drifters, adventurers, and "wrestlers," certainly made up a not-insignificant part of the *early* settlement years immediately after opening up the drylands in 1908, many of those who abandoned their homesteads during the 1920s were made up of people who had either initially settled the region in the early days or who had come up in the years after 1914. Mr. Anton Huelskamp of the RM of Mantario or Mr. Phillip Konschuh should be taken as average examples: both farmed in the drylands for about six years before being beaten-to-staggering by the heat in 1923.

It might be argued that the abandonment was caused, in part, by the tendency of settlers to "stake all on one crop," and this certainly contains more than a little truth. Auld certainly believed that farming for the mere pursuit of cash through the growth of wheat crops was one of the problems that perpetuated the abandonment because "when that crop failed the year's operations were a total loss."[251] Auld had always fervently supported diversification: cows, poultry, hogs, "even some bees." "Our slogan," he wistfully told a radio audience in the winter of 1926, "might well be 'a sideline on every farm.'"[252] True enough and indeed there is much to commend Auld's assertion that it was neither wise nor good farming to grow wheat to the exclusion of all else.

Auld did not acknowledge, however, the results of a Department of Agriculture report from 1925, which pointed out the excessive costs of diversification. The committee listed six hopelessly obvious reasons to diversify, such as "increased income," but it found eleven formidable reasons that would prevent diversification. These reasons included the high costs associated with purchasing cattle or chickens, the money required to adapt existing infrastructure, and the high cost of the equipment associated with diversification.[253] For settlers whose average yield per bushel between 1917 and 1927 lay in the five to ten bushels per acre range, for settlers who were busy working on road gangs to feed their families and pay off relief debt, diversification sounded good but repeated monotonous crop failure always kept it just out of reach.

Auld would change his mind when the greatest calamity of all would descend a few short years hence. In 1934, with relief aid spinning out of control into millions, Auld admitted that much of the crisis of the 1930s could have been avoided "by land settlement policy which would have prevented occupancy of sub-marginal lands."[254] With the repeated crises on the south plains, Auld said "we must, finally, judge a locality on its ability to sustain life" and the drylands were insistent on proving they would not.[255] But Auld's epiphany was still a few years in the distance and even then it was provisional, contingent.

At the end of the crisis of the 1920s, ensconced in the pleasing glow of progress and brief prosperity, a persistent and telling sense of disquiet evidently nagged at Auld for he took the unusual step of writing Stanford University in California asking their thoughts and opinions on the south and west plains. Professor C.P. Wright admitted to some confusion. He said the presence of prosperous farmers located next to thousands of abandoned farms "pretty nearly leads one to confess ignorance on the whole situation there."[256] Why should some settlers succeed where thousands of others fail? That remained, for Auld, a question to which there seemed to be no mathematical, structured, logical answer.

And so the 1920s roared. In the late 1920s, the future once again held all of the possible. Deputy Auld, his fellow mandarins, the burned-out settlers, and the beleaguered rural municipalities would be given a few short years respite, a few years of warm and pleasing comfort in which to bask, contented. Ragged and tattered hope would nervously reappear in 1928 (as it did in 1915–16), when pioneers grew one of the biggest crops in the history of Saskatchewan. But then the exception would exit and make place for the rule. Hope would then exit the south plains for very nearly a full decade, making room, as it did in 1917, for "hardship, misery … and gloom." The rehearsals were over. The roof caved in. The wolf finally arrived at the door. The bill had finally come due.

Before the "Dirty Thirties"

CAPTAIN JOHN PALLISER, YOUNG, LEGGY, AND IN HIS PRIME (SAB
R-A4962, C. 2).

Captain Palliser, 1852, after his first visit to western
Canada to hunt buffalo (SAB R-A1563, c. 1).

"THE MEANEST MAN IN CANADA" FRANK OLIVER IN AN UNDATED PHOTO (SAB R-A12958).

The Deputy resplendent in Mason regalia (SAB R-A7884).

DOWNTOWN HATTON IN BETTER DAYS (SAB R-B9178).

A VIBRANT ESTUARY DURING THE AFTERNOON OF AN ANNUAL
SPORTS DAY (SPORTS DAYS WERE USUALLY FOLLOWED BY A DANCE IN
THE EVENING); ESTUARY WAS NESTLED IN A VALLEY ON THE BANKS OF
THE SOUTH SASKATCHEWAN (SAB R-B11592).

"Each room has a Brussels Rug." The refined Palace Hotel in Estuary before it burned down in 1923 (SAB R-A23358).

They were amongst the first to leave. Settlers fleeing the Vanguard area in south-west Saskatchewan and "moving north" in 1919; note the telephone pole (SAB R-A2727).

Philip Konschuh, his wife Marie, and young son David.
Courtesy of *Memories of Cluny* (Winnipeg: InterCollegiate
Press, 1985) and Stanley and Haddie Konschuh.

The Konschuhs fleeing the Fox Valley district 1923. Adam, or perhaps it is young David, is taking a rest. Courtesy of *Memories of Cluny* (Winnipeg: InterCollegiate Press, 1985) and Stanley and Haddie Konschuh.

Proof that grain could be grown in Mankota country. The 1928 harvest before the construction of grain elevators (SAB R-A506).

Interlude:
A Collection of Absurdities

Absurdity existed everywhere and in such large quantities on the south and west plains during the dry years that it's a shame no one tried to farm it. Like Russian thistle and gophers, absurdity was everywhere between 1914 and 1937. Absurdity's handmaidens – insanity, suicide, drunkenness, and general idiocy – were also present. It may strike one as insensitive to draw attention to these elements of life but they remain just that, elements of life and they are just as real as happiness, courage, sadness, persistence. The good, the bad, the tragic, the profoundly sad, the wonderful, the silly, and the ridiculous are all part of one piece.

There are things that occurred on the south plains that can only either bring a tear to one's eye or reduce one to helpless laughter because the border between infinite desperation and infinite absurdity was crossed so often and with such enthusiasm by so many people and officials during the crises of the south and west plains that it is hard to tell where the misery ends and the ridiculous begins. We might begin with insanity.

Insanity is defined as a "derangement of the mind," and it seems that many settlers had been going insane before proving-up their homesteads: so much so that government officials quietly amended section twenty of the Dominion Lands Act to ensure that only the cultivation requirements of settlement duties (i.e., keeping a certain amount of land under cultivation) need be satisfied "in the event of any person ... becoming insane or mentally incapable."[1]

That a disproportionate number of south plains settlers had lost their marbles trying to farm was in fact one of the chief findings of a study undertaken by University of Saskatchewan professor E.C. Hope. Hope was a "professor of soils" who travelled throughout the south plains in the mid-1930s. Hope considered the histories of thirty-nine abandoned farms in the RM of Wood River. The average number of owners for each farm was three and the average length of operation was ten years. Hope also came to the unfortunate realization that a number of the occupiers of these lands "either committed suicide or went insane."[2]

Of course, defining insanity was fraught with difficulty. There was "a man by the name of Dahl" who apparently went insane on the drylands. It seems some neighbours were riding by his place one evening in the early stages of the 1914 crop failure and heard noises. Dahl was inside his house "tearing the whole inside out of the house and generally smashing things up." Restraint evidently proved useless because "he had the strength of five men." His neighbours tried to subdue him but in the course of this "he [Mr. Dahl] had torn off most of their clothes as well as his own."[3] Serendipitously, a doctor was nearby and walked into the room full of grunting, wrestling, half-naked men: he took one glance at Dahl and "pronounced the man insane." Mr. Dahl was carted off to Regina.

Suicide back in the crisis years was still front page news. Entirely lacking any and all sense of the delicate (and one can only assume that being delicate on the south plains was something upon which generous frowns were proffered), the editors wrote that a man accomplished his grim task by the following means: "[he] put two shots from a number twelve hammerless shotgun into his head."[4] Another man in the Glidden district located very near the RM of Happyland, "had been depressed about drought conditions" in the terrible year of 1937 and killed himself. He had survived the Boer War in South Africa.[5]

Although no formal academic studies have been done, drunkenness, too, was likely a not-insignificant element of settler life during the worst years of the crises. There was the constant drink-inducing threat that one's aid relief would be terminated if one was found to be drinking, and in the 1930s, in a small community or RM, it would be very hard to hide drunkenness, which likely led to grim and infrequent bouts of solitary boozing. But serendipity smiled. A cure for drunkenness was developed in the midst of the first absolute crop failure in the drylands in 1914. "Alcura #1" was sold for a dollar a box. It helped "build the system [and] steadies the nerves."

This wonder-drug could be administered by "any wife or mother wanting to restore a dear one to health and usefulness."[6]

The RM of Pinto Creek was brutalized terribly during the droughts of both the twenties and the thirties. Councilmen there tried to restore their settlers to health and usefulness by shutting down the bars and beer halls during the crisis. "The government beer stores" council assured a worried population would "serve the needs of the public very well."[7] Anything, one must suppose, was better than sniffing ether.

There was a certain "Edward Pim, Inventor," who dabbled in "experimental research" involving "ether." He claimed in the drought years of the 1920s to have found a cost-free way to generate electricity by using gravity. Pim tried to interest Premier Charles Dunning in his discovery because it was, according to Pim's own estimation, "one of the greatest discoveries of modern times!"[8] Gravity-made electricity was hailed as the energy that would enable farmers to wash clothes, do chores, cook meals and, generally speaking, make all of life "really worthwhile." Pim's invention might have actually gone over well with the women of the south plains. According to the Rowell-Sirois commission, it seems that there were very few "domestic conveniences" available to women during the dry years. In fact, one of the few labour-saving devices to be found in most south plains homes was "some sort of washing machine," which was apparently "operated by a small gasoline engine."[9] For women wishing to upgrade from gas-powered laundry machines, gravity-generated electricity would have had a natural appeal. Pim, like ace rainmaker Charles Hatfield, was one of the last of the nineteenth-century snake-oil salesmen who preyed upon Naïve Credulity before it met its match and ultimate death at the hands of Cruel Irony.

In addition to drunkenness, credulity, suicide, and insanity, there was also no shortage of delusion. D.C. Kirk was a settler who "farmed" land very near to the Great Sand Hills, the informal and unofficial border between the west-central and south-west drylands. Kirk explained in a letter to Premier Dunning in the summer of 1921 that he "awoke and found himself sitting up in bed" one evening because he had "seen a vision of what will in time take place" in the drylands.[10] Kirk had dreamed of a colossal construction project to develop lakes and canals for irrigation in order that the drought and soil problems might be solved absolutely. Swift Current council also dreamed up a similar project in 1937 and tried to interest the province in damming up the Swift Current Creek, but it was less delusional and driven instead by desperation. In Kirk's fevered estimation, however, such a project would cost roughly $15 million ("the best money ever spent") and it would ensure "splendid crops and millions of bushels," which he not unreasonably suggested "would be a wonderful asset in paying off our national debt." The project, as Kirk dreamed it that hot sweaty evening, would be "the greatest enterprise in the history of the dominion."[11] Kirk, along with "hundreds of others," was on the verge of losing his farm, though whether he could be "pronounced insane" or even delusional is a matter for debate.

The care of the deranged, the insane, the delusional, and perhaps even the alcoholic fell, not surprisingly, to rural municipalities. The tiny community of Burstall, located just south of the RM of Happyland, paid fifteen dollars to Ferdinand Zeitner of Leader (formerly Prussia) for the upkeep of one Jacob Grentz, "a feeble-minded person of no fixed abode."[12] It seems that no one was left to care for Mr. Grentz and so that responsibility fell to the RM whose councillors indelicately recorded that Mr. Grentz was "a proper subject for a mental hospital."[13]

Insanity, suicide, drunkenness, delusions, and idiocy all formed a part of what passed for life during the worst of the several crises to hit the drylands. There were often even combustible, highly emotional over-reactions to even the kindest and gentlest of measures. The province, for example, passed a 1936 Act, which evidently afforded some small measure of protection to the hated and detested coyote of the south plains. But two Swift Current councillors had others ideas. Councillors Koch and Dyck both moved a motion declaring the coyote "a pest" and, furthermore, "rather than being protected should have a bounty put on its destruction"[14] That bounty finally came years later in 2009 when Saskatchewan's popular Agriculture Minister Mr. Bob Bjornerud announced the long-awaited twenty-dollar bounty. Proof of a kill was required in the form of coyote paws, which were to be cut off (all four of them) and handed in to grateful administrators at the local RM office.

In 1934, when the crisis was at its peak, and relief had become a part of daily life, the Saskatoon *Star-Phoenix* wrote a story about the closure of that city's relief office. It was closed to save money: an "economy measure" it was called.[15] The story quoted a common saying of those dying days of the frontier: many settlers joked that they have "come into the country with nothing and still have it."

It was lunatic laughter; crying and laughing at the same time.

John King had hard times in the drylands. He had strange times. He and his friend Pete Kuczek came up to the south country in 1913 and, judging by the laundry list of things which went wrong, one can safely assume that he was pleased when the droughts finally forced him out ten years later.

Like many pioneers, Mr. King built a shack upon arriving at his homestead a little west of the Great Sand Hills. In the spring, both he and Mr. Kuczek went looking for the stakes but found that "my shack was on another guys land."[16] Mr. King's difficulty in locating his homestead stakes may have had something to do with rancid, embittered cattlemen who were known to alight on dark evenings to tear up homestead stakes and throw them away, angry at the loss of their lands to the mossbacks.[17] Or the stakes could have just been buried under the snow.

At any rate, Mr. King asked his neighbour, Marty Solberg, to help him pull the shack to the right location, and when Mr. Solberg showed up the next day, the oxen broke through the harness because the house was so heavy. Mr. King removed the dirt he had used as insulation and the next day, when harnessed to the suitably lightened house the oxen "nearly ran away with it." This was Mr. King's first memory of the drylands. From here on in, things just stayed weird.

While working in Alberta, he paid a neighbour forty dollars to plough his land, but "all he done was to run down the land with one furrow."[18] Later on, this same neighbour had Mr. King co-sign a note for "$27.00 worth of chickens," but the neighbour defaulted. As Mr. King ruefully recalls, "[the neighbour had] eaten the chickens so I had to pay the note."

Another neighbour entered into a contract with Mr. King. It was a fifty-fifty crop share agreement. Mr. King went back east for work with his chum August Ingenthron, but when he came back in the fall, "[the neighbour] had sold my share of the crop." Discussion occurred; threats were general. Later, settlers John Koch and Joe Kuntz asked Mr. King to help dig a grave. When he asked for whom the grave was being dug, Mr. King was advised that he would be digging the grave for the man who still owed him 50 per cent of that year's crop.

Another neighbour, Jack Fleck, used to let his cattle run wild on Mr. King's fields. After chasing them out, Mr. King observes that he "was not a good neighbor after that."

Mr. King and Peter Hafitook were hard at work, digging a well when Mr. Hafitook "decided to go for the mail." John kept digging until dark when, with a rope, he finally had to haul himself out of the hole by himself. "Pete never did come back," a wistful Mr. King remembered.

Mr. King was permanently blinded in one eye when shards and sparks flew from a plough share that he was sharpening.

On a fine summer day, Mr. King and his friend Mr. Harry Keeble were on their way to a picnic when a storm blew up. When they arrived at the picnic, Reg Nelson told them he had been hailed out. So too, it later turned out, were Mr. King and Mr. Keeble – "In fact, the storm killed quite a few of Keeble's chickens."[19] It wasn't just Keeble's chickens but chickens generally who were subject to the brutal and capricious fate of the Heavens. Daryl Moorehouse from down Aneroid way recalls that one year, they lost not only the crop to hail but also "all the chickens in the yard."[20] It would appear that chickens led short, brutal, violent lives in the early settlement years. Alma Mutter, daughter of Gustav Mutter, recalls that the hail storms during the 1930s were so bad and the hail was so big that it "broke the chicken's legs and sometimes smashed their heads."[21]

And so it went for Mr. King. He hired the Coderre boys for harvest one year and had to watch to make sure they were not putting the wheat and the chaff in the same bin.

The Coderre Boys were apparently not very bright. Mr. King recalls that they could not find the money to patch the tires on their car so they filled the front tires with cement.

Mr. King mentored the local one-room school teacher who was having a tough time with some of the lads at his school. Some "tough boys" wanted to "gang up on him." Under Mr. King's tutelage, the teacher resolved the situation by carrying an axe.

Mr. King summarizes his years farming on the west plains between 1913 and 1923 thusly: "there was only about three years that I might say I had a crop out of the ten years that I was farming."

Hard Times

Dignity: (noun) the state or quality of being worthy of respect. From the Latin *dignus*, 'worthy.'

Indignity: (noun) treatment or circumstances that cause one to feel shame or lose one's dignity.

Agony: (noun) extreme suffering. From the Greek *agon*, 'contest.' – *Oxford English Dictionary*

The Dirty Thirties is what it is because of its gruesome soul-destroying quality. It is this element of the crisis that causes us to remember that decade when it is remembered at all in these modern times. And while Saskatchewan people may no longer have a very strong appreciation of what that period actually meant then or means today, it still forms a basic part of the prairie mind. The descendants of settlers have all heard tales from their grandmothers and grandfathers of what it was like during those years. Often as not, these tales are endured by young prairie kids whose only fault lay in not being quick enough to escape the nimble and remarkably virile clutches of their elders who merely wish to remind the desperate child of the struggles of the early years (in addition to imparting to the youngster the value of a nickel, which in their day could feed a person for a week, or so they said). But even when we re-enter the Dirty Thirties from the safe and comfortable distance of seventy years, we are still struck by the intense levels of frustration, futility, and despair, and it is this affective element of the crisis that defines and characterizes the Dirty Thirties. Bruce Hutchinson was a journalist who travelled throughout the south plains during the worst years of the Thirties. He characterizes the Dirty Thirties this way: "people lived worse than the poorest peasantry of Europe."[1]

The Dirty Thirties also contains an element of which most people seem unaware: absurdity. It sidles up slowly and silently between 1914 and 1924, making brief appearances here and there, and then, after 1929, it leaves its impression on virtually everything it touches. So while there are undeniable levels of the sad and tragic, there is also this strange parallel dynamic of the sublimely ridiculous that courses through the entire decade and at which one must either laugh or cry. One so frequently crosses despair and finds oneself surrounded by so much of the sublimely ridiculous that it is hard to believe that it was tolerated for one year, to say nothing of ten years, or twenty-five. Absurdity casts a very long shadow (or, perversely, brightens its battleship-grey colours) over the entire decade.

Principally, though, the 1930s were grim beyond measure. And while there were positive elements in abundance like strength, courage, determination, and persistence (above all, persistence), the primary colours of the decade are negative, and this is the principal reason why we remember the event when we remember it at all, anymore: it was a massive assault on and test of the self-respect, dignity, and pride of the people of Saskatchewan. The Dirty Thirties implicitly asked these questions: how long can a man retain his pride and dignity and walk with his head up when he is compelled to ask the village council to provide him with underwear? How long can a man resist the all-too-human temptation toward contempt for the man who asks to be supplied with underwear? At its most basic level, the Dirty Thirties was a soul-destroyer. It was also ridiculous.

The "unholy mess" of the 1930s was produced by the confluence and convergence of several elements all at once. As historian John Archer puts it, "drought, insect pests, erosion, low prices for produce and high winds occurred simultaneously."[2] A quick year-by-year sketch of the 1930s supports Archer's characterization: 1929 to 1931 featured crop failures and "black blizzards" (dust storms); 1932 was not so bad in some areas and a crop of sorts was even grown in some areas of the drylands; 1933 and 1934 were so bad that "for the first time in living memory" summer fairs were cancelled; 1935 moderated; 1936 was "a disaster," and 1937 was worse than 1936.[3] Indeed, the drought of 1937 would prompt the last of the great evacuations and abandonments of that decade. Saskatchewan, according to Mr. James Gray, had the worst of it all: "worst drought, worst grasshoppers, worst rust, worst cutworms and worst hail."[4] In sum, and speaking of the south and west plains, Mr. Archer explains that "the weather was bad all of the time and worse sometimes."[5]

For all the importance of drought on the south plains between 1914 and 1937, however, there is a fairly broad body of thought that places the drought second or even lower on the myriad list of minor and major problems that afflicted Saskatchewan during the 1930s. Historian Bill Waiser, for example, argues that "the real challenge" in the 1930s was "not trying to grow enough wheat but getting a decent price for it."[6] He notes that the 1932 harvest was the largest crop since 1928 but settlers were only paid thirty-five cents per bushel for it.

In addition to the obvious conceptual problems associated with using a single year as a stand-in for an entire decade, this approach to the Thirties emphasizes the economic problem ("The Great Depression") at the expense of the drought and all its attendant misery, and thus Dr. Waiser glides by the fact that depending on where a settler lived the principal problem was in fact very different. Indeed, if all sources of information were removed from the sod and paper shacks of south and west plains settlers, they may not have ever even known that in addition to drought they were also caught up in a global economic crisis.

Simply put, there were vast areas in Saskatchewan that were not affected by the drought at all, and thus for them, yes, commodity prices and the economic problems associated with the Great Depression were the principal concerns. The life-sucking drought did not register for these lucky ones and thus Dr. Waiser's argument applies only to something like half of agricultural Saskatchewan. The rural municipality of Pinto Creek provides a wonderfully challenging example of what did *not* occur in most of Saskatchewan.

Located south-east of Swift Current, settlers in this RM grew five bushels of wheat in 1929, three in 1930, zero in 1931, four in the good year of 1932, one in 1933, one in 1934, eight in 1935, three in 1936, zero in 1937, and six in 1938.[7] When the Prairie Farm Assistance Act was passed in 1939, the federal government settled on what we will call the 'five bushel benchmark': if a crop district fell below five bushels per acre, it was a disaster zone requiring aid. Essentially, Pinto Creek was a drought-induced disaster zone for ten years. This same level of failure occurred in RMs throughout the south and west plains. Happyland, 200 kilometres north-west of Pinto Creek, grew an average of six bushels per acre between 1929 and 1938.[8] The same was true in Mankota, Swift Current, Maple Creek, Clinworth, Reno, White Valley, Big Stick, and in all the RMs that surrounded them.

The eastern and northern grain-belts simply had a much different ex-perience during the Dirty Thirties. The RM of Sliding Hills in the Melville district grew an average of fifteen bushels per acre during the 1930s, as did the RMs that surrounded that district. Carrot Valley, the home riding of Prime Minister R.B. Bennett's federal agriculture minister, Robert Weir, grew twenty-three bushels per acre in 1931.[9] By contrast, the RMs of Reno, Pinto Creek, Mankota, Big Stick, Maple Creek, Swift Current, and Deer Forks grew between zero and four bushels per acre in 1931. The eastern RM of Fertile Belt went four years without any rural relief aid and even when it received it in the worst year, 1937, it still only amounted to $115,165.[10] Mankota and Pinto Creek received just over $3 million in direct relief and seed grains during the decade.

Saskatchewan's Department of Agriculture divided the province up into nine crop districts and the worst of the drought was limited to just four out of the nine. The land abandonment crisis of the 1920s registered *only* in the south-west and west plains of Saskatchewan, and the drought of the 1930s was essentially an extension of those basic lines. In 1929, the drought spilled its banks as it were and flooded down onto the Regina Plains and into the extreme south-east corner. Crop districts one (Oxbow-Carlyle), two (Weyburn-Radville), three (Moose Jaw-Mossbank), and four (Swift Current-Maple Creek) were struck the hardest in the 1930s. In addition to the drought that periodically hammered away at much of the south-east corner, there was also a continual problem in that region with rust, both of which scourges ruined crops with equal facility.

But north and east of this region, crop districts averaged between eight and fifteen bushels per acre and the yield averages stay well above ten to fifteen for the entire decade when one gets into the northern grain-belt of Preeceville, Star City, Saskatoon, and North Battleford. In 1932, the good year, crop district nine in the North Battleford-St. Walburg area averaged twenty-three bushels per acre while crop district two around Weyburn averaged one.[11] Even in the worst year, 1937, while crop district five in east central Saskatchewan grew a quite respectable fifteen bushels per acre, crop district four in the south-west grew nothing. Literally nothing. In 1933, crop districts three, four, and seven (Kindersley-Leader-Swift Current-Maple Creek) grew just 7 million bushels of wheat in a province that grew 128 million.

So certainly, for some settlers, the problem was in fact pricing. But for those luckless souls on the south and west plains that make up roughly half of agricultural Saskatchewan, there was simply nothing to sell. The wheat had been burned to a crisp and where in good years a proud and healthy four-foot-high stand of wheat could be seen (even five and six feet, depending on the variety of seed used), in the bad years the crop was a scabby, scrubby, sparse field of failure that would be lucky if it grew six inches. The settlers in the RM of Pinto Creek, whose existence during the thirties was characterized by desperation and starvation, could only dream about having the problems of the RM of Sliding Hills.

The drought was bad enough, but what made it punitively worse were the dust storms. It is this element of the crisis that gives it its grim countenance, its resonance. The dust storms were not the cause of the drought but rather one of its symptoms. Under repeated instructions from the Department of Agriculture, settlers had hammered away at the soil with the summer-fallow method until nothing was left. Yes, it was a wonderful way to conserve moisture, and yes it killed weeds like nothing else could, but it would grind and granulate the dirt and thus in dry years "the pulverized, fibreless topsoil was ready to fly with the first wind."[12] And that's exactly what it did. W.R. Motherwell and Angus McKay and the other dryland farming advocates of the early settlement years could only sit back silently, stunned at what their admonitions had wrought.

Dust storms are a very foreign concept today, difficult to grasp, and even harder to appreciate because they are so rooted in a specific time and place. They occurred so very long ago and have not occurred on the same magnitude since. We apprehend dust storms only in books, family legends, and local myth: they are an abstraction. It is a commonly told story that the skies blackened and day seemed as night. Former Hatton resident Laura Phaff affirms that early settlers "often had to light their kerosene lamps in the middle of the day" so that they could see.[13] Dust storms of this size and enormity have not occurred since, and so the idea of one is strange, foreign almost. It is worth quoting at length the words of one observer who witnessed these spectacles:

> No one who has not experienced one can possibly imagine the depressing and nerve-wracking effect of a really bad dust blizzard. Something happens to the farmer himself as he sees, year after year, black clouds of dust sweeping over his fields and in some cases carrying away the top soil and with it the seed he has sown or in other cases cutting down and burying beyond recovery the grain that has succeeded in surviving the drought and has begun to give some promise of a possible harvest ...

these storms have often continued for days and while they were in progress they produced living conditions that were almost unendurable, even to the most courageous.[14]

With less finesse, though perhaps with more accuracy, one settler recalled that "the winds came and blew the goddamned country right out from under our feet."[15]

Kathleen Meyer nee Armson was the daughter of George and Margaret Armson who had come to the south plains from Manitoba in 1910. They settled in Shamrock country just north and west of Mankota. She recalls that "when the skies began to darken" her father would send them into the cellar for safety. She feared the dust storms but even then she never realized their full import: "I didn't realize the devastation it meant, nor the worry it must have been for our parents."[16]

The first dust storm in Saskatchewan quite possibly occurred on 24 May 1929. Frank Ulm of the Aneroid area remembers that day well. "A huge ominous black cloud" came rolling across the south plains. "It grew larger and uglier by the minute. I remember my parents looking at each other with worried looks." Mr. Ulm's father told his young boy to run as fast as he could and help his neighbour unhitch his team and help get the horses in the barn. After accomplishing this, "we all went to the basement. In a very few minutes the wind was really howling and it became so dark that we lit the old coal oil lantern ... little did we realize that this was the beginning of the Dirty Thirties."[17] Mr. Ulm is recalling a dust storm that occurred in the early spring of 1929, and this reinforces the point that these black blizzards were a consequence, a continuation, of what had occurred in the 1920s. The soil did not magically become sand in 1929: there was a problem *long* before the Dirty Thirties hit.

Mrs. Marjory Malcolm recalls a dust storm that struck in 1930 and, for three days and nights, the family was holed up inside the house with the windows and doors closed up, the lamps burning, and wet cloth on everybody's faces so they could breathe. The house was full of dust, so much so that "you could write your name in the table," which Mrs. Malcolm likely did.[18]

Writing one's name in the dust that had settled in the house after a dust storm is a unique and novel experience but there were also other ways in which one could enjoy a calamity. Ida and Charlie Fleck's little boys "enjoyed the fun of playing with dirt on the floor which had blown through the cracks of the house," although finding fun in playing with dirt does certainly seem to suggest a certain poverty of choices for other types of fun.[19] Dirt, however, was one of the very few things that settlers had plenty of. (Grasshoppers and wind were the other two.) It has been estimated that farms lost from one hundred to one thousand tons of earth from their lands in dust storms.[20]

It is easy to forget that dust storms, at least in the early years before they became a natural part of the climate of the south plains, actually caused a deep fear and worry. The sense of panic in the memories of the storms is palpable. It is a panic and fear similar to that caused by a tornado or a hurricane. Dust storms were unknown, strange, and violent, and so it is likewise easy to bypass the idea that they were also beautiful. Very nearly every natural occurrence contains within it some sort of beauty or, perhaps better stated, an element that mesmerizes, stuns, and leaves one staring, mouth agape in wonderment. Dust storms were like that. "When you were in one" a settler wrote, "they were terrible; when they were on the horizon, they were beautiful."[21]

These dust storms, a by-product of summer-fallowing, were even news all the way over in England where a certain newspaper columnist by the name of A.G. Street, no doubt taking delight in the convulsions wracking the pained body of the mother country's former colonial possession, argued that the storms were a kind of cosmic fair-play, that they were in some divine way punishment for the settlers' barbaric insensitivity to the earth. He blamed the settlers for the storms, alleging that farmers had "mined the land" taking out all that was good and then put nothing back.[22] It was a fairly harsh and certainly ill-timed criticism (one never needs to be reminded that one is to blame for a disaster while the disaster is occurring), but it was certainly a criticism that contained some merit, at least where his identification of the cause of the dust storms were concerned.

South plains Wood Mountain Member of Parliament T.F. Donnelly was stung by this criticism (that it came from an Englishman likely made the sting worse), and he argued in the House of Commons that "no article could be more misleading."[23] Deploying a fairly simple-minded syllogistic logic, Donnelly argued that if Street's cross-Atlantic criticism were correct, then central Canada would have no crop and the west "would be having crops" because the older parts of Canada "would be mined and would run out first … but the very opposite is true."[24] One admires Mr. Donnelly's defence of his settler constituents but the point must be grudgingly conceded to Mr. Street on this exchange.

Dust storms, then, represent many things. They were an allegorical expression of the many thousands of lives that came unravelled in the droughts. They were hard and brutal proof of the peculiar nature of the south and west plains ("black blizzards" did not happen anywhere else in Canada). As one settler observed, dust storms were evidence of nature on the loose, of nature gone mad. Dust storms were the practical consequences of poorly thought out, misguided ideas. Dust storms represented in a way nothing else could the absolute and total destruction of the south and west plains wheat economy. And if one were so inclined, as the biblical prophet Jeremiah certainly was, one could see dust storms as divine punishment for placing faith in the sub-marginal ideas of man, ideas from men like Mr. Motherwell, Mr. McKay, and Mr. Oliver. Jeremiah 17:5: "Cursed be the man who trusteth in man for he shall be like the heath in the desert ... and will not see when prosperity comes but will live ... in the wastes, in a salt land, not inhabited."

On the south and west plains, then, the dust storms wreaked their strange and bewildering havoc while in the north and east areas of the province, global commodity price failures stretched the farmers of those regions to the breaking point. Thus it was that Saskatchewan achieved something very few jurisdictions on the planet ever did during those years – as historian John Archer notes, agricultural incomes in Saskatchewan dropped into minus figures, an achievement "unmatched in any civilized country."[25] Saskatchewan was the country's wheat-growing paradise, its pride. The Breadbox of the World claimed the promotional literature. Saskatchewan gambled everything it had on wheat. And as Dr. Waiser writes, Saskatchewan, having staked everything on wheat, was "helpless" – utterly and completely helpless.

Given the high absurdity quotient in the drylands, it is fitting that the crisis of the Dirty Thirties was preceded by one of the most bountiful, successful crop years ever experienced in the history of Saskatchewan. Like the elevator-jamming harvests of 1915/1916, which preceded the crisis of the 1920s when evanescent Hatton became, for a brief time, the largest grain-handling point in the west, 1928 broke wildly loose and stomped all previous records. Deputy Auld was ecstatic: "all records were shattered by the crop of 1928."[26] The province produced an astonishing 312,215,000 bushels of wheat and what's more, all districts contributed. When people on the plains speak of the Roaring Twenties, it is likely something like this they have in mind. These production figures also happily lay to rest some rather extravagant claims by American historians. Mr. Timothy Egan wrote and fine and compelling history of the American Dust Bowl. But he succumbed to the siren temptations of gross, over-heated hyperbole when he wrote of the sturdy but unexceptional 250 million bushel harvest of 1930: "In all the history of the world, no country had ever tried to grow so much grain."[27] Saskatchewan routinely grew such amounts, even in bad years. So, so much for that.

Naturally, a year in which settlers were 'dizzy with success' led to thoughts of more of the same to come. It is a general rule (one wishes to employ the word 'principle') that a farmer will do one of two things when flush with cash from a good year: he will either buy more equipment or buy more land. Historian Gerald Friesen notes that the expansion of farm holdings in the province during this period implied that farmers were prepared to "take greater risks in their annual bets against soil and climate."[28] 1928 buffeted this expansion and indeed made much of it possible. Expansion was a gamble, true, but the overflowing successes of 1928 made it seem like a safe bet. A south-west Saskatchewan farmer recalled that he bought $11,000 worth of new equipment in 1929: "thought nothing of it; paid cash for it" recalled Mr. Hearns.[29] After ten years, ten harvests, and ten droughts, the equipment didn't stand up so well anymore. Mr. Hearns ruefully noted in 1937 that his equipment was in such sad shape that he thought he "ought to throw the whole lot of junk out." It is more likely that Mr. Hearns moved the detested equipment into the tree line and allowed ubiquitous and fast-growing Caragana bushes take care of the rest. This is, or was at any rate, a common fate of old and unused machinery in rural Saskatchewan.

The crisis of the 1920s was overshadowed and likely all but forgotten in the whirlwind of the successes of the late 1920s when the province produced an annual average of 350 million bushels of wheat. By comparison, settlers produced an average of just 230 million bushels during the 1930s.[30]

In the late 1920s, farmers were getting an average of a dollar per bushel for wheat. A settler with 320 acres who grew a thirty bushel crop (not unusual, especially up north) meant that he stood to earn, before inputs, almost $10,000, a small fortune in 1929. That same farmer on that same field, though, who grew a thirty bushel per acre crop in 1932 earned at even the high price of sixty cents per bushel $952, or an income drop of just over 90 per cent. And if that same farmer grew a wheat crop of five bushels per acre on a quarter-section that was the general rule on the south and west plains, then he would earn forty-eight dollars.

In the worst of the bad years of the 1930s, several rural councils throughout the south plains petitioned both the federal and provincial governments to establish a minimum price for wheat of "not less than seventy cents per bushel." This impulse toward minimum pricing was indeed the seed that would ultimately germinate into the Canadian Wheat Board in 1935. But that was yet to come. First the tipping point had to be reached, and the province and the people of Saskatchewan needed to be pushed from the edge of the abyss down into it.

1930 repeated the failure of 1929 and made the bushel-busting harvest of 1928 seem a distant memory. Deputy Auld grudgingly conceded in 1930 that, for the second year in a row, "drought conditions prevailed in much of the south central district."[31] One-seventh of the provinces municipalities needed relief because of the crop failure and "in the south and south-west, much [of the] crop was blown before it could take root."[32] But in 1931, with little or no fanfare, though likely with a distasteful tang of umbrage, the deputy finally arrived at his inevitable epiphany: "it is now apparent," Auld confessed after guiding and shaping Saskatchewan agricultural policy for twenty years, "after more than a quarter of a century of agricultural development in the western and southwest third of the province, that periods of drought may be expected at intervals."[33] One fights the impulse to stand and applaud. The guarded and very carefully worded admission of Auld, however, did little (in fact, did nothing), to change his actions. Though he walked with the settlers every step of the way, accompanying them on their long dark ride, he never really had any belief or faith in them, though. Not much at all.

The province's J.T.M. Anderson government moved quickly on the problems created by the drought and the depression. Shortly after his famous promise made in Yorkton in the winter of 1930 that "no one in Saskatchewan will starve" (a promise that many times came near to being unfulfilled, were it not for the generosity of other provinces in confederation) Anderson's conservative Co-operative Government set up the Saskatchewan Relief Commission (SRC). With the south plains burning and north and east Saskatchewan tangled up in the economic crisis, it was plainly evident that something extraordinary needed to be done and the SRC was the answer, at least for a few years.

Operating under Chairman Henry Black, Anderson established the SRC on 25 August 1931 with the sole purpose of providing relief aid to Saskatchewan's stricken rural population.[34] Over the three years of its existence, from 1931 to 1934, the committee spent some $19 million providing aid to rural Saskatchewan settlers.[35]

Under the SRC, the maximum allowance for food allotments per month was ten dollars per family (plus a single ninety-eight-pound bag of flour).[36] Additionally, under the SRC's stringent regulations, "no purchase of fruit of any kind or of vegetables ... were permitted." Though again, one must caution against judging the SRC too severely on this point because no one in 1931 could have ever guessed that the problem was going to drag on implacably for another seven years. In the SRC, regulations were merely another reflection of the desire to keep firm limits on the amount of charity that was distributed.

When the SRC was shut down in 1934 and its responsibilities were farmed out to various other government departments, the monthly food allotment was increased to as much as $20.20 per month in 1937 and the Bureau of Public Welfare allowed the recipient a choice in whether or not he or she would purchase fruit or vegetables with the aid.[37] Given the refusal of the SRC to finance fruit and vegetables during the dry years, it should not be surprising then that, as was the case during the droughts of the 1920s, medical men reported numerous cases of malnutrition, "especially among children in the drought area."[38] There were fourteen deaths from starvation between 1929 and 1938 and, as we will soon see, many dozens of deaths from rickets, scurvy, pellagra, and beriberi.[39]

But for all the SRC did and tried to do (and again, most reports suggest it holds a very respectable record[40]), it was nowhere near enough, a single drop in an ocean, as it were. The Dominion and provincial governments would ultimately spend $186,585,898.81, or just under a quarter of a billion dollars on aid for rural Saskatchewan alone.[41] $10 million would be spent on road work throughout the province, though principally the work occurred in the south. The $18 million spent by the SRC, then, for all its help to the settlers, seems rather more like a gesture, an indication that something, anything, was being done, when compared to the total sums that were ultimately spent trying to keep rural Saskatchewan alive and breathing.

The establishment of the SRC was also a tacit acknowledgment that RMs could not stand the financial strain of the crisis on their own.[42] The SRC operated within three defined regions. Area A was the hardest hit and had experienced three crop failures in a row.[43] Area A was shaped like a triangle with its principal point just south of Watrous, and the base extending from Lampman in the southeast to Eastend in the south-west. The triangle should only be used as a rough guide though: it was only used for three years and in addition it did not include the RM's in the area of the Great Sand Hills, the core of the desert. Area B included seventy-seven RM's within the west and east-central regions of the province. Area C, what amounts to the entire area north of Watrous, experienced one year of crop failure.

This is the territory within which the SRC worked, and it roughly, though very imperfectly, corresponds to the drought areas outlined by the Department of Agriculture. The designation of Areas A, B, and C was important for the purposes of distinguishing levels of responsibility. For example, the Dominion government agreed to pay all relief aid for Area A, 50 per cent of relief aid for Area B, and nothing for Area C. In addition, the Dominion government contributed 50 per cent of the costs for relocation programs, of which there were very few.[44] In the first year of the commission's existence, the SRC appointed a relief official to each RM. This official was responsible for taking applications and administering aid. By appointing an outside official to administer aid, the SRC hoped to avoid any "influence of municipal politics or local prejudices."[45]

Avoiding "local prejudices" was very difficult because those prejudices could be rooted in any number of feelings and express themselves in any number of ways. Prior to the establishment of the SRC, for example, Deer Forks council in 1930 agreed to give George Engleman ten dollars in aid per month, but Mr. Engleman thought this a pittance, an insult, and he evidently went about the town of Burstall complaining. Burstall back then (and still today) only had between two and three hundred residents, which means that Mr. Engleman knew the councillors personally and they knew him. Mr. Engleman's complaining did nothing to endear him to council because a visibly irritated councillor Henry Rutz suggested that "if he [Mr. Engleman] continues to complain, this help may be cut down to $8.00 per month."[46] It was this type of local politics the local SRC appointees worked diligently to avoid. Mr Engleman, by the way, apparently heeded councillor Rutz's warning because, in 1933, council gave the indignant settler shoes and "two pair of underwear."[47]

Relief aid included everything from underwear to seed grain. In total, 14 million bushels of seed grain were distributed to settlers during the 1930s.[48] The mind boggles at this amount: it could well have been used to seed up to 16 or even 18 million acres of land. The seed grain was meant to ensure that a farmer whose crop had failed would have enough seed to plant a crop the following year. The amounts were generally doled out in 100, 200, or 300 bushel allotments, but a settler was not guaranteed seed grain allotments, especially if he was a big farmer, and here again we see local politics at play.

Deer Forks area farmer Leonid Lomow appeared before council in 1933 in the final year of the SRC's mandate and asked for 470 bushels of seed grain. There is absolutely no reason to think Lomow was unlike all other farmers on the south plains. We can assume that he summer-fallowed and so seeding an estimated 470 acres suggests that he had another 400 acres lying fallow, and in addition, he had land that he maintained for his cattle and horses. Mr. Lomow and his family were by most standards well-established and represent the classic case of immigrant settlers adapting and making good. But council refused to grant him the seed grain he had requested, likely because they felt he was doing well enough without it.[49] Mr. Lomow fled Deer Forks shortly after.

Mr. Lomow was one of fifteen family members who experienced an incredible journey half way across the world only to see that journey come to a pathetic end in a tiny little council room in a tiny little town lost somewhere in the middle of the drought-stricken west plains. The Lomow journey began in Russia where, Leon's brother Alex writes, "a generation caught at the cross roads of history by an emerging nation soon to feel the onslaught of violent revolution" in 1917 had two choices to make: "stay and face certain lifelong turmoil and annihilation" or leave.[50] Leon Lomow and fifteen members of his family left.

Their escape from the bloody pitchfork and machine gun reforms of the Bolsheviks took them from Odessa to the Baltic port of Lebova. After a brief stay there, they alighted to Denmark and from thence to Liverpool. The Atlantic crossing took thirteen days, during which time Leon and his brothers enjoyed themselves: "[we] fought, danced and sang our way across the stormy North Atlantic." With Halifax port iced in, they landed at Philadelphia, where "negroes" threw rocks at them and called them names, though one wonders at the provocation that caused this: there were no "negroes" in Russia and the rustic, provincial Russians may have felt obliged to offer some remarks upon seeing a "negro" for the first time.

Fresh from their introduction to the United States, they headed for the straight-laced and staid atmosphere of Toronto, across the Canadian Shield to swamp-dwelling Winnipeg and from there they took the train to Canada's windiest city, Lethbridge, to inquire in badly broken English about land. The family got a tip on a region that had a heavy Russian immigrant population and so finally ended up in Burstall via Maple Creek. The road out would be much easier.

The Lomows ran a very successful farm. Flush with cash from the grand harvest of 1915, they bought seventy-five head of horses for later re-sale. They even raised cattle but "drought quickly finished them off." During the 1920s "the exodus of the Lomow's began" when two brothers left. Alex recalls that "we stayed on the farm for a while in the early thirties but every year kept getting worse," and so they, like many thousands of others, moved to eastern Saskatchewan: the Russian Lomows, unfortunately one must think, chose the heavily Ukrainian settlement of Kamsack.

There is a tinge of bitterness in Alex's story. Deer Forks council rejected his brother's aid application in 1933 and the Lomow's left soon after. One cannot but assume that the two incidents are related. Leon had been ready and willing to go into debt on more than four hundred bushels of seed grain, but council would not approve the request perhaps because of the fact that the Lomows had been, to that point, very successful. Envy often colours the perceptions of farmers.

Alex understands that they were merely one of thousands who fled. "Many" he writes, "gave up and never returned." The Lomow's visited Burstall a few times over the remainder of the 1930s where they retained some lands. Alex writes that they wanted to "view this awesome spectacle" of a world falling apart and he adds that they always returned to Kamsack "broken hearted." Their homestead was torn down in 1942.

The Lomow's were not the only ones subject to "local prejudices." The administration of relief aid in Saskatchewan reached deep down into the tiniest parochial corners of envy, and dislike. The nature of farming, for example, was in the process of changing during the 1920s and 1930s. Oftentimes, one might have seen a tractor being used in a field next to a neighbour who was still working with horse and plough. It is widely recognized that farmers are *terribly* sensitive creatures when it comes to the equipment used by their neighbours. The harmless though ostentatious displays farmers today make of their equipment likely had some sort of rough equivalent in the 1930s. A successful settler might perhaps park his mechanized equipment – his "tractor" – near the access road for all his neighbours to see. Sensitivity to these displays, not too very far removed from envy, likely caused Deer Forks council to restrict aid to these modern farmers. Deer Forks councilmen vowed that "no gasoline whatsoever" would be advanced to what they called "tractor farmers" and the sense that an irritated council deployed this phrase as a pejorative is palpable.[51]

Thus it was that the crisis of the Thirties refracted through the tiny little prejudices, emotions, and idiosyncrasies of rural Saskatchewan. "Tractor farmers" and successful hard-working Russians provide just two examples of the target of "local prejudices" that the SRC tried to avoid or mitigate. But despite council's reluctance to provide aid to "tractor farmers," it was a reality that could not be avoided for very long. Grease, oil, gas, and repairs became staples of relief aid in the 1930s. "Tractor farmers" in White Valley, for example, received a fulsome 615 pounds of grease for their tractors in 1935.[52]

When councils weren't wrapped up in aid disputes, they were often trying to keep their settlers warm. Coal was a crucial part of life in Saskatchewan. The prospect of spending a winter in a homestead shack on the open plains while impoverished, penniless, and relying on food from friends and neighbours is a hellish and frightening vision if one adds to that the simple absence of heat to stay warm. Historian Pierre Berton once observed that the CPR learned one crucial and important lesson from building a rail line across the country: a man can tolerate a great deal of discomfort and misery if his belly is full. That tolerance is proportionately though greatly reduced if a person is not only starving but also cold.

Much of the heating coal used in the Thirties came from the coal fields of Estevan and Lethbridge. There were alternatives to coal: Deer Forks council asked and later received the then necessary approval for settlers to trek the twenty to thirty miles to the sand hills or the river to cut and pick what wood they could find.[53] But coal was primary and because it was primary, settlers went to great lengths to ensure they had it. And "great lengths" in the Dirty Thirties actually meant great lengths – no italics are necessary here.

It seems that the SRC wanted to keep a tight reign on relief costs and so advised the settlers in Mankota to use their own nearby coal fields to access heating supplies rather than having it shipped in from other areas. With winter's chill in the air, the night cold, settlers trekked out of tiny Mankota under the sad, grey skies of October to the distant coal mines, which were in the coulees of what is today a Prairie Farm Rehabilitation Administration (PFRA) pasture. By moonlight they made their way through the hills and draws of one of the most desolate regions of the south plains to wait "many times overnight with no shelter or accommodation" to get their coal allotment.[54] Council begged the SRC ship in coal from Estevan and restrict the use of the local mines to "those living within eight miles" so as to save the settlers from this thirty-mile moonlight trek in which the pioneers would find shelter in a shallow draw or a ditch and sleeplessly wait to get their ration of second- or third-rate coal with which to heat their shacks for the coming winter. It was people like the Mankota settlers that historian James Gray had in mind when he wrote that "their clothes had worn thin, their stoves and heaters were wearing out, they were short of bedding and as half the people lived in flimsy sub-marginal housing [farming sub-marginal land], the business of keeping warm occupied most of their waking hours" during the winters.[55]

The Konshuch family provides a good example of what Mr. Gray meant. After fleeing the drylands, the Konschuhs found life almost as tough as what it was for those down Mankota way. Adam, the son of patriarch Phillip, would routinely get up around four o'clock in the morning in the winters and "start out on those bitterly cold mornings for the [coal] mine and return about 5pm." According to Adam's daughter, the horses had as tough a time as Adam – even though her father would frequently walk behind them in order to stay warm, the horses arrived bedraggled and frozen "with icicles hanging from their nostrils."[56] Thus Mr. Konschuh, as part of his winter routine, spent thirteen hours on cold winter days gathering coal to keep his family warm.

There was, then, no money for coal. There was no money for gasoline, oil, or food. Neither was there money for clothing; thus, it seems normal, almost natural, that the problem of relief fraud developed.

According to one commentator writing about the rural Saskatchewan merchant and the once ubiquitous but now non-existent general store (the last of these stores were torn down or moved into museums in the 1980s and 1990s), the attitude that "most strongly characterized" his business was "the belief in individual initiative" and in the owner's qualities of "natural leadership."[57] There was also, apparently, the sense within the rural business community that anything that might "undermine the economic position of the businessman" was considered a "threat to society."[58] These observations give us slight bearing on how relief fraud developed amongst rural Saskatchewan merchants.

As with any system that lacks proper checks and balances and has also been hastily assembled and is unwieldy, the relief system was abused. Clothiers and general store merchants would sometimes charge if not extortionate prices then at least prices that were inflated because the government was footing the bill. And this abuse appeared quite early on in the crisis. Pinto Creek council was quite disturbed by this development and agreed that "relief orders will not be issued to such merchants" who inflate prices.[59]

This problem of inflated prices appeared up the road from Kincaid, which was the seat of the RM of Pinto Creek, in the now non-extant village of Ferland, where Mr. Joseph Morin had been overcharging for his wares if they were purchased with relief aid. But likely because there were very few merchants in the area who could provide such items, Mankota council backtracked on its previous censure of Mr. Morin and moved that he be "reinstated [as a] dispenser of relief food and clothing" because whatever he had done in the past had been apparently put right and, given the absence of other vendors in the region, council found that he was a man who now was a "conducting a straightforward business."[60]

The province, as a way of shoring up local business during the decade, required all relief clothing to be purchased locally, as opposed to, say, mail order or from communities nearby or even one of the cities. And merchants actively courted those families brought to their knees by the crisis. There was no shying away from it either: destitution was out in the open and a natural part of life in the dry years and something about which one need not have felt too embarrassed. C.W. Baker was one of Kindersley's first dry-goods merchants and he stumped shamelessly for relief business. He placed a half-page ad in the Kindersley *Clarion* in the terrible year of 1937 in which he observed that many people will be receiving relief, "some of you for the first time," he helpfully noted. And when these relief orders came in, it was Mr. Baker's earnest wish that "we hope you will decide on our store."[61] He urged mothers to bring their children because there was something for everyone.

Merchants, like settlers, did what they had to do because, like the incomprehensible drop in farm income, the merchant too saw a precipitous drop in his revenues. In Saskatchewan, merchants' revenues fell from $265 million in 1928 to $104 million in 1933 and stayed there until the end of the Second World War.[62] So it may appear unseemly to stump for government relief orders or to fraudulently overcharge, but, survival being what it is, it was simply one way in which costs could be made up without hurting anyone but the government. With life re-ordered to a basic and very low-level form of existence, defrauding the government was likely viewed as a victimless crime.

The development of relief fraud also points us toward an element of the Dirty Thirties that has never been explored: the collapse or corrosion of the moral code of the day. This code, one's sense of right and wrong, went through some profound changes during the drought but, as mentioned, it is an issue on which there has been very little study and research. There has been none, in fact.

Isabel Winterstein was one contemporary who noticed the changes and in 1937 she briefly reflected on what she had seen during those years as part of her address to a gathering of the United Farmers of Canada.[63] Winterstein claimed to have observed in the years prior to 1937 a collapse of moral values especially amongst young people. She claimed that they had "come to regard ordinary moral standards with impunity" and this produced what she called "fatal results."

Part of the reason why those morals changed was the role, better yet, the non-role that the church played during the crises of the dry years. For centuries, the church has stood as that mediator between good and evil, right and wrong. It has guided people towards what it felt was appropriate behaviour. But during the crisis of the 1930s, the church ceased to play the prominent role it had played prior to the droughts and desperation. Most clerics during the 1930s spent the majority of their time dispensing relief aid or caring for the sick and the poor rather than conducting services. The Reverend Mr. Gawthorp in Pinto Creek, for example, spent the early years of the drought not ministering to his flock but instead undertaking a survey of family needs in the district and distributing clothing in advance of the winter of 1929/30. He also assisted with dispensing a $5,000 "relief grant" for road work.[64]

A post-drought survey from 1938 found that more than 50 per cent of 425 ministers polled stated that participation in Sunday service and general church activities "decreased considerably" during the 1930s. The reasons cited were mixed: some indicated they had no money for the collection plate; others suggested that they had no means to get to church, while a few contrite souls cited "a lack of suitable clothing."[65] Clerics then were busy handing out food, settlers were occupied with getting coal, or failing at farming, still others felt embarrassed at appearing in church with clothing patched up and shot through with holes. Under these circumstances, it is natural, normal almost, that questions of right and wrong become less important.

The matter of clothing on which the survey respondents touched was actually a very perplexing one for many settlers. It was called the most "aggravating feature" of the drought because in the first instance, there was no money for clothes and, second, the clothes that one owned had to be continually patched up. As one farmer indicated to two reporters from a Saskatoon newspaper in 1934, he had to put patches over areas already patched "only to find that the garment had given away somewhere else."[66]

Since there was no money to buy clothes, expedients had to be found. Sean Kelly was a little fourteen-year-old Irish kid from Player, and he was so short of clothing that he wrote Prime Minister Bennett in 1932 to ask for a suit. After duly noting his size ("chest 34, waste 32, size 7 shoes") he told the Prime Minister that needed the suit because "we are going to play at a picnic."[67]

Mrs. Clarice Glascock of Shamrock received parcels of clothing from her aunt in Ontario, but rather than using the clothes for herself, she would cut up the materials and makes clothes for the kids. Mrs. Glascock is universally remembered in the Shamrock district as a kind and giving woman.[68]

One of the legendary tales of the Thirties is that children wore potato sacks during the dry years. And while dust bowl kids went about in potato sacks, women sometimes opted for flour sacks. Robert Hammond came up to the south plains from Sandusky, Ohio, and settled near Swift Current. He claims that a woman who had cut and bleached a one-hundred-pound flour bag evidently didn't use enough bleach because the words "Pride of the West" appeared on the backside.[69] One winter, Eunice Hayward recalls the trainload of clothes arriving and she was desperately hoping for toques and mittens to stay warm. But what she and the other settlers got was "high button boots, whale bone corsets, satin and crepe dresses." All of this in addition to receiving "fancy hats."[70]

There was actually a kind of black market system set up for clothing in south plains communities that directly bordered or were very near to America, places like Coronach, Mankota, Orkney, and Climax. Mrs. Hayward, from down around Hart Butte near Coronach, recalls that since fancy hats were not appropriate, "any new clothes were often smuggled." Americans and Canadians along the border would frequently meet by the Goose Creek in the summer for Sports Days and the Yanks would bring clothes and cloth because they were much cheaper than Canadian materials. Mrs Hayward recalls that "many a parcel changed hands behind the scenes at Sunday picnics."[71]

Settlers engaged in black-market smuggling, merchants over-charged for dry-goods and thus it was that a tiny corner of the moral code of the day was corroded, warped. We can see further evidence of this warping when we turn to the matter of relief aid.

It was commonly suggested back then (as it still is today) that farmers should look after themselves. In the 1930s (but less so today), aid was considered "repugnant" to "self-respecting men" and thus the sense that they should provide for themselves was extremely strong. Journalist Mr. Bruce Hutchinson tells the story of a settler called Mr. Hearns who farmed south and west of Regina. In the worst of the bad years, Mr Hearns did not have a whole lot about which he could have felt proud: the house was stripped of paint, the barn sagged "as if the wind had been too much for it," and a family of chickens wandered about hopefully in what had once been a garden casting nervous glances skyward. It was, as Mr. Hearns observed, "not as bad as most." Mr. Hutchinson noted that "nearly all the farmers in this district were on relief" and Mr. Hearns validated that point when he said "You see them houses up the road? Everyone of them is on relief."[72] Mr. Hearns went on to insist that he had never been on relief and he was "mighty proud of that."[73]

There is here a sharp and pointed moral distinction being drawn here by Mr. Hearns. He took pains to point out that he had never been on relief while all around him his neighbours were and in this he took a great deal of pride. Not accepting relief was, for Mr. Hearns (or just "Hearns" as Mr. Hutchinson refers to him) an issue of pride, of ethics, of moral fibre. Mr. Hearns' story may be doubtful, but it certainly illustrates the interesting idea that those who took relief were frequently considered to be somehow wanting in fortitude, wanting in strength, wanting in toughness. Relief at that time was considered "repugnant" and something to be rejected at all costs by men who had any degree of self-respect and this perspective is at its core incredibly, irredeemably moral and it withered in the droughts.

Mr. E.W. Stapleford was an adviser to the federal government and he wrote a summary of the Dirty Thirties in 1938 for the House of Commons. He noticed a quite peculiar though basically human development where relief aid was concerned. Over time, settlers stricken by drought developed a sense of *entitlement* to relief aid. Stapleford found that this dependence developed in three stages: the first stage was characterized by reluctance, the second featured grudging acceptance, and the third was expectation. If we are to believe Mr. Hutchinson, then Mr. Hearns successfully resisted moving past the first stage.

Stapleford's observation may wound the pride of some because it is antagonistic to the image we have of the Proud Settler doing all in his power to carry the load by himself. While Mr. Stapleford's observation is indeed an unattractive one, that does not make it any less true. In fact, the crumbling of the moral code of the day may have started precisely at this point, the point at which relief was sought and readily accepted. This moral corrosion started in the family and radiated outwards: the crop failed, relief was accepted, pride was wounded, excuses were proffered, rationalizations formed, comforting lies told, moral and spiritual weights increased, weakened spirits collapsed, corrosion followed. The man's family watched the corrosion. The community watched the family.

Both Stapleford and Winterstein are suggesting that the personal moral code of settlers was ruptured in the droughts of the Thirties. The ready acceptance of relief aid, and as we will see in due course the even more enthusiastic willingness to disregard the repayment of that debt, is just one way in which this corrosion expressed itself – relief fraud and black market smuggling were other ways.

Perhaps the most compelling evidence to support the idea of a moral rupture can be found in the matter of sex. Mrs. Winterstein suggested in 1937 that the "moral code" of young people had been abandoned and that people had "come to regard ordinary moral standards with impunity" with "fatal results."[74] For his part, Mr. Stapleford toured the south and west plains and came to the sad realization that the poverty induced by year after monotonous year of drought produced serious consequences for young people. They were "thwarted in the normal desire to marry [which] create[d] a serious social problem."[75]

Neither Winterstein nor Stapleford explicitly state or name the issue to which they referred, believing instead that their readers would be at once familiar with the context and content of the comments. This suggests that the problem was widespread and well recognized. In all likelihood, it had something to do with the enormous surge in premarital sex, illegitimate births, and unwed mothers.

The number of illegitimate children (as they were tenderly called in those days) shot through the roof during the Dirty Thirties. Between 1914 and 1918, about 100 to 150 illegitimate children were being born each year in Saskatchewan.[76] But by the end of 1921, one of the worst droughts of the 1920s, the number leaps to 225 and never again does it retreat below that 200 level: there were only more and more illegitimate children produced each year, most of them, as we will see, were produced in the rural areas by the Germans.

A total of 344 illegitimate children were born in Saskatchewan in 1924.[77] There were 551 born in 1929, the first year of the drought. At the close of 1932, some 680 illegitimate children had been born in the previous twelve months. The peak was hit in 1934, when 746 illegitimate children were born in Saskatchewan.[78] Thereafter, the levels retreat and the number of illegitimate children falls to 665 in 1938, the lowest number in almost ten years.[79]

Rural municipalities were apparently hotbeds of sex of both the illicit and premarital variety and this was especially true amongst the German settlements (many of the rural German settlement blocs were on land located exclusively on the south and west plains of Saskatchewan; think here of the Schuler-Hatton-Leader [Prussia] corridor along the west side of Saskatchewan). In the 1920s, the Department of Public Health began keeping statistics on which areas of the province were producing the most illegitimate children. Of the 551 produced in 1929, for example, 250 or just under half were born in rural municipalities. Just 128 children were born out of wedlock in the cities.[80]

The age and racial origin of the young mothers was catalogued upon the birth of all illegitimate children: the mothers were always young, frequently German, and they usually lived in remote rural areas. In 1929, three girls under fifteen years of age (two Ukrainians and a Pole) had illegitimate children. But 227 were born of young girls between the ages of fifteen and nineteen, the age group from amongst which the highest number of illegitimate children were born that year, indeed in most years.[81] Approximately fifty of these mothers were young German girls, which made them the ethnic group with the highest rate of unwed motherhood that year.[82] The next closest ethnic group was the Scots, who produced thirty illegitimate children in 1929, although those children were born from amongst women in the twenty- to twenty-four-year-old age group, a demographic that produced 204 illegitimate children that year.

The total numbers of illegitimate children born to young mothers in Saskatchewan is staggering. Between 1914 and 1920, 1,044 illegitimate children were born; between 1921 and 1930, 4,856 were born. And in the Dirty Thirties proper, 5,508 children were born to young mothers out of wedlock. Thus 11,408 illegitimate children were born between 1914 and 1938. Fully half of those children were born in rural areas in the 1930s.

As suggested above, unwed mothers likely took their moral cues and sexual behaviours from their parents, whose lives were then in the process of crumbling in response to pressures like the drought. Divorces that cite adultery as the cause increase at a shocking rate (shocking because of the modern conceit that assumes that people who lived in the decades prior to the thoroughgoing full-on social and sexual revolutions of the 1960s did not have illicit sex – this conceit is *vastly* inflated when the subject of study is the sex lives of pioneers because the word "pioneer" itself is so irredeemably and inextricably linked to our grandparents) and these numbers also feature a very surprising twist: more women than men were committing adultery.

In 1921, just three husbands who divorced their wives cited adultery as the cause, as compared to forty-nine women. There is a comforting familiarity here. This was the usual way of things: the men strayed and the women left. When divorcing, men and women could choose from amongst several reasons but adultery was usually the most frequent. There was: "adultery," "adultery and cruelty," "adultery and desertion," "adultery with cruelty *and* desertion," "impotence."[83] In 1921, of a total of seventy-nine divorces, fully fifty-two cited just plain old adultery (there was only one claim for impotence and nine for adultery and cruelty). This 1921 level remains essentially unchanged for the next few years: there is a rough average of five to seven men who cite adultery as the cause for divorce, and roughly thirty-five to forty women each year who do the same. But then the Dirty Thirties arrive.

At the end of the first excruciating year of crop failure in 1929, twenty-nine men cite adultery as the cause of their divorce as compared to thirty-four women, out of a total of seventy divorces.[84] The number of men filing for divorce because of adultery in 1932 reaches thirty-three as compared to twenty-six women, and this trajectory continues on in this way until the end of 1938 when fully *seventy-seven* men that year file for divorce from their wives because of adultery as compared to just *forty-one* women.[85]

There was clearly not only a corrosion of the moral code but also a deep and wide rupture in the intimately related matter of sexual mores: in just ten years, the instances of illegitimate children very nearly quadrupled from 227 in 1923 to 746 in 1934, an almost four-fold increase in just ten years. The number of women having illicit affairs as cited in divorce records increased from four in 1921 to thirty in 1929 and all the way on up to seventy-seven in 1938. Indeed, the total number of divorces went from a low of twenty-seven in 1924 to 120 in 1938.[86]

Mr. Stapleford, then, is more than a little correct when he suggested that there was something in the soul of the settlers that was altered, or twisted, or disturbed by the drought and we ought to treat his observations as basically unexceptional. After all, need we be surprised, he asked, "that with year after year of such experiences, human endurance sometimes reaches its limit and something snaps?"[87] Settler Albert Stahl grew up at Hatton. He still has family buried in the English cemetery (the German cemetery is a mile away on what would have then been the other side of town), and he definitely recalls the stresses and pressures of the dry years. Mr. Stahl wrote that living in such a "hostile atmosphere can do strange things to a man."[88] Chastity, sexual mores, and modesty, the church, moral codes, and proper behaviour: all quite pointless in a starving, dry, dusty land.

A settler named W.H. March certainly felt that his south and west plains peers lacked moral fibre. March argued that many of the drought problems could have been resolved if the stricken settlers simply provided for their own needs by growing gardens. "It can be done" he argued, but the problem was that "so many people in this south part never even try."[89] March's assertion tends to support Stapleford's idea that "apathy" was one of the side-effects or by-products of the drought. But starvation usually trumps apathy, and so the argument that the absence of gardens can be attributed to laziness, lethargy, or apathy is probably not the best view of things.

The growth of even a small garden in the drylands was as equally as difficult as growing a crop. Explaining that the yields in the Swift Current region have been "ranging from nil to five bushels an acre" for some years, council observed that the drought of 1933 also had another practical result: "all garden stuff has been destroyed by grasshoppers." Thus it was that council petitioned the SRC for more aid because settlers "were unable to provide" for their families and the RM itself was "unable to give any assistance."[90]

In the village of Bateman, the administrator informed the Department of Municipal Affairs about the "decided lack of vegetables" in the village.[91] And in 1933, Pinto Creek had to remind the SRC, which was at that time considering a food allotment reduction, that there has been "no crop or gardens in this municipality for five years" and would it please reconsider the reduction.[92] In the end, it is not entirely fair to say that settlers should have just "grown a garden." One is reasonably sure that the starving settlers of Mankota or Pinto Creek at least gave it some thought.

Mrs. Eunice Hayward's family had a garden, although their experience demonstrates that it was not an easy proposition. The Hayward's grew a garden every year in the Thirties, with the notable exception of 1937. The success of the garden was not easy though and was achieved only as a result of "carrying pails and pails of water" to and from a nearby stream.[93] But on the south plains, there were many thousands of settlers who did not have access to water. Many thousands in fact lived right next to rivers and smaller lakes that had simply dried up. The Haywards were also doubly fortunate to have had hogs, which they would spend all day and half the night killing and processing into food before finally going to bed tired, exhausted "with the smell of rendered lard hanging over all."

Young Madeline Glascock was a school girl during the droughts in Shamrock just north of Pinto Creek, and she recalls the daily life of a starving school kid without garden stuffs. Children would often walk to school barefoot and without food. Those who did have lunches were perhaps worse off than those who did not because those lunches often took strange and exotic forms like "lard sandwiches" and in other instances, for variety, "salted lard sandwiches."[94]

It was not just an absence of garden vegetables that Mrs. Glascock recalls but in particular the absence of fruit: "we never saw a piece of fruit for many years. It was a very special treat when, at Christmas, each of the children in our family received an orange."[95] Receiving fruit in one's Christmas stocking is still very much a tradition in many south and west plains families and this peculiar rite might just trace itself back to the hungry years of the Dirty Thirties when once-ubiquitous fruit was then the most precious of gifts. Fruit indeed became a kind of currency in the RM of Shamrock: a quarter section of land was once traded for a box of apples at a local store.[96]

There is the old frequently told tale that youngsters in the drylands grew up in the Thirties never having seen a piece of fruit or a vegetable. Tales like these are listened to today with no small measure of post-modern disbelief: the mind balks at the silliness of the idea. But on the ravaged banks of Pinto Creek or on the hot plains at Shamrock, when lakes and rivers dried up, when hoppers ravaged every bit of food and drought ravaged every bit of hope, it very well could have been true – children were dying in the dozens because of nutritive deficiencies.

Beriberi, scurvy, rickets, and pellagra: all of these diseases develop as a result of vitamin and nutrition deficiencies. Rickets, for example, is caused by a lack of calcium and vitamin D. It results in the softening of the bones, which itself leads to easy bone fractures and painful physical deformities. Between 1929 and 1938, seventy-eight people, mostly children, died from rickets. An additional six perished from scurvy, two from pellagra, and one from beriberi, of all things.[97] The children who were dying from these diseases were generally under fifteen years old.

The highest instances of death from rickets came in the first two years of the drought, 1929 and 1930, when fifteen and twelve children died respectively. The eight deaths the following year correspond to the establishment of the SRC and the numbers drop to two in 1934, the year it was disbanded. Thereafter the numbers climb, peaking at ten in 1936 (although twelve children died that year – the other two died from scurvy – and all were under fifteen years old).[98] Thus eighty-seven people died from nutritive deficiencies in the thirties at least as noted in the records of the hospitals: the number of children who died outside the sight of a public official was likely much higher than eighty-seven and this is to say nothing of the thousands who suffered, but did not die from, nutritive diseases. So yes, children likely did go for weeks, months, perhaps years at a time, without ever having seen fruit.

The dearth of both fruit and vegetables was mitigated by the by-the-ton donations of food funnelled into the drought area of Saskatchewan by railcar in the 1930s, although in the early going, making a donation wasn't as important as making money. In 1931, the Deputy Minister of Agriculture in Nova Scotia (with a back-slapping familiarity entirely out of place considering the context), wrote informally to "my dear Hedley" (Deputy Auld) and laughingly noted that "judging by press reports, you people in Saskatchewan are likely to starve this winter."[99] He informed the Deputy that Nova Scotia had apparently lost out on a contract to supply potatoes to pre-Castro Cuba because of tariff increases. Thus it was that Auld's Nova Scotia counterpart came knocking with a smile on Saskatchewan's front door trying to solicit the sale of between 50,000 and 60,000 barrels of potatoes – this to a bankrupt province whose children were dying from malnutrition and in some instances starvation.

In right and proper fairness to Nova Scotia's deputy, he likely had no idea how bad it really was. Mr. James Gray has pointed out that even at the time of the national Red Cross appeal for relief in 1931 (the same year in which Nova Scotia's deputy was soliciting business in Saskatchewan), "nobody outside the Palliser's Triangle was told much or knew about what was going on inside."[100] The people of Canada knew it was dry, they knew the settlers were hungry, they knew there had been a crop failure of some kind, but no one really knew how far and how deep the rot had spread. Thus the Nova Scotia deputy likely did not know that two children died from pellagra in 1931. He did not know that thirty-five children had died from rickets in the first three years of the drought. He did not know that between 1929 and 1931, 298 men, women, boys, and girls killed themselves.[101]

There was one foodstuff shipped from the east coast which was universally reviled. But the stature of this commodity in Saskatchewan history has reached the status of genuine legend: every regrettable metric ton of it. One is compelled to stop and linger on this matter of cod for wherever it was distributed it provoked strong almost emotional reactions.

Mr. Harry Forkert landed in the drylands in the early 1920s. He came from the Saxony region of Germany and he had served in the Kaiser's army during "The Great War." He recalls food being shipped into Saskatchewan from points all over Canada. "One can still remember" he wrote, "the rail cars loaded with apples from B.C., the vegetables and baled hay from Manitoba, the big round cheddar cheeses from Ontario." These are not idle reminiscences: by November of 1936, fully 782 carloads of food had been shipped into south and west Saskatchewan from all across Canada and these cars included fruits, vegetables, beans, cheese, and "dried fish."[102] And it is this "dried fish," the cod, that Mr. Forkert distinctly recalls and in his remembrance one can still see the grimace of distaste: "those awful dried cod fish from the Maritimes."[103] Mr. Edward Keck shares this distaste. He was appreciative of everything Saskatchewan received from the rest of Canada "but the fish, they were something else!!!"[104] Mr. Carl Albrecht recalls nailing the cod to the barn door and letting the cows have at it as a salt-lick.[105]

Much of the distaste with cod surrounded the flatlander's basic confusion of what to do with it. Mrs. Eunice Hayward's family came up to Coronach country from South Dakota in the early years and she too says that "the Cod was not welcome."[106] And even though her mother Lena eventually learned to prepare delicious meals with it, "hundreds of pounds were thrown out by other people."[107] There is the old joke in south and west Saskatchewan that settlers put the cod on a board, cooked it, threw away the cod and ate the board.

While the cod seems to be universally though affectionately condemned as "awful," it certainly had some competition, and here one can see Newfies squirm in their seats. Some settlers apparently took to eating gophers but in all fairness this is not as tragic and stomach-turning as it might seem (and here one must certainly guard against making the suggestion that settlers preferred fried gopher over dried cod). Gophers could be, and evidently were, prepared in a number of ways: there was "stewed gopher, canned gopher, gopher pie, smoked gopher, and pickled gopher" in addition to the bachelor-friendly "fried gopher."

Gophers, according to James Gray, were "used not infrequently for food."[108] But the resistance to eating these particular rodents is a deeply rooted impulse in Saskatchewan. While those who ate gophers were "in a very decided minority," they were eaten. But since, as Mr. Gray notes, "the people of the prairies are almost pathologically squeamish to esoteria in food," the gopher was allowed to live free and plunder wheat fields, at least for so long as the kids at Shamrock Primary School didn't get a hold of them. Mrs. Barbara Chai's family landed in Shamrock from the green hills of England in the 1920s. Her schoolyard was overrun with gophers "so at lunch time and at recess we drowned or clubbed gophers."[109] Not just at lunch time. But at recess, too.

It seems that much of the fun to be had by youngsters in those years revolved around gophers. There were annual gopher hunts in which young lads would be rewarded for their efforts with one penny per tail. In one instance, Mr. Orville Lien recalls that there was even a provincial contest in which a pony was offered as a prize for the destruction of the most gophers. Young Mr. Lien set about the undertaking those basic tasks that will be instantly familiar to any young prairie lad who has hunted gophers. He installed gopher traps, laced poison with wheat, made binder twine loops, and poured water down the holes to drown them or flush them out. But for all his work and effort, Mr. Lien did not win. And of all the things about which a man might feel bitter it is the indignity of not winning the pony that he most remembers:

> By fall, I had over a thousand gopher tails. [I got] $10.00 in new quarters but no Shetland pony. I don't know who won but what I do know is that I had more gopher tails than anyone in Aneroid. If the first prize had been restricted to our town alone I would have won the pony. There is no doubt about that because for a long time there were no gophers on our land, not until the following year anyway.[110]

Mr. Lien's family survived ten years in the drylands before fleeing.

It was not just gophers on which settlers focussed, but rabbits too. Rabbit culls were frequent and acted as both a pest eradication event and social event all in one: thus did culture develop in Saskatchewan. Mr. Reinhard Marks recalls these drives (he calls them "social occasions") in which pioneers would meet at an infested area. They would then spread out in a line and rattle rocks in cans to scare the rabbits who would then be corralled into a pre-fabricated fenced-in area where "the grisly job of killing the rabbits was undertaken."[111] He does not provide details, but in the Coronach history book, there are four pictures that accompany this story and the last picture shows a smiling man armed with what appears to be an axe handle.

The Felix and Lawrence Warken brothers somehow managed to kill 1,500 rabbits over the course of three days and they were paid three cents a hide by Art Friedman. Mr. Marks recalls that winter was the best time to hunt rabbits because "the crunch of the snow seemed to bring the rabbits out in the best way."[112]

While the fact that settlers were reduced to eating gophers and "lard sandwiches" (salted or otherwise) may lead some to question the efficiency of the SRC, its record remains impressive, despite the fact that it was shut down in 1934. It was disbanded by Jimmy Gardiner's Liberals. Long a personal bugbear for Gardiner, he felt the SRC was a political tool wielded with enviable success by the Anderson conservatives and so thenceforth there would be no relief commission and instead those duties would be farmed out to various government departments.

In 1935, William Patterson assumed power and he continued the policy direction set down by Gardiner. The Patterson government was known then and is known to history as "the do-nothing" government.[113] Patterson was cheerlessly renowned for being "conscientious and fiscally prudent" and for "[maintaining] government credit in the face of adversity." This was the man who oversaw the second half of the greatest crisis in Saskatchewan history.

RM councils across the south plains were shocked when they found out in 1934 that they were, once again, to be responsible for aid distribution and in fact "would share equally" in aid costs beyond federal relief grants.[114] Exactly how the RMs were supposed to "share equally" was very likely never fully comprehended by municipal administrators, reeves, and councilmen. The crisis of the 1920s very nearly bankrupted many RMs in the drylands and here both levels of government were steering course back to that system against which Big Stick had so ardently railed in 1924. But this was the course and the RMs pushed forward through the dense thickets of desperation that had enveloped their lives and, although they may have been groping blindly through these thickets, the settlers in the RMs still managed to scrape together something that roughly approximated life.

The Dexter Clan down Coronach way has some fond memories of the Thirties and their efforts to enjoy life. Don Dexter, for example, "was a violinist and played for country dances ... we also had card parties in homes and visited our neighbours as often as possible."[115] The local barber shop (shops that used to appear in every Saskatchewan town right up until the 1980s but then, like pool halls, disappeared – "salons" took their place) often served as a cheap form of entertainment. There were two in Aneroid in one of which an apparently popular fellow by the name of Leo Olmstead "often held court," recalls a family member of Laughlin McKinnon.[116] And there were of course local billiard halls that could provide some entertainment, but, as Fred Maier's experience in Hatton demonstrates, these places were frequently viewed with heavy social disfavour. The Aneroid pool hall solved the prejudice toward pool halls by establishing "a library" in the front of the pool hall and thus people, especially young lads, were able to enter "with impunity."

But sometimes, no matter what the fun, food was always primary. Sports Days were a common feature of plains life, which, like pool halls and barber shops and general stores, persisted right up until the 1980s when they too fell out of fashion. Mr. Murray Powell recalls the dances that were held in the evening after Sports Days and the fact that women would always bring their own lunches to these events "so you would always try to pick yourself a partner for a supper waltz and hope she had brought a good lunch."[117] It is quite possible, then, that love in the Dirty Thirties began over a "salted lard sandwich."

Still there was no getting around the dire situation that faced RMs. Swift Current council, for example, borrowed $75,000 in the spring of 1935 for seed grain to ensure that farmers would have the resources to plant a crop that year.[118] This was an enormous amount of money in 1935 and some historians have downplayed the role played by the RMs. H. Blair Neatby comes very close to dismissing the efforts of the RMs when he says that, yes, "it is true" that RMs had to "assume some financial obligations" to provide aid, but he is insistent on reminding us that the majority came from the federal or provincial governments.[119]

With the depressing writing on the wall, RM begged for a continuance of the commission's mandate. Mankota's councilmen pleaded for "all allotments [to] be made out of Regina." Deer Fork's Abe Yacower suggested that the problem was "not nearly over" and urged the SRC to continue its efforts. But it was a political decision, not a practical one and thus Gardiner disbanded the SRC and William "Do-Nothing" Patterson frog-marched the RMs back to the front lines where they simply did not belong. For all their worrying, though, and for all that the RM's had gone through, there still remained the sense in 1934 that the councillors of the many small rural councils that steered the south plains through the crisis of the 1930s were "made of pretty good stuff." Two Saskatoon newspaper reporters took a tour of the south plains, spoke with the councillors and administrators west of Mankota, and concluded that "The leaders appear prepared to make a dollar go as far as it can be stretched."[120]

The disbandment of the SRC meant that councils once again became responsible "for all distribution and collection" of relief aid and loans and that the matter of relief became primarily a local responsibility.[121] Each councillor was responsible for the distribution of relief in his division.[122] The SRC had always feared that a less uniform and less equitable relief system would result from placing all these matters in the hands of local council and that is just what happened. Councils spent "many weary hours" dealing with related problems and deciding who was deserving of relief allotments.[123] We have seen such in the case of Mr. Engelman and the threats to reduce his aid if he didn't stop complaining. Added to this was the fact that many councillors might be on relief themselves; it was thus feared that they might become either "extravagant or even unfair."[124]

There was one "Mrs. Peel" in the Mankota district who had applied for aid but, for various reasons (pride or fear likely chief amongst them), she refused to disclose her monthly income. She was refused aid and then went about complaining to people in the community about the councilmen. She did this to such an extent that council was moved to suggest, almost dare her, to come in and fill out the proper forms and "if she really needs aid then we will grant same."[125] R.S Thompson in Swift Current was graciously granted a double order of groceries in May of 1936 but it was solely on one condition: "that no further relief be granted either him or his family."[126] One can only guess at the conflict that lay beneath those words.

The councillors of the RM of Shamrock kept a sharp eye on who was getting relief aid. Over time and quite naturally, they became a little intolerant of "the indigents who didn't work and wanted to sponge off the municipality."[127] These indigents could have been those men who were passing through on their way to somewhere else. Mr. Al Forsythe was one such man. He stopped at the Robinson farm in the Shamrock district looking for work and food. Obviously they couldn't pay Mr. Forsythe because, as the Rowell-Sirois Commission would later find, Saskatchewan suffered a greater income decline than any other jurisdiction in the world during the 1930s. But the family offered to let him stay and work in return for food. This was an instance in which everything worked out well – Mr. Forsythe remained with the Robinson's for fourteen years "with adjustments in salary of course."[128]

Local Shamrock lads Otto and Adolph Arnold were two of the many who took to the rails in the Thirties, but their experience proved that it wasn't as dramatic and exciting as it might sound. They shuffled over to the Wymarck area looking for work and were offered "the fantastic sum" of five cents per acre for stoking oats: they caught the next train home.[129]

While the Arnold boys shuffled round the south plains looking for work, local councils sunk deeper and deeper into debt, and there was a growing reaction to the responsibilities that RMs had to assume. The RM of Big Stick had long been a critic and active petitioner against what it felt was an unfair aid system. This was the case in the 1920s and councilmen raised their battle standard once again in 1936 when they protested against the "unfair aid system" for exactly the same reasons it had petitioned in 1924. After somewhat disingenuously pointing out that the council alone had been providing aid for five years, Big Stick councillors suggested that it is "absolutely necessary to change the system [because] problems of this kind," councilmen wrote, "we consider a national responsibility and should be treated as such."[130] And really it is hard to take issue with that statement and the allegations of unfairness. Shortly after the cancellation of the SRC mandate in October 1934, the federal and provincial governments each provided $23,000 in aid and Big Stick coughed up its share by taking out another loan of $20,000.[131] All told, Big Stick received $308,531 in aid during the crisis and paid back just $9,531. The government cancelled $226,040.[132]

To get a clear and defined picture of the role RMs played, it helps to consider the month by month expenses incurred. Clinworth, for example, spent $1,800 on relief and "agricultural re-establishment" in January 1935; $5,000 in June; $3,500 in May; $3,000 in July; $3,000 in September, and $1,800 in December. In the year of the big failure in 1937, Clinworth spent fully $28,551.05. Thus very nearly $50,000 was spent on aid and resettlement by just one RM. In addition, Clinworth received $551,972 in relief "advances" and paid back $26,245, and the province was moved to finally cancel $302,307.[133]

The total bill spent by the provincial and federal governments to keep rural Saskatchewan alive and breathing during the crisis of the 1930s was $186,585,808.81.[134] 1937, the worst of the bad years, cost the federal and provincial governments $47,800,000. As further evidence of the intensely regional nature of the drought, the drylands proper (not including the Weyburn-Regina district and south-east area of the province), received the majority of the aid, almost fully half. Crop districts three, four, and seven from present-day Grasslands National Park north and west to Macklin and from Moose Jaw west the Alberta border received $80,037,211.23; this figure does not include the millions collectively spent by the many rural councils of the south and west plains.[135] And since all of this money was in principle an "advance," it was always and throughout the crisis a question of how to get the money back, but it was a question with no easy answer.

The basic and guiding principle that compelled governments to spend nearly one quarter of a billion dollars in rural relief aid was actually quite simple and echoes all the way back to the crop failure of 1914, a year that cost fully $8 million in relief aid.[136] Government officials were building a province and the millions in aid were meant to ensure that no one abandoned their land and left the province, because that would have put at risk the very life of the south and west plains of rural Saskatchewan. The government in the 1920s, and then again in the 1930s, veered wildly away from formal evacuation policy plans as such, although there were special programs in place and settlers were relocated but they were relocated only as a *consequence* of a policy that never had as its primary aim the removal of settlers. It was the reclamation of land that was primary; the removal of settlers was incidental. Mr. J.G. Gardiner, the federal Agriculture Minister in the 1930s, would say even in the hardest year of 1937 that it is not the purpose or goal of the province to remove settlers from the drylands.

The very logistics of an evacuation policy were "mind-boggling." There were an estimated 30,000 families straddling the drybelt on the western side of the province, and a further 100,000 families living in the south plains of Palliser's Triangle proper. Helping remove 130,000 families (which could amount to well past 300,000 people) was obviously not a can of worms the province willingly rushed to open.[137] And while one senator felt that the whole region "should have been left to the cows," A.D. Rae also understood the rock-and-a-hard-place position in which everyone found themselves. Evacuating settlers and returning the land to the cattleman, he felt, "would solve nothing."[138]

The relief system then served much the same purpose as a respirator does for a comatose hospital patient: it kept the dying body breathing. Historian John Archer notes that as the drought and economic conditions worsened "policy choices were eliminated." Relief became policy and thus government's role became a simple if still difficult matter of "preventing the collapse" of large areas of rural Saskatchewan.[139] It was thus that the provincial government essentially became a distribution agency for federal assistance.[140]

While the relief aid kept the body Saskatchewan alive, it did not arrive in time to save the spirit of Saskatchewan. Mr. Archer is keen to suggest that the crisis of the Thirties "ennobled" rural Saskatchewan, that "the privations shared in common re-awakened the older spirit of co-operation" that had marked the early years of settlement. Historian Bill Waiser comes closer to the truth when he writes that "the once vibrant rural society buckled under these conditions."[141]

Surviving the crisis was the principal thought on the minds of most people. From the lowliest settler through the local RM councils and on up to the Minister of Agriculture and the Premier, each participant did what he or she thought was necessary to survive it. These actions included land, grain, and property seizures, fraud, and lies told to get relief. When Big Stick council wrote settler Archie Murray and informed him that "unless he settles up with the RM we will have to repossess [his] land," there wasn't any spirit of co-operation in their words: the RM was trying to survive by seizing land and Mr. Murray was trying to survive by not paying his bills.[142]

Perhaps, though, this spirit of co-operation did exist but maybe it did so in a way that reflected the wider moral confusions and corrosions of the time. During the 1920s, the settlers were often held in contempt by those charged with providing aid. The RM of Clinworth spent themselves broke helping the settlers before proclaiming that they "would not carry them any longer." Big Stick council suggested that settlers were a "burden to the municipality." These statements point toward an animosity that was created and generated by having to care for helpless settlers who, through no real fault of their own, were unable to provide for themselves. But during the 1930s, there was very little if any of that contempt expressed by the councils and rural municipalities. So, in a way, the spirit of cooperation that Archer is keen to suggest guided Saskatchewan through these stormy waters may in fact have actually manifested itself in a restraint or even a reluctance to berate settlers because those who would do the berating were themselves receiving aid. The drought was a great equalizer.

The existence of a widespread spirit of co-operation is a difficult proposition to accept for another well-documented reason: debt collection. Debt collection and notions of cooperation cannot and will not stand in the same room with one another. The animating spirit of both is completely antagonistic toward the other.

Debt collection was the ultimate fact of life on the south plains and the Dirty Thirties produced some fantastically Saskatchewan ways of debt collection, and it is in this that residents may choose to take a kind of perverse pride. In the 1920s, RMs were ready to "seize any buildings on skids" or any farm equipment they could get their hands on; collection agents were busy chasing after the grain stocks of the widow Catherine Slovak; Big Stick councillors, suffering from a curious miasma, were "shooting horses" on the grounds they were a "public nuisance;" the Huelskamps fed porcupine stew to the John Deere collection agent who visited their farm and, to the likely amusement of the Huelskamp household it was a concoction on which he apparently gagged. All these elements and stories of debt collection have a very frontier Saskatchewan feel and stories of this type continued into the 1930s.

In the Thirties, local elevator agents were placed on the front lines of debt collection. In addition to their regular duties of adjudicating the quality of wheat, they also assumed the tertiary duty of collection agent for the RM and were charged with the task of seizing grain grown with seed relief.[143] The agents were issued collection books, which detailed the name of settlers in any given RM who had grown a crop with relief seed and how much of that crop was payable to the RM. In principle, a settler was allowed to keep a maximum of a hundred dollars of any crop grown with relief seed and, at least according to myth, if farmers could not cover the lien with what they grew (and who could when the average wheat yield in the drylands was often zero bushels per acre, or one, or two) then, at least according to historian H. Blair Neatby, "an extension was readily granted."[144] But one must wonder how accurate Mr. Neatby's statement is.

Prefacing its intentions to seize grain at the elevator, Clinworth officials noted that, in principle, they "favour blanket compulsory seizures." It was thus that council resolved to seize any grains delivered to an elevator whose grower owed money to the RM either in the form of back taxes or relief: "all elevator agents" Clinworth council advised, "have lists and authority to issue cash tickets to the RM."[145] It requires little effort to imagine the conflicts produced by these efforts at collection. After all, the same man who seized a settler's grain (and hope) in the morning would be the same man across from whom the settler would sit at coffee row in the afternoon.

Clinworth didn't stop at empowering elevator agents to seize grain. In 1935, it planned a major Seizure Offensive. A list of 260 ratepayers was drawn up opposite the amount of money they owed and "distress warrants" were issued and the collection agent was ordered to "seize the goods, chattels and growing crops" of those who owed money in the form of taxes or relief.[146] One is only faintly surprised to learn that Clinworth churned through at least three collection agents during the first half of the crisis, between 1929 and 1934.

Collection agents were paid handsomely for their efforts. Councils likely understood that such distasteful work needed to be rewarded somehow. Clinworth's first agent was hired during late autumn, 1929. The man worked strictly on a commission of 8 per cent and was charged with collecting on "all unpaid relief seed accounts and unpaid taxes."[147] He lasted until 1933, when council hired R.A. Young. He received a commission plus "10 cents per mile necessarily travelled" to collect and seize.[148] Mr. Young went straight to work trying to collect on $2,000 owed by six different men. James Howes was into the RM for $488 in back taxes and Louis Tumbach owed $9.70 for coal. Mr. Young lasted just two years when council hired on Vernon Ross as collection agent at fifty dollars per month and, a sign of the times, just a 2 per cent commission.[149]

The secretary treasurer of the RM often did double-duty as community collection agent and this almost prompted open revolt in the RM of Deer Forks. In the cold miserable dead of a 1931 winter, in a hall full of people assembled for the purposes of relief aid, a resume for the position of secretary treasurer was handed to Councillor Gus Angerman. The councillor read through the application, considered it, and immediately understood its implications. He dared those settlers assembled in the room: "if anyone [has] anything against the present secretary let him speak up now." The matter was dropped when Angerman saw that "no one had any charges to make."[150] The RMs who hired collectors from outside the district likely did not run into the conflicts associated with having the local secretary-treasurer (which is to say a neighbour or friend) seize the "goods, chattels, and growing crops" of settlers.

The unnamed secretary treasurer defended by Mr. Angerman was, in addition to being paid $120 per month, also being paid a 6 per cent commission on all he collected and was authorized by council to "distrain and make seizures whenever he thinks necessary."[151] That is a considerable level of arbitrary power granted to an unelected man and it would have had the smell of illegitimate authority to the settlers whose lives and property he was seizing and "distraining." Certainly it would have seemed that way to David Riehl who had 300 bushels of grain stored away but which were seized by the agent and, according to Councillor Ira Robbins, "totally applied to his relief account."[152] Thus Mr. Riehl had to stand by and watch a man who may have been his neighbour seize the very little grain he had been able to grow in one of the worst droughts of the century. Indeed, Riehl was at risk of being struck off the relief rolls for storing grain. "Secret hoards of grain" were one of the four principal reasons why a settler would be removed from the relief rolls; alcohol use, non-disclosure of income, and refusal to accept work (likely road work) were the other three.[153]

As philosopher/historian Isaiah Berlin pointed out, any solution to any problem creates its own unique set of problems, and it can be said that the relief system of the 1930s continually generated problems equal to or greater than those it solved. Nothing demonstrates the cyclical absurdity of the relief system like the circumstances surrounding the unfortunately named Mr. Peter Lose.

Mr. Lose appeared before council in late 1932 to ask them to refund a portion of the value of the property and grains the RM had earlier seized and which had left him penniless. The debt to the RM had been settled but in solving that problem it created another one: it left the settler broke, thus requiring more relief aid. Mr. Lose was likely a little shocked when "after due consideration council refused."[154] Lose claimed he had nothing left and was likely being at least somewhat honest for he would not let the matter drop. He re-appeared a month later to again plead his case in November. Council again refused. But finally, on the eve of the Christmas season, serendipity smiled and, due to "hard circumstances," council agreed to grant an eighty-five-dollar refund of the amount that had been seized by the collection agent, though it was a narrow vote as two councillors, unmoved by the spirit of the Christmas season, voted against Mr. Lose's request.

Property and grain seizure was such an omnipresent fact of life that Saskatchewan's Attorney General was obliged to spell out in a formal pamphlet who could seize what and at what times could the seizing be done. T.C. Davis explained that, yes, RMs "can seize for taxes without notice" and can seize for relief aid with advance notice (think here of the distress warrants issued by Clinworth).[155] The document also reflects the debt moratoriums that had been introduced in Saskatchewan as Mr. Davis issues a call for restraint and encourages creditors to give settlers time to pay and room to breathe. This is precisely the approach that the Saskatchewan government refused to take in the 1920s because of the possibility that investors might be scared away. Davis noted that "the government will refrain from pressing for payment of debt" and, indeed, he fires a shot across the over-zealous bow of rural collection agents by politely noting that "I am sure municipalities … will co-operate … in trying to reach this end."[156] Some of them did.

Pinto Creek hired a collection agent in 1932 but, given the fact that they lived in a disaster zone and would continue to do so for another seven years, they agreed to restrain the agent and would let him loose to seize "only under instructions from council," which is a distinct, and for the settlers welcome, departure from those RMs that favoured the "whenever the collection agent deems it necessary" approach.[157] Swift Current went through both phases of this general arc. It hired M.J. Knapp in 1932 as a collector for arrears of taxes and relief, but, opting for the style adopted by Deer Forks and others, certainly Big Stick in the 1920s, they granted Mr. Knapp "the power to make seizures when it is considered necessary."[158] Deer Forks considered it necessary to continue with its approach right up until the end of the crisis when, after granting $200 in aid to fifteen people, council again moved to make seizures "in any case where the circumstances warrant it."[159]

No matter how much debt was collected, it was never enough for the dozens of one-room schoolhouses in the rural areas. Like settlers, the schools in each RM often subsisted on government grants and relief aid. In 1930, it cost about $16,000 to operate a school for one year, but, by 1935, that amount had fallen to $8,600.[160] Teachers' salaries had fallen to an average of less than $600 per year and, by 1938, unpaid teachers' salaries had climbed to $1,303,004.[161] As was the case in the 1920s, it took no time at all for schools to be steamrolled by the drought of the Thirties. In 1931, the government determined that it would need an immediate grant of $30,000 just to keep rural schools open and would need a further $1.5 million to keep them in operation until the end of that year 1932.[162]

In Swift Current in 1930, for example, it cost the RM $3,200 for the Wymark school district; in 1932, the cost was down to $985.60, such was the trimming of services, the lowering of wages, and the absence of school children. In the disaster zone of Pinto Creek, the Dixie School District cost $1,850 in 1929 and $1,350 in 1931.[163] Desperate to maintain some control, Big Stick urged its school districts "to keep their bank borrowing to a minimum."[164] And as the crisis slowly wound its way past the half-way mark in 1936, Clinworth, despite all its productive efforts, found that it was twenty-one months in arrears to its schools and dejectedly stated there were "no prospects of collecting taxes" that year.[165] Provincial cuts to school grants began early on in the 1930s. Fully one third of the education grant was cut in 1932. But as the crisis dragged on and on, the cuts went deeper and deeper. In 1921, a rural one-room schoolhouse teacher made $1,388 per year; by 1936, that salary had fallen to $407.[166] As of December 1936, the total unpaid salaries of one-room school teachers was $937,594.11.[167] Rural school teachers, a Dominion government adviser correctly observed in 1938, "[bore] the full impact of the distress."

Mrs. Ethel Schmidt made a career out of working in the drylands through the worst years in the history of this province. She began as a teacher in the tiny community of Liebenthal, which is just down the road from Leader (formerly Prussia) and although there are still a few (literally a few) people in this hamlet, the school, the store and the post office in Liebenthal were finally shut down in the 1980s.

Mrs. Schmidt's pupils ranged in age from six to sixteen and the highest grade was six. Given the very hit and miss nature of education in those days, having sixteen-year-olds in a grade six class is not surprising. Mr. Frank Ulm, down south at Aneroid, recalls that, in those early days, some kids were reaching nine and ten years old without ever having set foot in a school.[168] And further reflecting this trend of education being inconsistent and highly uneven even at the best of times, there was the story in Alberta about the young fellow who "spent the happiest four years of his life in grade six, was given a farm by his father on his 21st birthday whereupon he forthwith married the teacher."[169]

Mrs. Schmidt taught a total of thirty students but what really disturbed her was the fact that fully twenty of her charges could only speak German.[170] This language barrier caused the young Mrs. Schmidt no end of distress: "I was really in a dither," she recalled and "didn't think I could stand it." She was lonesome and homesick and stuck in a one-room school full of young Germans and she was "sure they were talking about me."[171] As a first-time teacher, however, it is quite possible that Mrs. Schmidt's biggest problem was her classroom management skills. Mr. Carl Albrecht was a German who came from Romania as a boy and settled on the Krupp Flats, north of Maple Creek and his English was terrible. In the yard of the school he attended, there was a large boulder and "at recess and noon hour we kids that couldn't speak English would run behind this rock and talk German until the bell rang."[172] This suggests that Mr. Albrecht had a teacher who refused to allow German to be spoken in the classroom.

In the end, though, Mrs. Schmidt didn't stand it. Even though she met some people at local barn dances, she "got discouraged" and she "couldn't hack it any longer," in part, at least, because "there was no library worth a hoot" and finally felt that she had to quit. Mrs. Schmidt was actually correct in her assessment of the school library. The Rowell-Sirois Commission found that most libraries in the drought area "suffered severely" during the dry years because there was simply no money for books. One must conclude that the intellectual life of most drylanders suffered as much as the physical, economic, and spiritual side of their lives. But Mrs. Schmidt did not quit teaching, nor did she quit the drylands. She taught at a few schools in the region before finally leaving for Saskatoon in the 1940s. Where her salary was concerned, she recalls that sometimes she had to "wait a year or two" to get paid.

Even hospital bills had to be covered by government grants. Since "the crop in this municipality [Clinworth] is a total failure" (it was zero bushels per acre in 1937), council asked the province to foot the medical bills for the district.[173] Pinto Creek, which had throughout the late 1920s and early 1930s made concerted efforts to attract a physician to the district, found it couldn't pay him once he arrived. Council pleaded for the ratepayers to "pay at least a few dollars" on their 1933 tax bill or the doctor would leave.[174]

For all its antagonistic but effective nature, debt collection still had its limits. After all, how does a settler pay if he hasn't grown anything that he can sell? But when collection failed, some RMs had no choice but to start writing off bad debt. Clinworth, for example, cancelled $14,059.59 in unpaid taxes on twenty parcels of land in 1933, likely because the land had been abandoned and no collection could be achieved.[175] Before reaching that point, however, councils tried the carrot-and-stick approach.

Swift Current felt it "necessary to grant a compromise" and thus cancelled all penalties on the 1931 tax arrears if they were paid by a certain date.[176] In Mankota, hundreds if not thousands of dollars in relief loans and back taxes were lost when council, adjusting itself to the peculiarities of life in a dust bowl, stopped pursuing that to which it was legally entitled and instead adjusted itself to the infinitely broader and roomier idea of pursuing what it could reasonably expect to get. Mr. J.H. McCleary had gone through six years of crop failure in a row and owed the RM $800, but council agreed to accept $600 and thus cleared the slate. Mr. Armand Masse owed $412, but council accepted $340 as full payment. Mr. Charles Lagarre owed $2,040, but council cleared his bill after he paid $1,595.[177]

The Saskatchewan government was certainly not insensible to the plight of its municipalities. Debt and credit always was and continues to be the motor that drives agricultural Saskatchewan. Credit is necessary to farm: that was true then and it is true today. Saskatchewan had always borrowed money. Settlers borrowed to farm and merchants borrowed to stock their stores; thus credit was Saskatchewan's backbone: "the depression broke that backbone."[178]

The province made every effort to soften the hammer blows of the drought in the south and the depression in the north. The Anderson government, for example, introduced a two-pronged effort for tax consolidation and debt adjustment early on in the Thirties. This 1931 Act allowed municipalities to cancel annual tax sales, and it allowed indebted rate-payers the opportunity to stretch out the repayment of those debts to the RMs over the course of five years between 1933 and 1938.[179] This plan was optional for each RM and it was a short-sighted measure because it was "predicated upon a quick return to prosperity." There was always the assumption that it couldn't get any worse, that it had to get better.

The tax sale, as we have seen, played a huge role in the crisis of the 1920s and it was a not-insignificant factor in allowing settlers to expand their holdings. The tax sale also allowed the RMs to recoup some of the massive losses they had incurred through non-payment of taxes and relief loans. To give an example of its potential importance, Pinto Creek had annual expenditures in its operating budget of just $23,932 in 1933, but its tax arrears as of 1934 were $135,967 and that is not counting money owed for aid and relief seed. The possibility of making money off land sales to satisfy municipal debt was one of the operative principles of the tax sale, even though in the 1930s such sales often could be justifiably viewed with some anger as a settler watched his land being purchased by a neighbour. But still the tax sale became a problem. Even though "a great many taxpayers are forced to allow their lands to go through the tax sale … owing to drought conditions," Big Stick council, in the early years of the crisis of 1931, decided not purchase these lands.[180] And indeed council finally stopped holding the sales in 1935 because there were not any buyers attending, the RM could not get a decent price anyways, and selling abandoned land laden with liens posed a myriad of problems.[181] Under these conditions, the Anderson government's cancellation of the tax sale as a protective measure for settlers has all the appearance of a grandiose bow to an empty theatre.

Clinworth stopped holding its tax sale in 1932 with the apparent purpose of mollifying the growing resentment in the community and instead agreed to "make an earnest appeal to all ratepayers to pay at least one year's taxes."[182] Swift Current was among the earliest to abandon the sale of seized or abandoned lands when in 1931 it asked the Department of Municipal Affairs for the authority "not to hold a tax sale."[183] Pinto Creek, always gentle when it came time to apply the rough and hard hand of collections, granted land seizure postponements to eight settlers in June of 1932 and another six in July.[184] But still, councils assumed title to land whether they wanted to or not because in the developed/developing west of the 1930s, someone had to own the land; it simply cannot lie ownerless. So, Big Stick in the winter of 1937 assumed title to an unspecified number of parcels of land "which, in the opinion of council, are sub-marginal or unfitted for agriculture or which have been abandoned."[185]

Big Stick was always a little different from the other RMs in the drylands. It was far more aggressive in its collection efforts during the 1920s, and it was also far more strident and willing to express its opinion on the state of agriculture, its views on settlement policy, and how it felt about the relief aid system generally. It was one of the few RMs to be consistently and actively vocal about the broader issues connected with local crises. It may have in fact been councils like Big Stick that the world-weary scribes of the Swift Current *Sun* had in mind when they poked fun at RMs who passed wordy, obfuscatory resolutions which, for all their depth, had no practical effect. "In Germany" wrote the editors of the *Sun*, "the people say 'Heil Hitler!' in Italy its Hosannas for Il Duce; over here it's 'therefore be it resolved'"[186] Still, Big Stick was not afraid to leap into the fray and give voice to its opinions.

In 1935, Big Stick council gave the province a bit of a history lesson (albeit using the clunky and unappealing format of a municipal resolution to get their point across – there are in these resolutions, as the *Sun* scribes suggested, lots of "whereas" and "therefore be it resolved"). RMs, councilmen explained, could not provide the services expected by the ratepayers because the ratepayers were not paying any money for taxes or relief. Council could not collect taxes because no one was growing anything. The banks were insisting that the interest on previous loans be paid by the money from future loans and, furthermore, were only lending 50 per cent of what RMs were allowed to borrow. It had been this way during the crisis of the 1920s and was so again in the 1930s. All of this was a preface to asking the province to "assume the ultimate loss of relief loans."[187]

The resolution touches a number of important points that it is profitable here to reconsider and summarize: the RMs could not function because no one could pay taxes. Settlers could not pay taxes because they weren't growing anything. RMs were seizing what the settlers had grown, thus necessitating more relief. The province spent a good majority of its relief money for rural Saskatchewan on seed grain implicitly insisting that the settlers grow something. When nothing grew and no taxes could be collected, the RMs were compelled to employ collection agents to collect on the useless seed relief loans, but there was no money to collect because nothing grew. When something did grow the RMs seized it to satisfy tax arrears, once again necessitating more relief. The government introduced a moratorium on contracted (bank) debt but yet insisted that payments be made to itself.[188] The Anderson government allowed settlers five years to pay off their municipal debts, which drove the RMs further into penury, thus increasing the demands on the settlers to pay something, but they couldn't because they were growing nothing in a land where the government kept insisting they try again.

This ridiculous circus is profoundly, deeply astonishing. That it dragged on for ten years, and, in some jurisdictions, twenty to twenty-five years, saddens one very nearly to the point of laughter. In all of Canadian history, there is nothing quite like it. At no time have Canadians engaged futility and absurdity with such devotedness, sincerity, and enthusiastic earnestness. The decade is tragic, yes, but it cannot fail to bring a kind of grim laughter.

Nothing quite captures the ridiculous essence of the Dirty Thirties in the same way as road-gangs. Rural road-gangs in the Thirties became institutionalized. They became a part of the Saskatchewan landscape. Road-gangs and road-work relief camps played an important role during both the depression and the drought, but to this point far more scholarly attention has focused on the camps for the urban unemployed. The urban camps usually employed young single men and are remembered mostly for the fear they induced in governments who thought that unsavoury (read:

communist) political machinations were occurring within their confines. Precious little attention, no attention in fact, has ever been paid to the rural settler road gangs, which were a ubiquitous presence on the plains between 1914 and 1937 but particularly so after 1929.

It is the slight but very real suggestion of the penal-punitive nature of road-gang work that makes these camps compelling. It sometimes seems as though all that is missing is leg irons. Here we have the spectre of desperate, impoverished men with starving families unceremoniously put to on heavy-labour work details to pay for seed grains with which to fail at farming. The futility of the existence is awesome. But still the men went to the road-gangs and what's more they did it willingly, or that is to say, they viewed the labour as an opportunity to work instead of asking for relief and thus road-gangs also explain much about what it meant to be a man on the south plains at the close of the frontier in western Canada.

Saskatchewan-raised novelist Wallace Stegner grew up in Eastend, not too very far from Mankota, in the early years of dryland settlement between 1914 and 1920. His world as a boy in those years mirrors the world of the settlers of the 1920s and 1930s. And even though, when Stegner identifies what he admires in the men of the south plains he is speaking of the cattle ranchers and cowboys whom he encountered, his reminiscences still suit our purposes admirably because they point us in the general direction of the kind of man who would lose his crop ten years in a row or fifteen out of twenty, would have the spirit to stay, and, what's more, would go to work on heavy-labour road-gangs.

Stegner says he and his friends admired "good shots, good riders, tough fighters, dirty stories," but, even more than that, they admired "stoical endurers of pain."[189] Endurance is what counted on the south plains – blissfully, "feelings" did not matter. No one ever asked settlers how they *felt* about the problem – the question was how settlers would *deal* with the problem, a quite marked contrast to the culture of our own age.

A failed settler working on a road-gang, then, was nothing if not a stoical endurer of pain. Being a sickly child, Stegner grew up "hating [his] weakness" and thus found some measure of comfort in this principle of stoical endurance, what he later termed an "inhumane and limited code."[190] As we have seen earlier, at no time were settlers very much respected amongst the cattle ranchers and cowboys of the region ("moss-back" and "sob-buster" were not terms of affection), but, still, there were some basic philosophical similarities between ranchers and settlers: the life of both revolved around individual freedom. The cowboy found freedom riding a horse in the middle of nowhere while the settler found freedom from the servitude of Old Europe, or freedom from the tenant farming endemic to the American west. Settlers and cowboys were what D.H. Lawrence famously called "masterless men." This much they shared in common.

At bottom and despite all he despised about the frontier world ("the prejudice, the callousness, the destructive practical jokes"), Stegner admired the ranch hands and cowboys who lived and judged life by what he called "the same raw standard." These men honoured "courage, competence, and self-reliance," and Stegner adds that "it was their absence not their presence which was cause for remark."[191] This point needs to be emphasized: it was the *absence* of courage and self-reliance, of stoical endurance, that caused remark and thus it was naturally assumed by most people, the settler included, that if his crop failed then he *should* go to work on a road-gang. That was just one of the enormous expectations placed on men of that day and if a settler refused (and there were likely a good many who did), then that meant a settler lacked those very qualities that were held in such high esteem in the frontier days of early Saskatchewan, qualities like courage, honour, and self-reliance.

Stegners thoughts on being a man find an echo in remarks made by the head of the Northern Saskatchewan Resettlement Branch (NSRB), a government agency hastily established in 1935 and which helped to evacuate settlers from the drylands. Its chief, Richard Matte, was explaining to a radio audience in 1938 what it was the NSRB had done and was doing. And he noted that their efforts at removing settlers were designed to get him and his family off of relief because, in Matte's words, "we all agree that relief is the most repugnant form of assistance to the self-respecting man."[192] Absolutely nothing of the sort could be said today, at least publicly anyway. Western culture is engaged in a full-on retreat from anything that even resembles a strong moral judgment despite the fact that most people, deep somewhere in their heart of hearts, still agree with Matte's words.

There was, then, a heavy emphasis in the early settlement years on being a man of courage, resilience, strength, and persistence. On a cultural level, these sentiments would not survive the 1960s and were instead deposited into a moral junk-heap at the earliest opportunity in favour of self-esteem and the expression of one's rights and "feelings" and entitlements. Indeed, today, when words like courage or strength are deployed, they are often accompanied by quotation marks indicating that, at least at the level of public discourse, we no longer share those ideals and indeed are somewhat embarrassed by them, though perhaps embarrassment is the wrong word. Perhaps men today know that they do not quite measure up to the men of the early settlement years and we escape this knowledge by taking refuge in sophisticated cynicism and irony and the distant comfort provided by quotation marks and inverted commas. Honour, courage, self-reliance: quaint, archaic thoughts that withered and died in the moral corrosion of the 1960s.

There were huge expectations of men in the frontier world and they were expected to perform abhorrent tasks without complaint and do so gladly or if not gladly, then, as Stegner notes, without complaint. And by and large it would seem they did so, although, since people are generally the same in all times and at all places and since the expressions of desperation and despair do not really change over time, we can assume that, at least once or twice when a settler's head was bowed down over his shovel whilst .plying his grim and futile trade, a tear or two fell into the dust and hot asphalt.

Road-building in Saskatchewan has always been an important element of rural life. How else is one to get to his field if not for roads? Deer Forks council held a special meeting in the sunny, happy spring of 1914 to "discover ways and means" of building roads.[193] One smiles at the earnestness with which they considered this problem because it would be solved for them through no effort of their own that very year. Indeed, drought would be practically the only thing that would ensure an adequate supply of money and labourers to get the work done. If you have ever wondered why it is that Saskatchewan has the most roads of any province in confederation, you might trace the answer to that question to the dry years on the south and west plains and a certain Colonel H.R. Matthews.

The Colonel was selected by the province (his title probably gives a good indication of why he was chosen for this line of work) to oversee and administer the road-gang camp system, which was similar in nature to the famed urban relief camps that were established across Canada during the Great Depression. Very little is known about the Colonel – he is one of those shadowy figures who drifts into the pages of history and then exits upon completion of his assignment. At any rate, the Colonel's camps were set up not just in the drylands but right around the province, though as one may suspect, most of the work was done on the south plains, and, of that work, the largest amount occurred in the Kincaid-Mankota-Gravelbourg-Assiniboia districts.

The Colonel worked out a wage scale for those who would do the work. The foreman for each camp got six dollars per day; labourers got four dollars (minus one dollar for meals) and "the straw boss" received five dollars.[194] Men were expected to bring their own plates, forks, and spoons, much to the likely displeasure of their wives because it raised the prospect of lost cookware and cutlery. The settlers were able to work up to $100 in earned wages, after which point they were ordered to step aside and make room for the next man. So, at four dollars per day they could conceivably have work for about four or five weeks.

Rural municipalities operated on a somewhat different system than the Colonel. They would make application for a project (and the minutes of the RM meetings show a *constant* application for "road-work relief"), the Department of Highways would review it, and if the project was suitable, the money for the work would be granted.[195] This system was different from the Colonel's set-up in that there were no camps for the settlers. RM projects were by and large local day work "so as to make it possible for the farmers employed on the work to return home at night."[196] Mr. Frederick Hartman was a German who had come to the south plains from Russia in 1911 and he regularly did road work for the RM in the Richmound district. His reasons for it are pretty simple: "anything to earn a dollar to clothe and feed a family of nine and pay the taxes."[197]

Letting loose thousands of starving, impoverished, and destitute settlers to build the highways and byways of a new province is not exactly what the founding fathers of Saskatchewan had in mind when the province was born in 1905, so a crew of road inspectors was hired to oversee the work being done by the settlers on the RM jobs. These inspectors did not bother with the road camps: evidently, the Colonel was his own authority.

The inspectors checked to make sure "the men come to work when required" and that the quality of their work was acceptable. They also handled all complaints of "discrimination" or even the "improper use being made of relief moneys." There were forty-two camps in 1930, the first year of the program, which continued for much of the decade, and a total of $1,131,090 was spent in that first year on both camp and RM projects. Road work in 1931 employed some 9,000 men.[198] Over the course of the 1930s, $10 million was spent on relief road work, which employed roughly 40,000 men.

In the early years of the 1930s, before it became an institutionalized government-directed affair, relief road work was a simple and straightforward proposition. A.W. McLaren of Swift Current worked off $98.70 in relief "in lieu of construction of a road to Bode school."[199] It was a simple problem with a simple solution. John Hardy in Mankota received twenty dollars worth of groceries early in the crisis and thus also received "$20.00 worth of road work" with which he "repaid" his loan.[200] But the problem grew more complex as the thirties worsened.

The payment or non-payment of wages for work on the day jobs, for example, was often at the discretion of council. After decreeing in the summer of 1930 that "no cash be paid for road work where the parties owe for taxes," Big Stick council softened its stance and, in the fall of that year, decided that only 50 per cent of wages needed to be "turned in on municipal debt."[201] Big Stick, like many other RMs, was not paying a princely sum in wages: it couldn't. A road-work labourer was given forty cents an hour and over an eight-hour day that works out to $3.20, about eighty cents less than a worker would receive on the Colonel's road-gangs. Pinto Creek councillor George Stribell even managed to win a vote in which the wages that council was (at least morally) obliged to pay the settlers were withheld until such time as settlers could clear either their relief or their tax account. When that didn't happen, those settlers lost their wages, which were "applied to 1933 municipal taxes, relief interest, or hospital and medical aid as the case may warrant."[202] This, of course, necessitated more relief.

Alberta municipalities were likewise in the same bind as their counterparts in Saskatchewan. The President of Alberta's provincial municipal association, Mr. John Gair, told his organization's membership in the early years of the drought that, when councillors had been elected to office, their primary consideration had been the construction and maintenance of roads. But by the 1930s, Mr. Gair noted, there was much that had changed: "you now all realize that the financial condition of your municipality is your first duty and road building is more or less a secondary consideration which, in many cases, is now carried on only as a relief measure."[203] For municipalities in both Alberta and Saskatchewan, then and today, placing road work second on *any* kind of priority list was a fundamental inversion of and offence to a very basic and natural order. Roads come first in rural Saskatchewan and Alberta; everything else is second.

What makes the road-work element of the crises intriguing is that the men volunteered willingly to the point that there were always backlogs and more applicants than there was work. Swift Current council had a hundred applications for road work even before there was provincial approval for either a road relief grant or one of the Colonel's camps: council "strongly urged" the province to set up a camp near Highway 4.[204]

Given the very few people who have travelled the highway between Kincaid and Mankota, even fewer would be aware of the troubled history of that forty-kilometre stretch of highway that detours into the town itself and stops there because there is nothing below Mankota except rock piles, snakes, and emptiness. The town is a last exit from Saskatchewan.

Pinto Creek had petitioned the government for a road camp to be set up on the number 19 in the late summer of 1930. But there was a bit of a problem because of the camp's location. The camp was closer to Mankota than it was to Kincaid, and, when the Kincaid men, armed with their shovels and picks and their wives treasured plates and spoons, arrived for work, the camp had been overtaken by Mankota men. The Colonel had sent "at least 150" men from Kincaid to the camp but upon their arrival they found ninety men in the camp already, with apparently another forty on the waiting list. The Kincaid men were "refused work and sent home."[205] There is no record of conflict between the two groups but men under intense pressure who are suddenly and capriciously batted about by fate do not simply "return home" without at first expressing their thoughts and views about the situation. The squabbling over scraps of highly valued heavy-labour relief work is a distinct possibility. Pinto Creek councillors even pledged to provide their own cook and bunkhouse if it meant the Kincaid men could get to work on the Nineteen. Didn't happen, though.

This potentially explosive situation was a natural outcome of the Colonel's rules. Actuated by some impulse toward arbitrary fairness and chance, the Colonel decreed that work camps were not for any single municipality but instead were meant for the men of three or four adjoining or nearby RMs.[206] It was simply the hard luck, in a land full of hard luck, that the Kincaid men showed up late, or rather not early enough.

It is not often that one is able to hear the voices of the men who worked in these camps. Reminiscences frequently concern the urban instead of the rural camps. But there was a man by the name of Mr. Pax Crowley who gives us a valuable if ever so slight glimpse into what it was like. Mr. Crowley worked on Highway 10. And in writing about the days he spent working in the camps, one finds that it wasn't all bad or rather there was at least a touch of light that brightened the dark edges. Between fifty and sixty men worked in this camp. Mr. Crowley recalled that the men would sing while working. In particular he remembers working out the ditty "Spring Time in the Rockies."[207] One might also assume that "Someone's in the Kitchen with Dina" was also given extensive treatment, popular as it was in that day and age.

There were also other forms of entertainment too. There were socials, dances, and "whist drives" organized with the help of local community clubs. And on the final night before the camp was shut down with the completion of the job, Mr. Crowley recalls that there was a dance at which an oldtimer known only as 'Old Blue' played the piano. No one knew his real name, Mr. Crowley remembers, or where he had come from, only that he was called 'Old Blue' and that he played all night.[208]

Highway 21 runs north-south, connecting Maple Creek to Leader, and it too was a relief project or at least its development, paving, and maintenance was (and anyone who has driven the 21 from Leader north to Eatonia will have no trouble believing that the last improvements made to that highway were done by settlers during the 1930s). But in 1935 with "total crop failure" looming (two bushels per acre in 1934, four in 1935, and one in 1930), Big Stick council asked that twenty-five miles of the Twenty One be resurfaced and that "settlers be given a chance to work."[209] If you ever find yourself in Golden Prairie, the seat of the RM of Big Stick, which sits at the halfway point between Leader and Maple Creek, please do not call Highway 21 "Highway 21." According to local historian and Irishman A.L. O'Farrell, "if you call it that, you will be marked as an outsider."[210] It's "The Big Stick Trail," he cautions, and it has been such for a hundred years.

Of course, and quite understandably at least from a modern perspective, not all men were willing to go to work on heavy-labour road crews, but there was the continual threat that one would be stricken off of the relief rolls if one refused. Settlers had several anvils hanging over their head at any given time during the crisis. For RMs it was always a matter of dollars and cents: the settlers owed money and the RM needed either money or work in kind and thus road relief solved that problem. But for the men involved, it was more a matter of the affective elements of life: of pride, of dignity, or even of laziness. The practical elements of life were at constant war with the affective. Swift Current council felt that settlers ought to be "allowed" to work off 50 per cent of relief or taxes and that, if they refused, "without a valid reason," they would be "cut off relief."[211]

As mentioned, an RM set its own rates and rules for road work. As part of a $2,000 road-work project granted in Mankota in the good year of 1932 (three bushels per acre that year) council limited the number of days worked to three, after which the "recipient" of the "aid" would step aside for the next man.[212] On a 1934 project, seventy men worked and were paid twelve to fifteen dollars and this project was one of the few times the name of a woman showed up out there working on the road-gangs. A "Mrs. George Jones" was amongst those working on the project.

The wages that were paid were necessarily a pittance, and one wonders how useful the "relief work" actually was. On provincial jobs, the wage rate was fixed at five dollars per day (less a dollar for meals) and on an eight-hour day that works out to about sixty cents an hour. But RMs, perhaps wishing to help more settlers by paying less in wages (or for even less appetizing reasons – recall the inspectors ensuring the proper use of relief money), paid their labourers quite a bit less. Mankota paid forty cents an hour as did Deer Forks and Big Stick, and it seems this was the top end of the wage scale on municipal projects. The poorest-paying RMs were Pinto Creek and Clinworth. Pinto Creek paid its men twenty cents an hour (later thirty-five cents) or about two to three dollars per day. Clinworth paid its men twenty cents an hour in 1934 for the spiritually destructive task of "burying weeds" in ditches. Swift Current started out at $2.50 per day (about thirty-five cents per hour) but dropped its wages to two dollars per day in 1931.[213]

All told, the province spent $10 million on road-work relief between 1929 and 1939, and 40,946 men received work on these various provincial and municipal projects. In the worst of the bad years, 1937, the province estimated road-work costs at $750,000 in addition to the $180,500, which to that point had not been completed from the projects of 1936.[214]

There was no escaping road work. If you lived in Saskatchewan during the Dirty Thirties, you or someone you knew was likely a member of a road-work gang. And that includes the northern grain belt where road work followed the settlers who had been evacuated and where "the building of pioneer roads" occurred.[215] It seems that road work up north was a tad more punitive than on the plains. Instead of the often-used benchmark of 50 per cent, settlers were obliged to hand over two thirds of their income to satisfy relief debt. "In this way," historian Mr. Blair Neatby thoughtfully explains, "the cost of re-establishing settlers was considerably reduced."[216] Good news.

The pay for settlers up north was less discretionary than it was on the south and west plains. The foremen were given lists of men and "[these lists] specified amounts each should be permitted to earn" and these earnings were not paid in cash but in "orders for supplies."[217] Thus it was that settlers stumbled through the trees and brush of the north country in the middle of winter, cursing the Last Best West while delivering firewood to train stations, which was another way in which relief debt/relocation debt could be satisfied. One wonders when settlers actually had time to fail at growing wheat.

It is profitable here to summarize. Settlers were put to work on road crews to work off relief debts. At twenty cents an hour, it would have taken two weeks to work off a debt of fifteen dollars. And since the money for which they worked was already spoken for, they would again need either direct relief for food or seed relief with which to fail at growing wheat in the following crop year, thereby necessitating more road work. But since there was such a clamour for road work, which reduced the amount of money a settler could earn, the relief debt and back taxes piled up quicker than one earned the money to satisfy the debt. Relocation to the north would result in relief work to pay back the cost of relocation and since in the north it could and did take between one and three years to get a piece of land productive, the settler would again be required to go on relief work while the bills piled up. In the end, for tens of thousands of settlers, the question was not "how can I pay my bills?"; the question was "how can I get out of here?" Thousands upon thousands settlers found what we must assume was an easy answer to that question.

Exodus

Abandon: (verb) desert or leave permanently; give up (an action or practice) completely. From the Old French *abandoner*.

Relinquish: (verb) willingly cease to keep or claim; give up. From the Latin *relinquere/linquere*, "to leave."

Quit: (verb) leave, especially permanently. From the Latin *quiescere* 'be still.'

Desert: (verb) leave without help or support; abandon; leave (a place) causing it to appear empty. From the Latin *desertare*, "left waste." – *Oxford English Dictionary*

By the 1930s, hope had fled from many regions of the south plains. Year after year of punishing physical labour on road gangs, year after year of spiritually ruinous dust storms, year after year of starvation and relief aid had come and gone and settlers made up their minds and voted with their feet. Tens of thousands of people fled and left behind whatever they couldn't carry. It is not much of a stretch to say that each rock pile located on pasture land in Saskatchewan, each derelict barn, each worn and weathered yard site can trace its unhappy history back to the 1930s. There is often the complaint in Saskatchewan that we have no 'real' history, that unlike Europe or Asia, one must go to museums to see the past. That is just not true.

The mass land abandonment phase began shortly after the start of the drought in 1929. It began as early as 1931 and continued on down to 1938, at which time it slowed and instead of abandonment it became what we politely refer to today as consolidation, or a *general* movement of people away from the farms and into the cities, rather than hyper-speed abandonment. The difference between consolidation and abandonment is merely one of scale and speed. Consolidation is a gradual, scarcely noticeable drift of people away from the land, whereas abandonment, at least within the context of the Thirties, is a harried and frantic mass stampede. The difference between the two is largely a question of degree, of numbers. Consolidation may see a hundred people leave an RM over the course of a decade, but, in the 1930s, hundreds if not thousands fled every month. Abandonment certainly catches one's attention but consolidation (of people, of schools, of towns, of hospitals, of railways, of banks, etc.) remains the Great Theme of Saskatchewan history.[1]

The difference between the abandonment of the 1920s and the 1930s is also striking. Despite the curious absence of records on the land abandonment crisis of the 1920s, for example, we do know that it did not assume its full import until three or four years of failure had hammered away at the spirit of the settlers in the drylands. People fled in droves only at that point when the RMs were unable to provide more relief aid and there was, finally, no other option but to flee. In the 1930s, however, the settler's response time was much quicker and the prolongation of abandonment was much longer.

In the 1920s, the crisis refracted through the prism of the decade's "roaring" nature, a time when prosperity seemed general, contentment was widespread, and thus the difficulties in the drylands, at least in the minds of officials, was only ever a local or a regional problem at best, even though an estimated 30,000 men, women, and children fled. Guided by Deputy Agriculture Minister F.H. Auld, the province simply could not regard evacuation as policy because the south and west plains region would naturally and inevitably collapse. Instead the province rationalized non-action by suggesting that there were no "dry areas" in the province and if there were no dry areas then there was in fact no real problem, and even if there was a problem then the settler likely had something to do with it: this was the poisoned seed bed out of which government policy developed in the 1920s. The 1930s, by contrast, saw almost immediate instances of either evacuation or abandonment, which naturally begs the question.

In the 1930s, the province could not wish or rationalize the problem away. The drought had burst its banks and flooded down fully onto the south plains. This thunderous rolling drought was accompanied by a disastrous global economic collapse. The world was falling apart and the province had to respond. It helps to view the matter as it stood in 1930: between 1914 and 1930, there were droughts or crop failures of varying degree for all except a few years (1915, 1916, 1926, to note the prominent few). Thus when the third round of drought and failure came knocking in 1930, complete with dust storms, locust invasions and terrible winds, many settlers simply ran out the back door.

At any given time in the thirties, the province had two or three agencies moving settlers, depending on their circumstances. But, as we will see, few if any of these agencies had the welfare of the settler as their primary concern. These removals grew out of larger practical or political issues and so the province's actions in the 1930s actually conform quite nicely to the grudging and reluctant policies of the 1920s. As former Saskatchewan Premier J.G. Gardiner phrased it in 1937 when he was federal Minister of Agriculture, "moving farmers ... is the very thing we are trying to avoid."[2]

The province rarely seemed interested in or indeed even guided by the moral imperative to help. It is true that organizations like the Land Utilization Board (LUB) evacuated settlers, but they did so only because the LUB was charged with the unhappy and horribly belated task of classifying lands as suitable or unsuitable for settlement (they were about twenty-five years late on this) or had already been abandoned. One cannot simply take a settler's land and leave him and his bewildered family standing there: common sense dictated that they be moved somewhere else. It seems that the moral imperative in the 1930s got lost somewhere in the dust and heat.

And so, with or without government aid, settlers fled the south plains by the tens of thousands. Historian Barry Potyondi notes in his brief study of the history of Palliser's Triangle that the south plains "were the last to be settled ... and the first to be forsaken."[3] Forsaken is an excellent choice of word.

Historian Bill Waiser estimates that *in total*, 45,000 people are thought to have fled the drought area for destinations other than the south plains during the Dirty Thirties. He suggests that two-thirds of that number (about 15,000) fled between 1933 and 1934.[4] Dr. Waiser's numbers actually come in pretty light.

There are other estimates that hint at hundreds of thousands. Renowned Canadian historian Gerald Friesen argues that fully one quarter of a million people left the prairies between 1931 and 1941.[5] But, in the same way that one must deploy caution as guard against the myths that arose in this period, like little kids being scared by rain, or of children not seeing vegetables until maturity, one must be careful with the numbers and statistics of those who fled or were removed because those numbers can easily tip over, like the crisis itself, into absurdity.

Friesen's use of the figure of a quarter million is a catch-all number that certainly lends a sense of high drama to the period, but in the end it explains nothing and says nothing: it is too big, too abstract. It is too much. Additionally, many of the people included in that number might have left the prairies as a result of the war that began in 1939 or into cities to work in urban industry as a result of the conflict, or may have been urban dwellers that drifted across Canada on rail cars and for whom the plains were never really home at all.

Further muddying these waters was the effort to settle the more northern reaches of the province over whose land and resources Saskatchewan gained control in 1930. This "back-to-the-land" movement, as it was called, resulted in the shipment of some 35,000 to 45,000 people to the northern areas.[6] Historian James Gray calls this ill-considered and impractical movement "one of the wildest brainstorms of the depression."[7] Most of the people involved in this movement were from urban centres, like the forty-two Saskatoon families who went to Loon Lake to farm in 1931.[8] In this vast movement, there were undoubtedly south plains settlers but this program remained essentially an urban program created to deal principally with the problems associated with the Depression and not the Drought as such, and so one cannot comfortably include them in the total number of those who fled the south plains. Most of the dryland evacuations were hastily set up and quickly carried out, whereas by comparison the "back-to-the-land" movement had, as one of its principal goals, the colonization of the north, marking for the first time that "internal colonization became active within the borders of the province."[9]

For all the lessons of history that should have been learned by 1930s, it is depressingly astonishing to see what occurred in this effort to colonize the northern part of a former "colony of a colony." As though taking a page from the play book of discredited lands boss Frank Oliver, the Saskatchewan government established basic rules and regulations for settlement up north: a person had to have five years residence in Saskatchewan and their own capital and equipment to make a go of it. But there was a land rush of sorts and the government "did not take the time" to do soil, climate, and topography tests, thus resulting in the absurd situation in which "many pioneers were allowed to settle on marginal lands."[10] The gross and costly failure of the 1908 amendment received an encore up north.

Determining the number of settlers who fled the south plains of Saskatchewan because of the drought, then, can only ever be responsible guesswork. The best and most responsible guess, though, should be based on information provided by people who were directly and intimately acquainted with rural Saskatchewan. The most accurate source to use is the records of the Department of Municipal Affairs (DMA). The DMA was the agency responsible for administering the acts under which rural municipalities operated. RMs and the DMA were (and still are) joined at the hip. Each year, municipal government officials sent into the department estimates of the population of the RMs based on tax rolls. It must be noted that the figures quoted herein do not include cities, towns, villages, or hamlets: they represent *only* rural Saskatchewan. Using the best estimates of the local administrators, we arrive at a figure of 39,995 settlers who fled the rural areas of the south and west plains between 1929 and 1939. If we add the estimated thirty thousand who fled during the crisis of the 1920s, we arrive at a figure approaching seventy thousand just for the south and west plains. So, we now know with acceptable precision how many people fled the drought area – but determining how they left is another entirely frustrating matter.

There is a cargo manifest in the archives building in Regina that details the numbers of settlers the Department of Agriculture had grudgingly agreed to move between 1930 and 1932 under an unnamed program. The manifest is thirty-eight pages long with roughly thirty names per page and it shows that, at least in the early years, most of the people who were shipped out of the drylands fled to east-central and north-east Saskatchewan. The settlers went to towns, villages, hamlets, and sometimes places loosely described as "settlements," which, generously defined, were likely nothing more than a collection of huts by a railway siding somewhere. The settlers went to strange and exotic places: Dumble, Dummer, Dilke, Neeb, Pelly, Togo, Gronlid, Prongua, Crutwell, and Lurgan. All of these communities are located outside the drought area in the northern and eastern regions of the province. One can only assume that Mr. A. Perron of Sedley got on the wrong train because the records show he was "evacuated" to Fox Valley in the RM of Enterprise, a neighbour of Big Stick and Clinworth in the very middle of the worst areas of the drought, right next door to the RM of Happyland.[11]

This particular record shows the movement of 1,140 men. Assuming they took their families, which may have constituted a wife and a child, one can reasonably suggest that Auld's Department helped evacuate over three thousand people in the early years of the drought between 1930 and 1932, though under what program or for what reason, the manifest does not say. In 1933, Deputy Auld noted that the chief "relief activity" of his department had been "the transfer of settlers who had decided to move from drought affected districts." The railways, he observed, helped with "special low rates," but there are no details on how many people they moved or where they were coming from or going to.[12]

The fragmentation of the record is everywhere. In the files of the Department of Agriculture, for example, officials record the assistance given to seven men and their families from the RM of Mankota between October 1934 and September 1935 at a cost of $693.[13] Oftentimes, the only record that settlers were removed is a leftover list indicating the number of rail cars used to move personal effects and this too only suggests or hints at the number of people who followed. Between 1930 and 1935, for example, 3,880 carloads of settlers' effects were shipped out of the dust bowl. If we use the two-railcar-per-family minimum, which was standard procedure in the 1920s, then it is possible that 1,940 were shipped out, which translates (husband, wife, child) into 5,820 people. This same record shows that a further 200 applications for shipment of effects were, for obscure and un-stated reasons, rejected.[14] In 1931, a year when crop districts two, three, and four (Weyburn to the Alberta border south of Moose Jaw and north from the U.S border to a point just south of Kindersley) averaged three and a half bushels per acre, Auld noted that the evacuation of settlers "was resumed." The Department of Agriculture shipped north 1,089 people who "went into residence on crown lands."

If the files of the Department of Agriculture are a haphazard hit-and-miss affair, the records of the Northern Saskatchewan Resettlement Board are happily less so. The NSRB was one of a handful of acronyms involved in settler relocation and it was governed by Richard Matte. He claimed in a mid-winter radio address in 1939 that the North Battleford-Prince Albert-Melfort districts increased in population by 20 per cent between 1935 and 1939.[15] And, tellingly, going back to the crisis of the 1920s, he said that, between 1921 and 1936, the population of the northern grain belt had increased "no less than 50%." There were fourteen RMs in the North Battleford district that grew by 25,000 people in the 1930s.

Matte explained that, in his experience, most men and women who abandoned their lands "had reached a stage approaching hopelessness and despair."[16] Matte, a sage old drought-hand by this time, claimed he had seen all types pass through the NSRB. There was the poor and destitute settler all the way up to the wealthy one "who had seen his hundreds of acres ... turned overnight into a drifting sea of sand."

Matte suggested that the NSRB had moved 5,200 families between 1935 and 1938 at a cost of just over $1 million, which, if one family unit contained husband-wife-child, would mean a figure closing in on 16,000 people, and it was a figure achieved in little bits and pieces from all over the south plains. There were, for example, eight late-1934 relocations that cost $9,000.[17] The NSRB was set up in 1935 to bring some form and organization to the messy business of relocating thousands of families to the northern areas of the province, to gather up "the human debris that was scattered about by the violence of the storm," as James Gray observed.[18] So of our total of 40,000 people who fled the rural areas of the south and west plains in the 1930s, an estimated 16,000 were removed by the NSRB.

This impulse to remove settlers to the north country was not an idea that was universally supported. Alberta's Peace River Member of Parliament R.A. Pelletier likened the movement to a short-term band-aid solution to which no real thought had been applied. He felt the settlers were simply "being taken out of the dried out areas and dumped somewhere in the northern bush" with little or no knowledge of how to get along in this vastly different region.[19] And while Pelltier's opinion was not shared by K.C. MacDonald, the Minister of Agriculture for British Columbia, who actively explored the idea of getting the refugees up in B.C.'s side of the Peace country "where they can get returns on their labours," Pelletier's feelings about northern settlement did, in the end, prove to be far more prescient.[20]

The province and the University of Saskatchewan worked closely during the crisis. Quite often, academics were sent out into the field to gain first-hand information on how the settlers were doing, not only in the drylands, but up north as well. There was a "professor of soils" who was dispatched to the north to report on how the settlers were doing in their new forested environment. Professor J. Mitchell, though, had some sad news. It seems the drylanders did not often take very well to the woodlands. The professor had to explain to Deputy Auld that, upon relocating to the north, the hapless burned-out settlers set about cutting down every tree they could get their hands on. Professor Mitchell noted that one farm "was as absent of trees as it would have been anywhere on the prairies."[21] In fact, the only growth left standing on this farm was "a low willow scrub near some sloughs."

Mitchell pleaded with Auld to relay the information to the bewildered settlers that trees do in fact contain value for agriculture and that a field need not necessarily be flat as a pancake and as clear as a billiards table as was the case on the south and west plains (humour about the absence of trees is common – "turn south [north/east/west] at the tree" or, "and when you get to the tree turn …" are both still very common forms of direction offered). In the years before it was understood by the settlers that trees can prevent wind erosion ("shelter belts," as they are today called), Mitchell had to ask Auld to explain this to settlers. He also pointed out that, in addition to soil-drift prevention, shelter, and firewood, trees also provide a "natural beauty," but it was a beauty to which the flatlanders, who had grown accustomed to seeing their dog run away for three days were not especially attuned. Even the Dairy Commissioner weighed in. Ed Ridley, too, admitted that many settlers were "over-zealous" in their practical application of boreal husbandry.[22]

Even though the province had organizations like the NSRB assisting in evacuation, we must remember that evacuation was not the preferred option, nor was it even considered a good option. Like the 1920s, when the province gave tepid approval for an evacuation plan only after some years of being badgered for it, the province approached settler evacuations with the same brand of enthusiasm in the 1930s. It remained staunchly and wholeheartedly wedded to the idea that evacuation would not become general.

There was a time limit on when settlers could obtain evacuation assistance. It seems that administrators and secretaries from a number of rural municipalities had been nipping at the heels of the government for information on its evacuation and re-settlement plans. Deputy Auld, in an open letter to all RMs, dated 1935, dampened their enthusiasm for removals by explaining that "there is no general movement of settlers now and there will be none."[23] Auld called the evacuations that had occurred to this time a "limited movement," and, in order to make sure the councils understood him on this point, he reminded them that May 15 was the deadline for applications for evacuation and that after that date "*new cases cannot be considered.*"[24] May 15 was likely chosen as a cut-off date because it was the start of seeding: anyone who had not committed to leaving by then would have likely had little choice but to "farm" for another year.

And if time restrictions were not enough to sour settlers on the idea of government-assisted evacuation, there was another substantial hurdle over which exhausted settlers were required to fling themselves. The province, according to Auld, would not pay for the inter-provincial shipment of settlers "until we have in our possession permission from the province to which he is going."[25] If the settler was unfortunate enough to choose Manitoba as the location to which he intended to flee, then he would require the permission of the Manitoba Relief Commission; if Alberta, then the permission of the Deputy Minister of Agriculture himself.

Trapped in his mind in the 1920s, Auld informed the RMs that there were only "some small portions" of land where there is soil drift and drought and that "in a few instances" abandonment may in fact be the preferred option. But, as in the 1920s, he would not allow evacuation to become the principal plan and thus would only assist settlers at the recommendation of the rural councils and only when there was some measure of success that could be expected from that abandonment. "The public funds," Auld argued, were wasted when evacuation assistance was offered with no guarantee of success down the road. And since "the public funds" ought not to be wasted, he urged the RMs to "use the utmost care in the consideration of such cases and in the recommendations that you make not only in the interests of the applicants but in the interests of the province as a whole."[26] Auld continued: "I am sure that you will have this in mind when making your recommendations." Auld then retired to his office and jealously fondled his public funds.

Small rural councils in Saskatchewan were repeatedly placed in the very uncomfortable position of always having to make some kind of moral or ethical choice – of choosing between what they knew to be right (get the settlers out) and what they were being urged to do (do everything possible to retain the settlers). For their part, the settlers usually just wanted a train ticket out. This triangular conflict between the settler, the RM, and the province colours the entire period of the crises between 1914 and 1937. There is a constant conflict amongst the province, which was focussed on the ideals of nation and province-building, the RMs, which had as their goal fiscal prudence and financial stability, and the settler, who wanted answers as to how best to respond to starvation-farming. The government pushed one way, the settlers pushed in the opposite direction, and the rural councilmen were stuck in the middle. Much to their credit, the RMs did what they could to help.

Clinworth council gave Jacob Bentz twenty-five dollars to "defray the costs" of taking up land in the northern grain belt.[27] Big Stick sent out the offer, whose tone was delightfully at odds with the province's stated direction that it would offer conditional assistance "to any resident who wishes to move out."[28] Mankota likewise approved a number of applications from settlers "seeking new locations" anywhere but there.[29] And Pinto Creek gave A.J. Wichens money to get to Tisdale, a frequent destination of choice in both the 1920s and 1930s.[30]

Sadly, though, and much to the consternation of Deputy Auld, "the public funds" were abused during the 1930s. Some settlers used evacuation assistance as a free ticket out of Saskatchewan, something Auld was likely aware of and something that may have blunted any softer sentiments for the noble settler toward which he may have otherwise been inclined. There was a settler named C.H. Tonks who had taken assistance to move north, but apparently he did not make good on any promises he made to either work the land or work off the aid debt because the Dominion government came looking him. They couldn't find him and eventually wrote the NSRB seeking "a refund of the amount contributed by the Dominion government to railway fares incurred on behalf of settler #203, C.H. Tonks."[31]

Not everyone preferred the less droughty climes of the northern grain belt with its trees and water. After desperately hacking away at trees for a year or two building "pioneer roads," some felt life was better spent on a road gang laying asphalt in a straight line across the plains and these settlers formed an apparent small-scale return exodus. Swift Current council wrote the province asking in typically Canadian fashion which level of government was responsible to "[provide] relief of those parties who have returned from the north."[32]

If a settler was naturally turned off of a life of hard labour on the south plains, the verdant valleys of the lower mainland of British Columbia might figure large in his night-time fantasies of where he might take his family if he could ever get out. Many hundreds, perhaps thousands, did just that, and they created just as many relief problems on the coast as they did on the plains.

Between 1935 and 1938, Lower Mainland Member of Parliament H.J. Barber said, "a considerable number of families from the dried out areas of Saskatchewan" had been settling in his riding.[33] This was a problem because the settlers went from a world mired in drought-induced relief aid to a world of relief aid created by an economic crisis. One wonders if the settlers had the naïve and simple hope that the economic crisis might be better than the soul-killing drought they had known on the plains. Once in the valleys of the lower mainland, though, they began appealing to the municipal offices for aid and, struck down by the depression, the municipalities on the coast were in no better shape to provide aid than were their south plains counterparts. Barber estimated that there were some 1,745 of "these people" in his area and that some municipalities were looking after groups consisting of upwards of 400 people: the flatlanders apparently congregated in groups just like their Okie cousins to the south did in California.

Barber was not taking negative issue with the south-plains refugees. Indeed, he said that "ninety percent of them would make good citizens if given the chance," but there was simply no money to get them established.[34] And that was his plea in the House of Commons: that relief aid follow the recipient. But it was not to be. There was no happy ending for the refugees; quite the opposite, in fact. Having no relief aid to supply to the settlers, many municipalities could only come up with one solution that has a dark tinge of the cruel and the ridiculous: Barber grimly noted "[municipalities] have been compelled to buy transportation for them and ship them back to the dried out areas."[35]

Barber, however, neatly sidestepped an issue that apparently caused some degree of trouble between the locals and the refugee flatlanders who had fled to the Fraser Valley. It seems that Saskatchewan refugees who washed up on the verdant shores of the lower mainland didn't care who they hurt in pursuit of gainful employment to feed their starving families. One local oldtimer recalled in Barry Broadfoot's collection of stories about the 1930s that if you had a job and there was a refugee from Saskatchewan nearby, "you had better watch out." According to this unnamed fellow, a refugee might come looking for a glass of water or some gas and "sometimes before you knew it, that fellow had your job, and his wife and kids was moving into your house."[36] While the teller of this tale may be stretching things just a little bit, it is not a stretch to suggest that these refugees would have worked for less money than the locals, and if that was the case then perhaps it becomes easier to understand why the Fraser Valley councils so speedily shipped the refugees back to the south plains.

David Foss was one of those refugees from the south plains who fled to the coast in 1936. Mr. Foss and his family left his farm to the care of "Humphrey and Hazill Gorrill" while his family took off to Creston, B.C., "to find a new way of life."[37] Presumably, it was not a happy train ride for the older boys who "rode along … and cared for the stock on the trip." After being stuck in a steaming, odorous cattle car for a few days, the Foss's stepped out into another world and "it was quite a change to us; everything was so green"[38] And while some members of the family found their way back to the south plains, Mrs. Foss stayed in Creston to the end of her days.

Mr. Barber was one of many parliamentarians in the House of Commons who addressed the myriad problems associated with the drought. Mr. Victor Qulech, an Alberta MP, farmer, and former soldier in the Canadian Army, spoke of the drought and his words drip with exasperation. "Year after year," he informed the house, "reports consistently warned against the danger of these dry areas being opened for settlement ... report after report by government engineers and surveyors classified these areas as unsuitable for grain farming," and thus, like Senator Rae, Quelch no doubt too felt that the region "should have been left for the cows." It is interesting to note that the impulse to imbue one's words with the heavy weight of history was a common one for many MPs during the 1930s. Many who rose to address the drought issue in the house frequently made use of the history of the region and of Captain John Palliser's assessment of it.

Some people did not just want to quit Saskatchewan; they wanted to quit the country altogether. Mankota council begged the province to pay for the transportation of two families back to England.[39] It seems John Woodcock and the ill-named (certainly ill-named for the rough south plains) Percy Breeze were destitute and their only hope and thought was to get enough money to go back to the Old Country. Council felt it was "the duty and responsibility" of both levels of government to see this through and added that they were "very desirous" that Woodcock and Breeze be moved out "at as early a date as possible," probably because it meant fewer relief aid cases. It was a common refrain on the western plains (common for dour, iron-hard Scotsmen like the present writer's great grandfather, at any rate) that Englishmen made the poorest settlers.

Breeze and Woodcock and Tonks and Perrin and the thousands of others who fled in this direction need not have felt guilty about their choice. Abandonment is another one of the terrible scars that runs across the history of the south plains and indeed stretches back in time to the nineteenth century. At that time, a Regina newspaper man recalled seeing a similar exodus of people to the northern grain belt. They were fleeing from the drought-stricken east Assiniboia region in 1890.[40]

It helps to instil in the reader a sense of what it was exactly that the settlers were fleeing. They were running away from drought, crop failures, relief aid, and failure, true. But understanding or *appreciating* what these things mean is another thing. It could have meant this:

> The land was as lifeless as ashes and for miles there was scarcely a growing thing to be seen. Where a scanty herbage had struggled up through the dust, flights of grasshoppers had apparently completed the destruction and then despairing of further sustenance, had flown to other fields.... Gaunt cattle and horses with little save their skins to cover their bones, stalked the denuded acres weakly seeking to crop the French

weed, which with malign persistence, seemed to be maintaining some kind of sickly growth ... the few people in evidence in the little towns appeared haggard and hopeless. For fully fifty miles of the region ... there did not appear to be one single field that will produce a bushel of grain or a load of fodder ... and as for the people themselves, God only knows what their extremity must be.[41]

This is a Saskatchewan we will never see, never know – a Saskatchewan many oldtimers just wanted to forget about.

From hamlets and villages and isolated homesteads, then, the people fled. They gambled on British Columbia, caught a train to Ontario, thumbed rides into Manitoba, begged for money for passage back to England. Some wandered west, or south, or anywhere. It was a formless shapeless movement of people from many different backgrounds, ethnicities, races, religions, and countries. They really had only one thing in common: by their thousands, they left their lands, homes, and whatever possessions they couldn't carry and fled.

The Canada census records the population haemorrhage in some fairly compelling numbers and statistics. Saskatchewan had eighteen census divisions. The census records 5,183 abandoned farms in Saskatchewan in 1931.[42] The regions with the highest number of abandoned farms were divisions seven, eight, twelve, and thirteen or the Swift Current-Rosetown-Kindersley-Leader area. But what is more compelling is the amount of abandoned land. There were 1,024,211 acres of land that lay abandoned in 1931 and fully 40 per cent of that land lay in just six of the eighteen census divisions and this sharply drawn regional picture would only get worse as the Thirties progressed.

By 1936, the south plains were exclusively out-performing the rest of the province in the numbers of abandoned farms and abandoned land. In 1936, there were 11,222 abandoned farms in Saskatchewan.[43] 5,804 of these farms, rather more than 50 per cent, were located in the area bordered by Weyburn, Maple Creek, and Kindersley. Swift Current had the worst rate with 1,488 abandoned farms; Melville, in east central Saskatchewan, had just 181.

Abandoned acreage increased as well. By 1936, 2,486,253 acres of land in Saskatchewan had been abandoned and 1,408,249 or about 60 per cent of those lands lay in the drylands. Swift Current fought a pitched battle with those lonely luckless souls in the extreme southeast corner of the province near the RM of Argyle for the records of highest abandoned acres: the Swift Current region had 347,868, while the south-east had 300,988.

The contrast between the south plains and the central-northern grain belts is striking: in the northern and eastern areas of the grain belt, the Hafford region had 43,919 abandoned acres, Humboldt had 45,455, Canora 57,197, and the Wynyard area, in central Saskatchewan, had just 23,793, or about forty-three sections of lands. There were 255,394 abandoned acres of farmland in the Mankota-Pinto Creek region and 171,918 in Big Stick-Clinworth, or 300 sections. There were more abandoned lands and abandoned farms in the six census districts of the drylands than all the others combined.

These census figures paint an intensely regional picture of the drought and are supported by regional production and aid figures for each rural municipality. The RM of Wallace south of Canora only once fell below seven bushels per acre and that was in 1937. It received just over 100,000 in aid for the entire decade.[44] The RM of Orkney, north of Yorkton, even went four of the ten years without aid and only twice fell below seven bushels per acre.[45] Argyle, in the south-east corner, fell below five bushels per acre and thus into disaster zone levels of subsistence farming seven times in ten years and received over $250,000 in aid.[46] Pinto Creek, as stated earlier, stayed at or below seven bushels per acre for the entire decade.

In rough terms, the northern grain belt was, for the most part, free the extreme drought-induced deprivations visited upon the settlers of the south plains. First and always, the settlers of the south and west plains were burned and brutalized to a far greater degree and more frequently than any other region of the province. There was more aid, more road work, more abandoned land, and more abandoned farms; more privation, more perdition. Part of the problem was caused, as Deputy Auld admitted, by the "periods of drought which may occur at unexpected intervals." Part of the problem was the land itself.

The province only slowly awakened to the regional nature of land quality and that quite late in the day, considering that land abandonment had been a chronic problem on the south plains stretching all the way back to 1890. Still, belated or not, the province dispatched a number of university professors to the south plains to assess the land. E.C. Hope, a "professor of soils" at the University of Saskatchewan, was a part of this effort. Hope's findings capture in miniature all of the dramatic elements of the crises, including the literal insanity of farming in the drylands. All of this was a part of an effort to study this "unholy mess" and the ultimate aim was to reorganize the agricultural economy "on a scientific basis."[47]

One of Hope's first stops was the RM of Chaplin, located midway between Swift Current and Moose Jaw. Figures from the Department of Municipal Affairs indicate that Chaplin lost 145 "resident farmers" in the 1920s (approximating some 435 people) in addition to losing about a hundred people during the thirties. Hope undertook interviews individually or in groups with 116 farmers, which in 1935 accounted for three quarters of all farmers in that RM. His first conclusion was that the RM was quite land rich. Council had seized and taken possession of about a hundred parcels of land, though in some cases, "arrears are so great that they would exceed the proceeds from the sale."[48] In fact, the liens on the land, Hope noted, extended all the way back to the 1914 drought and ranged from between $100 to $1,400 per quarter. The Konschuhs in nearby Fox Valley had worked up about $1,500 in liens in just a few years.

Hope classed the land he saw into two broad categories. The first type had been settled in 1913, was abandoned between 1918 and 1922, "and [has] never been occupied for farming since." The second type had been settled earlier, in 1910, and this land "has changed hands two or three times." He adds that, "until quite recently, a succession of operators have tried to farm these lands and failed. Here again, the mortgage companies have only kept the best of the poor sandy quarters; some of these … are wind-blown sand dunes and pits swept out by the wind."

Of the 116 farmers Hope visited, "not more than twenty" were making a success of things and he attributed this to three causes: 1) good farming methods and management, 2) large initial capital, and 3) outside sources of income. These points are not that much different than what separates good and bad farmers today. But the line between success and failure in the 1930s was excruciatingly sharp and those who fell on the one side were often quickly dragged down into bankruptcy and destitution, and that is the principal difference between then and now: in the 1930s there was absolutely zero margin for error.

Hope also allows us to see the inner workings and thoughts of the RM councils away from their formal meetings. Councilmen and their interlocutor met and discussed the problem and the councillors confided that they "do not really relish" the idea of selling the land to which they held title through seizure because it will just become another relief problem. So council, like so many others, had cancelled its tax sale. And Chaplin councillors had enough problems because there was the belief amongst the councillors that the RM "was bankrupt with no hope of ever pulling out."

After quitting Chaplin, Hope travelled down to the RM of Wood River, next door to Mankota and Pinto Creek.[49] This is what Hope found: "[settlers] hanging onto sand piles ... waiting for an opportunity to leave." Wood River was as bad as or worse than Chaplin. There were 227 quarters of land settlers had been trying to farm but it was made up almost entirely of "sandy loam," which means the dirt had more sand than soil. 128 of these quarters were occupied and ninety-nine had been abandoned. Tellingly, and like Chaplin, the majority of the abandoned lands, two-thirds in fact, had been abandoned in the 1920s and just thirty-two were quit between 1930 and 1934, which means that the seven years of drought in the 1920s had wrought more damage in Wood River than the first six years of the crisis of the 1930s. Of the 128 quarters still being farmed, one-third to one-half were owned by loan companies, and, despite a value of between $1,000 and $3,300, "they all appear[ed] quite hopeless."

Hope relays the story of one luckless settler. Mr. Knight had been farming in the area for almost twenty-five years, from 1909 to 1934. And as he figures it, for all the toil and work and labour that Mr. Knight put into his sandy loam, he had only seen a return of about eight and a half bushels per acre on average in those twenty-five years. Hope concluded that Knight's story "would be typical" of this area, as soil drift also was. There are many who believe that soil drift was a creature of the 1930s, but Hope found that the problem reached back all the way to 1918. Hope also discovered an element to dryland farming that had likely been whispered about by the locals but just as quickly swept under the proverbial carpet: it seems that an inordinate number of settlers in this RM had "either committed suicide or gone insane." Suicide in Saskatchewan was endemic in the thirties: fully 922 people committed suicide between 1929 and 1938. The worst year was 1930 when 127 killed themselves.[50]

The land owned by Mr. Knight was just across the border from Montana, and, though it is a different country, the land itself is the same as that seen by Professor Hope. Hope's counterpart at the University of Montana, Professor Wilson, explained that his country too was "in the throes of the worst drought Montana has ever witnessed" and that settlers were being supplied with relief from the federal government and the Red Cross. Like Wood River, Pinto Creek, Mankota, Chaplin, Clinworth, Big Stick, and Maple Creek, the professor observed that "wheat is a failure."[51] In fact, just as Professor Wilson was writing these words, the entire wheat-growing area of Montana, like its counterpart on the south plains in Saskatchewan, was experiencing an end-of-the-world-type thoroughgoing collapse. People were fleeing, and most of the towns were "folding" as a result of the drought: "the northern plains homestead experiment," writes Timothy Egan, "was a bust."[52] 1935 was certainly an opportune time to adjudge the quality of lands in the south plains because "generally speaking, the area adjacent to the Alberta boundary and in many sections of the southwest, crops was reported poor to practically complete failures." While the province grew 135,000,000 bushels of wheat, crop districts three and four grew just ten million.[53]

Professor Hope's investigative trip into the south plains was connected to the work of the provincial Land Utilization Board (LUB), which was formally established in 1937, a couple years after Hope went south. The board was composed of a representative of municipal government, a farm management professor, a "professor of soils," Deputy Auld, and others.[54] According to LUB boss, Mr. R.W. Neely, the organization had three principal goals: 1) to classify unsuitable lands, 2) to turn that land back to pasture, and 3) to move the settler somewhere else.[55] Please note the position of the settler on the priority list. The goals and purpose of the LUB reflect the spirit and substance of the recommendations of the Pope Commission of 1914, the Royal Commission of Inquiry into Farming Conditions of 1920, and the general tilt of south plains land-use policy for several decades prior to 1908. That substance and spirit was captured in the words of Senator A.D. Rae, who caustically observed that the whole region "should have been left to the cows."

The LUB worked in conjunction with the PFRA. At either the request of an RM or by provincial directive, the LUB fanned out across the south and west plains to investigate areas whose land was considered unsuitable. If the board agreed an area was in fact little more than a wasteland that was impossible to farm, and if the wasteland contained "not less than twenty five sections" of land, then the board would assume title to the land and cancel most of the arrears associated with it and establish a community pasture on it.[56] If there were still settlers living on that land, arrangements were then made to get them out in order to "get the use of their holdings."[57] LUB secretary Mr. E. E. Eisenhauer described the work of obtaining title to these blocks of land as "tedious," but it did pay off: in the first year of the board's operation, 185,160 acres of land were seized and sixteen community pastures were constructed.[58]

After the land had been seized and "reclaimed," the question for the LUB remained: what do we do with the settler? 'Anywhere but here' was the operative principle. The LUB moved eighty-seven families to "points in Saskatchewan not classified as northern."[59] F.D. Cameron and C. Becker of Mankota were moved, for example, to McClean and Balgonie respectively at a total cost of $140. It appears that many of the families aided under this scheme came from the south-west around Ponteix, Eastend, Ravenscrag, and Aneroid. They went to places like Pinkie, Oakshella, and Tuguske. 361 families were moved by the LUB to "Northern areas."[60] A.M. Rust fled Fox Valley for Freemont at a cost of $148; M. Bedard quit Ponteix for Doyle at a cost to the province of $61.70.

But most of the settlers who received the help of the LUB fled the province entirely. The LUB, having obtained the proper approval of the provincial governments to which these settlers were being shipped, then moved 827 families to "points outside Saskatchewan."[61] Most of them chose Ontario or Manitoba. R.M. Humphrey, for example, went from Smiley to Galt, Ontario. Smiley is about fifty miles north of Happyland.

In total, the LUB moved some 1,275 families approximating some 4,000 people. When this number is added to the totals from, say, the NSRB and the early removals of the Department of Agriculture, our figure reaches about 25,000. We can surmise that the majority of the remaining 15,000 who fled did so on their own.

The RMs worked closely with the LUB in this land-classification effort. In 1937, Clinworth judged eighty-six parcels of land as sub-marginal.[62] Swift Current classed seventy-five parcels of land as such.[63] And Big Stick, true to its bold form – as constant as the stars on the PRC flag – not only classified land as unsuitable but indeed wanted to chop off something like half of the RM entirely. It should not come as a surprise that Big Stick was way out in front of the LUB. In 1935, Big Stick councilmen passed a resolution that stated that, since divisions one and three of the RM did not "fit in well with the rest of the municipality," this region of the RM would be "allowed to secede." Secession suggests that there is an element within a region desirous of cutting itself off from the main body, which, in 1935, could hardly have been the case, but "secession" likely sounded better than calling the district what it actually was – an albatross.[64] Big Stick later retracted its motion and instead suggested that the land be offered as pasture and "the settlers living therein be given assistance to move to a better country."[65] The LUB would eventually do that very thing and thus save the RM from the pains of secession. Current Big Stick administrator Mr. Quinton Jacksteit was rather surprised to hear about all this talk of secession in his RM during the 1930s. He assured the author that divisions one and three did not secede but are still attached to the RM right where they should be, on its eastern edge, and on the RM map they are coloured in a gentle pink, which harmlessly designates a community pasture.

As might be expected, the province had very definite ideas about the results it wanted to achieve with this land-classification and pasture-establishment scheme. Deputy Auld discussed these matters at length with Mr. C. Evans Sargeant. It is one of those serendipitous happenings of history that Sargeant, the former Mantario secretary reappears in the historical record in 1935 as the secretary for the RM of Royal Canadian. The reader will recall that Sargeant was the man who sounded the alarm about the threats of starvation in Mantario in the 1920s, though one must wonder whether Mr. Sargeant was cursed with bad karma because the RM of Royal Canadian no longer exists: it was bled white by population losses during the 1920s and 1930s.

At any rate, Deputy Auld informed Mr. Sargeant that each council is to determine, as did Clinworth, Big Stick, Swift Current, and others, what lands it chooses to designate as unsuitable for farming.[66] Never missing a chance to fondle his "public funds," Auld informed Sargeant that this classification should have as its goal, not just the creation of a pasture, but also the guarantee that any farmer who wilfully remains and continues to farm such lands will no longer receive aid. Auld writes: "the definite responsibility [will be] placed upon the owners to provide any agricultural assistance … because of its continued use for grain production." Here, Auld takes absurdity to the highest heights it reached between 1914 and 1937 – absurdity never knew it could soar so high. Essentially (and the writer is respecting the substance and meaning of the original text), Auld was suggesting that anyone who knowingly farms sub-marginal land will in the future have to provide themselves with relief aid: a kind of backward, inverted, self-cannibalism.

Auld emphasized his point. Repeatedly. "Unless and until those problems associated with the occupancy of land of low agricultural value become through crop failure a matter of municipal or provincial importance, no reasons exists for developing public policy in connection therewith." Once again, one must wonder how much Auld understood his adopted province over whose agricultural policy he held so much control for so many years.

Auld explained that each RM should classify the land, remove the settlers, and reorganize infrastructure. This meant that schools would have to be shuttered, the children (if there were any left) would have to be redistributed, telephone lines would have to be taken down, and roads hopefully constructed by the early settlers would have to be ploughed up.[67] Creating a community pasture was not a simple task.

Sometimes, though, as in the case of Big Stick, it seemed some RMs were one or two steps ahead of the province. The secretary for the RM of Kindersley, Mr. W.H. Howse, explained to Auld that he and his council had developed a plan in 1935 for the rationalization of the land in their district. Howse and the councillors proposed two separate pastures, a small one of 3,200 acres and a somewhat larger one of 10,720 acres. Of these lands, the RM held title through tax sale to twenty-eight parcels. The men proposed exactly what Auld had suggested: classify, reorganize, depopulate. But they also went further and planned the fencing, gating of the pasture complete with the installation of "underground crossings," and, much to the likely pleasure of Auld, had written up a financial plan to make it work.

Howse explained that history had demonstrated one very sad thing about south plains settlement: it had always been "in the nature of an experiment." By 1935, though, the long process of settlement had come full circle and Howse's efforts, like those in Big Stick, and Swift Current, and elsewhere merely represent the first steps toward the consolidation of that settlement.

The RM understood the enormous drag on resources that many settlers represented, and indeed Howse happily greeted the removal of these relief-hobbled settlers existing on sub-marginal lands because "it will reduce materially the cost of carrying on the municipality." Apparently, some of the families that the RM had to move were squatters of a sort. Howse explained to Auld that there were fifteen families living on the poor lands but that there had been no grain production on that land for some twenty years and that, until the RM could remove these families and others like them, "we do not see how we shall ever entirely eliminate our relief problem."

Auld was supportive of Howse's idea for the removal of the settlers so long as it didn't cost anything and that they were assured of some measure of success in the location to which they were removed. Reservations about "the public funds" aside, Auld was ebullient about Kindersley's proposal. He "didn't know of any other municipality which was dealing so effectively with its land utilization problems" and offered the sobriquet that council is to be "very highly commended for its enterprize [sic]."[68]

The movement toward the reclassification of land was, as Howes' comments suggest, the logical endpoint of settlement policies that had only ever been experimental, carelessly experimental at that. There was a mass of humanity that was thrown at the wall, as it were, and there were many thousands who did not stick and they paid a terrible price. The settlement of the south and west plains, writes historian Chester Martin, "presents a truly appalling list of casualties." The entire province, notes historian John Archer, had to pay for development that was "too rapid and too random."[69] "Nature," Archer observed, "would demand the rationalization of agricultural methods if man would not ... and Saskatchewan paid the price." Part of that rationalization, perhaps the biggest part, was the formation of the PFRA in 1935, which was made a permanent body after the *annus horribilis* of 1937. But the PFRA, while certainly useful beyond measure, could not stop the crisis of the 1930s from advancing; the drought could not be legislated out of existence; it could not be controlled, it continued on its reckless, rambling, destructive course. While community pastures, land classification, and dugouts provided some measure of relief from the crisis, some small oasis of hope in a desert of futility, the worst was yet to come. For anyone in 1936 who was still "hanging onto their sand piles," 1937 arrived and blew them into oblivion.

During the "Dirty Thirties"

THE SOIL QUITE LITERALLY TURNED TO SAND (SAB R-A3368), (SAB R-A16398).

The Bountiful Harvest. The year's crop lay in the foreground "cut with a mower and raked into a pile." Undated (SAB R-B8275).

Mr. Alton Reichert and his family leaving the Chaplin area of south-west Saskatchewan in 1935. They were on their way to Lestock, located near the Touchwood Hills region of east-central Saskatchewan (SAB R-A8188).

"Moving north." Undated (SAB R-A8540).

Likely one of the Colonel's work camps. Three views of the settlers working in a hard-labour road gang in the RM of Shamrock. Note the cook-house and bunk-house in the background (SAB R-A7632).

The Last Best West. Settlers digging a drainage ditch in the 1930s (SAB R-A8578).

Original title: "Dust Bowl Kids." Three youngsters from south-west Saskatchewan in the 1930s, well-shod, clothes in one piece, standing before a clean and sturdy if ill-painted house. "Their last name may be Debler" (SAB R-B8272).

Settlers lining up for fodder. The line stretches into the distance (SAB R-A515).

Herbert men from south-west Saskatchewan getting their hands on the elusive "vegetable" (SAB R-A3341).

Aneroid men unloading one of the thousands of rail cars that were sent into south and west Saskatchewan loaded with food (SAB R-A6729).

LOOKING FOR WATER IN A DRY LAND (OR PERHAPS FLEEING THE RM
OF BIG STICK) (SAB R-A5213).

On the other side of the drought. In the end, things worked out for the Konschuhs in Cluny. The large and handsome Adam Konschuh brood, late 1940s or early 1950s. Courtesy of *Memories of Cluny* (Winnipeg, InterCollegiate Press, 1985) and Stanley and Haddie Konschuh.

Interlude: Public Health

The physical, sexual, emotional, and spiritual health and well-being of the settlers was grossly, almost unimaginably impaired during the droughts of the thirties.

We have seen that studies done in the 1920s on dryland kids showed extremely high cases of malnutrition, and in the thirties conditions only got worse. People were dying of rickets, scurvy, and beriberi. Between 1929 and 1938, seventy-eight people died of rickets, six from scurvy, and one from beriberi.[1] This suggests that hundreds if not thousands suffered from the effects of these nutritive diseases but did not die.

There were fourteen deaths from starvation between 1929 and 1938.[2]

The extremes of cold and heat were a natural part of life in Saskatchewan, and there were deaths because of it. A total of 130 people died because of excessive heat or excessive cold between 1929 and 1938.[3] The worst year was 1935 when twenty people died from exposure to the elements. In the following year, 1936, nineteen people died. The category of people from amongst whom the most people died from the cold was the over sixty-five and the widowed. Likewise, the majority of the nine men who died from heat (three) were over sixty-five.

Given the fact that sexual mores underwent profound stress and change in the droughts, it should come as no surprise that the Gentleman's Disease made a dramatic reappearance in the Dirty Thirties. Each year between 1929 and 1935, the number of deaths from syphilis hovers between twelve and seventeen. But in 1936, there is a sharp spike upwards to twenty deaths, peaking in the worst year of the droughts, 1937, at thirty-four.[4] Twenty-eight men died of the disease that year, as did six women.[5] In the majority of cases (nine), the men were married and in the forty-five- to sixty-four-year-old age bracket. There were, however, three young lads under fifteen who contracted the disease and died. Of the women, the majority (three) were married and between the ages of twenty-five and forty-four. Just one girl under fifteen died from syphilis.[6]

Deaths from syphilis frequently occurred in the winter months, when much of one's social activity was confined to the indoors because of the health risks associated with minus-thirty-degree winters (from which eight people died in 1937[7]). The majority of the men who contracted syphilis (five) died in December of 1937, four died in February, and four in April.

While men were dying of syphilis, women were dying by the dozens as a result of abortions. The number of women who died in this way remained fairly consistent throughout the 1930s: seventeen died in 1932, twelve in 1934, thirteen in 1936, and nineteen in 1937.[8] The majority of women dying were married and between the ages of twenty-five and forty-four, which tends to suggest that the pregnancy was unplanned and unwanted and the abortion pursued because there was no money left to care for another child.

At least twice a day, between 1929 and 1938, a woman died giving birth or because of complications brought on by pregnancy. In these years, 915 women died in this way.[9]

Murders were endemic to Saskatchewan during the Thirties. There were 122 homicides in Saskatchewan between 1929 and 1938, and again their occurrence roughly parallels the years of drought. The fewest murders committed (seven) came in 1932, the only year of the thirties when a crop of any substance was grown.[10] Three of these homicides, the majority, involved the murder of "persons one year of age and over by firearms."[11] The year in which the most murders occurred was 1929 when eighteen were committed. The majority of the victims that year (ten) were women. Four were shot, and six were killed "by other means."[12]

Suicide was a major social problem: between 1929 and 1938, 920 men and women killed themselves.[13] In 1934, for example, 105 people in Saskatchewan took their own lives.[14] This means that roughly about every three days, someone somewhere in Saskatchewan killed themselves. The majority of those deaths were men – eighty-two that year.[15] But there were twenty-three women who committed suicide and four of them were young girls between the ages of fifteen and twenty-four.[16] Eight women between the ages of twenty-five to forty-four also killed themselves.

Suicide followed an arc. It jumped from fifty-five in 1929 to 127 the following year.[17] There was a lull as the numbers drop to below eighty for the next couple years, and then they climb to ninety-three in 1933 and 105 in 1934, thereafter declining to a low of seventy-eight in 1938.[18]

Men killed themselves more often than women. In 1937, for example, there were eighty-seven people who killed themselves and, of those, sixty-nine were men. Eleven of them did it in August when they were supposed to be harvesting. But, in 1937, there was no harvest.

The majority of the men who committed suicide in 1937, twenty-three, were married and in the forty-five- to –sixty-four-year-old age bracket. The most frequent choice of death, probably because it was the quickest and most accessible, was death by firearms, which accounted for thirty-one suicides.

There were twenty deaths from hanging or strangulation, one by drowning, twenty-four people (twelve men and twelve women) ingested "poison or corrosive substances."

Early Saskatchewan was a gigantic safety hazard: in the same time frame, 2,432 people died from accidental drowning, accidental firearms discharge, accidental mechanical suffocation, "accidental crushing," and the like.[19]

As one might expect, alcoholism claimed the lives of many people in Saskatchewan. Fully 158 people died from cirrhosis of the liver between 1919 and 1938. The worst years were 1935 and 1936, when, in each year, twenty people succumbed to the cumulative effects of alcoholism, and here again we see a traditional gender reversal: in 1936, thirteen women died this way as compared to nine men.[20] The majority of these deaths (twelve), involved people over age forty-five.

Cirrhosis of the liver is one thing, alcohol poisoning is another. Seventy people drank themselves to death between 1929 and 1938.[21] The worst year was 1930, the second year of the drought, when fifteen people died in this fashion.

In 1929, the very first year of both the drought and the economic collapse, fourteen people died this way, of whom just one was female. The majority (five) were married men between the ages of twenty-five and forty-four.

Seven men drank themselves to death in 1937.[22]

5: The Wreck of '37

Disaster: (noun) a sudden accident or a natural catastrophe that causes great damage; an event or fact leading to ruin or failure. From the Italian *disastro*, 'ill-starred event.'

Catastrophe: (noun) an event causing great damage or suffering. From the Greek *catastrophe*, 'over-turning, sudden turn.' – *Oxford English Dictionary*

1937 was a bad year. A total of fifty-two rural municipalities in Alberta and fully 170 rural municipalities and local improvement districts in Saskatchewan became the "special care" of the government and thus the Dominion assumed "the entire cost" of keeping the people in those areas alive.[1] Down to the end of 1936, fully $110,600,000 had been spent by the Dominion and provincial governments on relief aid for the rural areas; $47,816,010 would be spent by the provincial and federal governments on relief in 1937 alone.[2] Drought decimated wheat crops in whole sections of Saskatchewan; whole crop districts grew zero bushels per acre that year.[3] The drought of 1937 was so bad down Mankota way that "even Russian thistles had a hard time growing."[4]

1937 was the worst of the bad years. The 1930s generally had administered a vigorous and bracing beating to the settlers of the south and west plains. The settler was like a boxer nearing the end of a fight – he was weak, bloodied, and helpless. The settler was utterly lame, unable to lift his arms in defence; his eyes were swollen shut from repeated hammerings and he could only throw wild windmill punches, swinging desperately at shadows he could not even see. 1937 was the final round.

The year was a high-water mark in many different and important ways. First and most importantly, it was the last year of the Dirty Thirties as such. After 1937, it was mathematically impossible for the situation to get worse: a farmer cannot grow less than zero bushels per acre. As well, 1937 was the year when the entire grain-growing region of the province keenly felt the painful sting of drought, although no one felt it quite so bad as those down south and west. The heretofore untouched eastern and northern grain-growing regions experienced only a small measure of the drought-induced pain that the south plains had endured for close on to ten years, in some areas more than twenty. RMs like Martin, Sliding Hills, Orkney, and Wallace saw their crop yields dip into critically dangerous territory: eight, seven and a half, five, and six bushels per acre respectively. But still, for as bad as it was, the south plains got it worse. Every RM whose municipal minutes were consulted for the purposes of this work (Mankota, Pinto Creek, White Valley, Reno, Big Stick, Deer Forks, Clinworth, Swift Current, and Maple Creek, representing south-central, south-west, and west-central Saskatchewan) posted yields of zero.[5] Absolutely nothing grew.

The final spasms of the big evacuations and abandonment also occurred in 1937. Never again would rural train sidings in Saskatchewan be crammed with thousands of settlers desperate to abandon all for which they had worked. Never again in western plains history would Saskatchewan lose so many people in one year.

And 1937 was crucial for another, conceptual, reason: the frontier world that settlers fled, the world of homesteads, horses, oxen, and ploughs, of relief aid, road gangs, and starvation, also came to an end after 1937. The wild and unregulated frontier world (oftentimes referred to with no small amount of truth as the "Mild West") became tame and regulated. But before all of this occurred, the settlers, the government mandarins, and municipal officials had to grind their way through the desperate and frantic wringer of 1937, and, fittingly, the year started out coloured by delicate little rosebuds of hope.

The Swift Current *Sun* perhaps got a little too carried away with this whole idea of hope (the scribes at most newspapers in most locations in the early settlement years got a little too carried away with just about everything – "boosterism," it was called), though they had at least some justification for that hope, leavened as it was by intermittent rains, which twiddled and flitted across the plains through the spring and early summer. Perhaps the editors of the paper were simply trying to shore up the sagging shoulders of the settlers. The writers thoughtfully enthused that "one cannot help but be carried away enthusiastically by the optimism people of this district are exuding."[6] The gleeful editors understood that, at the end of 1936 (and presumably every year in the preceding eight and most of the years in the preceding twenty), "people had come to the end of their tether." But the light spring rains had induced optimism and the editors felt it, or at least claimed to feel it. The gentle rains pattering on the tin roof tops of settler shacks across the south plains was hypnotizing because rain had been such a scarce commodity for nigh on a decade. And the *Sun* editors suggested that "we can have nothing but admiration for them [settlers]" because "they simply won't be licked."

The burned-out and bewildered editors of the Medicine Hat *News* turned logic on its head as they rooted and rummaged about for something, anything, to feel good about. The editors desperately latched onto the history of what was then known as Johnson Lake. Johnson Lake was an eleven by sixteen mile lake between Moose Jaw and Swift Current, which had evaporated in the droughts and was "completely dry" in 1937.[7] Rather than viewing the existence of dried-up lakes as something at which settlers should necessarily be alarmed, or indeed rather than pointing to dried-up lakes as proof that the region "should have been left to the cows," the editors instead reasoned that this lake had gone dry many times in the nineteenth century and, so the logic went, it had to fill up again; "therefore," there is reason for hope. The president of the Alberta Association of Municipal Districts and Counties, Mr. John Gair, was bemused by these efforts from certain members of the media. Addressing an AAMDC convention, he said, "it would be amusing, were it not so tragic, to watch our daily press trying to keep up the optimistic spirit."[8]

The province, too, even Deputy Auld, was feeling those little stabs of optimism, or as close to those feelings as a logician can get. Responding to a south-west farmer who had claimed that the south plains were "useless," Auld rolled up his sleeves and took his time in responding, pondering. Thoughtfully so. "I do not agree," he patiently explained, "that south-west Saskatchewan is useless."[9] The lush and pleasing rains of spring in whose sanguine beauty harmony bloomed were quite enough to bring out the Shakespeare in Auld. Relating to this burned-out, grizzled, drought-haggard settler on a level he would most assuredly not appreciate, Auld waxed poetic when he wrote that there will be times in every settlers life when "to sow or not to sow will be the question." Indeed, Auld persisted, "the farmer will soliloquize" (farmers don't soliloquize – never have, never will) whether or not it is best to continue the bet in the spring or to save money for the next game. Auld urged the settler to keep his spirits up because, really, there were no other options. The settler had evidently requested some form of assistance to help him and his family flee, but, in keeping with the policy Auld himself had helped establish, Auld informed the hapless pioneer that he would not consider the request because "it is physically impossible to make a wholesale evacuation of many thousands of families" in south-west Saskatchewan. Auld understood that another year of crop failure would "undoubtedly break the morale of many farmers," but he urged Mr. Robinson to stay put and keep at it. There's a good chap.

The badly worn and threadbare ideas of province-hood and nation-building that underscored the policy of non-evacuation were ideas widely shared in Saskatchewan, though as one might suspect they were mostly held amongst politicians and opinion-makers. The editors of the Saskatoon *Star-Phoenix* felt that Auld was correct in his approach and argued that "there is no need for such a movement."[10] The editors based this conclusion on those same light showers that had thinly padded the dust and sand of the south plains that year. These rains were apparently "indications" that "the dry period is coming to an end and a period of normal moisture arriving." The image of a little boy with his hands firmly clasped over his ears talking loudly to drown out something he wishes not to hear is irresistible.

In 1937, even the *possibility* of rain was frontpage news. The Medicine Hat *News* had the grim duty to report in 1937 that, while Edmonton received five and half inches of rain in July of that year, there was only a trace at the Hat, "although a cloudburst was reported at Elkwater."[11] Slim hopes, cruelly dashed.

But still, the view of Saskatoon's newspaper was the same as that of Auld and indeed the federal agriculture minister himself. Former Saskatchewan Premier Mr. James Gardiner was in Saskatoon that weekend in 1937 to attend a "drouth conference." Above all, Mr. Gardiner clung to three basic principles when it came to the crisis of the Thirties: 1) modified farming (i.e., modified summer-fallow) 2) water conservation (dug-outs), and 3) money in the bank to tide farmers over in the bad years.[12] One can readily share Mr. Gardiner's emphasis on dug-outs and modified ploughing, but the final plank in his platform is a silly little conceit because many settlers had likely entered the 1930s with at least some money in the bank to tide them over through the bad times for one or maybe two years, possibly three, but how many entered the decade with enough to tide them over for what, in 1937, was eight-years-worth of bad years? Broke or not, Mr. Gardiner, too was on public record, stating "there will be no wholesale movement from the stricken area."[13] Mr. Gardiner was unequivocal about this: "moving farmers … from one part of the province to another [is] the very thing we are endeavouring to avoid."[14]

Mr. Gardiner's thoughts about the policy of non-evacuation were shared by Mr. J.G. Taggart, the provincial minister of Agriculture. He felt, not without reason, that the problems that would be created by abandonment would necessarily be larger than the problems that would be endured by staying. He suggested that those who went north would be worse off than had they stayed, and, anyway, there was very little useable arable land to which the settlers could flee so they should stay where they were.[15] These were the thoughts of the policy-makers. The movement of the settlers in 1937 would suggest that they held wildly different views on what government policy should have been.

The three parties concerned (the province, the RMs, and the settlers) each had very different ideas about what the crisis meant and what should be done about it and this dynamic created much of the friction between 1914 and 1937. The Dominion government in 1937 explicitly recognized the special contribution made by south plains RM administrators in keeping a sinking ship afloat: as part of a $17,000 operational grant to 150 RMs harmed by drought in 1937, $3,570 of that grant money was designated as "a bonus" to 150 RM administrators. This works out to about twenty-three dollars for each administrator, a tidy little sum in those days.[16]

There were some justifications for the optimism of the early months of 1937, that the year might be a turning point (it was a turning point – just not *the* turning point). Oklahoma, from whose dusty, drought-riddled lands thousands of Okies had fled in the 1930s, proudly produced a prodigious crop of winter wheat in June of 1937.[17] It was front-page news in the Saskatoon paper. It was "the biggest crop since 1926." There was such an embarrassment of wheat that "the problem of transportation had become acute." It was, the reporter excitedly explained, "a harvest equalled few times in history." And, of course, with the rippling waters of absurdity coursing 'neath our entire 1914 to 1937 period, the very same statement about an unequalled harvest was true of Saskatchewan in 1937 – except in Saskatchewan, of course, it was inverted.

In a provincial total of 37,000,000 bushels of wheat produced in 1937, itself amongst the lowest amount of grain ever grown in Saskatchewan to that point, the drylands of the south plains produced just 600,000 bushels of wheat in 1937.[18] In the public report of the Department of Agriculture, under the heading "Unsurpassed Crop Failure," Deputy Auld explained that "1937 will long be remembered by the people of Saskatchewan for the crop failure caused by severe drought. In no previous year in the history of the province have average yields approached the low point of 1937."[19]

Not just individual RMs but whole crop districts covering hundreds of thousands of square miles produced absolutely nothing. Crop districts two, three, four, six, and seven (from Weyburn-Regina to the Alberta border and from the American border to the Macklin region north of Kindersley) produced nothing or the next best thing to nothing. To be accurate, it produced an average of 0.8 bushels per acre. The entire year was an abject and pathetic failure. Mr. Gardiner observed of the isolated and forlorn Mankota-Pinto Creek region that "a broad strip of territory just north of the U.S. boundary has reverted to desert."[20] Settlers in these south RMs were "clamouring for government aid to relieve distress and starvation."[21]

Like dust storms, it is easy to forget how bad 1937 was. It is difficult to conjure the state in which settlers lived, the climate in which they existed. It sometimes seems as though these people lived on another planet. E.H. Target was from Flaxcombe, a forgotten little town tucked in a little valley just inside the Saskatchewan border on the northern tip of the drylands. Mr. Target went on a tour in 1937 and provided a bird's eye view of the disaster for the Medicine Hat *News*. At every turn, "I see drought and desolation."[22] He continued: "I see the vitality of our farmers drained to its lowest ebb and the power of fighting back waning." The drought, he argued was a "national calamity." Mr. Target describes what it was like:

> As I write this letter at 11:30 am on June 28, I see crops of wheat seeded almost two months ago barely above the ground and now flattened and withered. A fifty mile an hour gale is raging and the air is laden with thick particles of dust, so much so that the day is turned to night and I have to light a lamp with which to see. At this time of year I visualize a green countryside whereas in reality, stark desolation sweeps the country.

Mr. Target quoted estimates that suggested the destruction of ten million acres of wheat in 1937. And, given such circumstances, the days of the wheat-growing industry on the south plains, he felt, were numbered unless irrigation was developed. "The cry" in western Canada, he wrote, "is for one thing and one thing alone: water."

Mr. Target uses the phrase "national calamity" about half a dozen times in his article. The press certainly picked up on this basic theme of calamity: newspaper coverage for the drought of 1937 assumed the quality of reports filed from a desperate last stand in some dusty, far-flung corner of the British Empire – Khartoum, say (and from a British perspective, one has to assume that Mankota is as equally as far-flung as Khartoum). On page seven of the August 16 edition of the Saskatoon *Star-Phoenix* of that year, a reader might have thought the world was coming to an end: "Crop Total Loss: Vonda Farmers Desperate"; "Elstow Farmers Securing Relief"; "Families Go East Till Drouth Lifts"; "Gravelling Will Start This Week."[23] From Dunblane south of Saskatoon: "the farmers are busy cutting Russian thistle for feed. No crop will be harvested; all the young men and farmers have left."[24]

Added to this gross mash of misfortune was the Hitchcockian fear that whole swarms of locusts (grasshoppers) were set to flee the ravaged south and descend upon the virgin north. They had been "hatching and swarming" from lands "whose crops are approaching a total loss" and whose farmers "don't care to do anything about it."[25] Swarms of locusts descended in biblical proportions to use a hoary cliché. There were millions, tens of millions, "and where they decided to stop all at once, then those farmers could just kiss that year's crop good bye, if he had a crop."[26] It was, a settler recalled, as though "nature [was] on the loose, gone mad."

The Harry Burton family of Maple Creek certainly recalls the hopper invasion with what had to have been wonder, certainly bafflement. After emigrating from Essex, England, to Ontario in 1911 (Mr. Burton "voyaged to Canada on an orphanage ship" with his two brothers), he came west in 1920 to work on a threshing crew. He married Julia and raised his family.

When the Dirty Thirties hit, the Burtons were one of thousands of families who adapted to the strange requirements and demands that were necessary for life in a dust bowl. Julia would usually put damp cloths on the windows in the house to catch the dust from the dust storms "so they could breathe."[27] One day Julia saw a "black cloud" coming and casually anticipated that it was merely another dust storm, but it turned out to be a hopper invasion. The hoppers stayed for about half an hour and, along with taking the garden and any wheat they could find, they also "ate the paint off the house."[28]

Young Joachim Wold left Norway at the turn of the twentieth century and bounced around South America. After spending time at Rio and Panama, where he very likely was employed in the construction of the Panama Canal, Mr. Wold arrived in Canada in 1913, where he learned how to poison grasshoppers. In the 1930s, when the hopper infestation was at its worst, Mr. Wold mixed together poison, sawdust, bran, molasses, and arsenic, placed it into a drum on wheels, and scattered it about his fields. This approach was actually quite common amongst settlers, and it proved "very effective" because, when he went out the next morning to look, "dead grasshoppers lay all over the ground where the poison fell."[29] There was an option to poison in which a large metal roller with a hood extending out over the top was dragged over a crop – when the hoppers jumped, they would be caught by the hood, fall, and then be crushed by the roller (dragging an metal roller through a wheat field would seem to put at risk any wheat that might have been grown, but brutally crushing the source of one's despair would certainly satisfy one's anger at nature and thus has its own inherent attractions).

Like dust storms, like drought, like the climate itself, locust swarms were an element of nature over which the settlers had no control. And, like dust storms, even locust swarms were possessed of a certain appeal. One settler who witnessed these hopper invasions was not just struck dumb, revolted by the sight – he also felt that "in its own way, it was beautiful, too."[30]

It is not an overstatement, or at least not much of one, to suggest that the world seemed to be coming apart at the seams in 1937. But the sage editors at the Swift Current *Sun* urged calm amidst the panic. The people of the province, they advised, must "face the situation squarely." Even though "there has been much talk of abandonment," the editors urged the settlers to persist because 1938 just might be the year everyone had been looking for. The editors were evidently basing their frantic optimism on the desperate premise that it couldn't *possibly* get much worse and argued that despite all evidence to the contrary, "it can rain in south-west Saskatchewan."[31]

A Swift Current-region rancher did not wait around for it to rain: after being pummelled year after year with drought and crop failure, a settler by the name of Mr. Aspinall, whose story is included in Barry Broadfoot's collection of reminiscences about that decade, said to one of his neighbours, finally, "to hell with this Mac. No more."[32] He sold the steers he had left for one cent per pound (he had hoped to get at least five to six cents) and with sixty-three dollars in his pockets fled the south plains for the Okanogan and he never came back and that was probably the good play. Mr. Gardiner, the federal agriculture minister, estimated that between 200,000 and 300,000 head of cattle would have to be shipped out of the south plains in 1937 because there was no feed. Settlers had actually turned cattle out into the fields so they could feed on whatever the settler managed to grow.[33]

The council for the RM of Swift Current was laughing the laughter of the damned. They threw up their hands in disbelieving frustration that the problem actually did get worse and asked the government to take over all relief, hospital debts, medical aid, and dental care: it declared the drought problem "a national one." (Swift Current was one of the 150 RMs that became the "special care" of the government during the crisis.) Council didn't even bother with chasing down delinquent debtors: "We [will] dispense with filing tax liens this year," as indeed happened right across the south plains in 1937.[34] The Dominion and provincial governments heard the desperate, frustrated cries of the rural regions and did what they could to alleviate the situation. An act was passed in that year in which all unpaid seed grain indebtedness prior to December 1934 was forgiven in addition to all fodder and feed grain loans up to March of 1935.[35]

That the problem was in fact a national one was the substance of a very eloquent plea for aid from the Dominion government made by Humboldt MP H.R. Fleming. Fleming's speech was a difficult one to make because, when he arose in the House of Commons in early 1938, hundreds of irritated and impatient eyes settled on him, knowing that he was going to ask for one thing: money. He knew this; they knew this. By that time in 1938, Saskatchewan had a terrible reputation within confederation – it was "the dog with a bad name." It was "forever camped at the national treasury begging for help." Saskatchewan, as Mr. James Gray put it, was "a rat hole down which millions of dollars taken from eastern taxpayers were dumped."[36]

The prejudice an easterner can feel for a flatlander is markedly different in quality than the prejudice a westerner holds for an easterner: in the east, the prejudice is rooted in paternal contempt, whereas in the west, the prejudice is rooted in anger and impatience at eastern feelings of contempt. Manitoba's Duff Roblin was correct in the deepest way possible when he referred to western Canada as "outer Canada." And so Mr. Fleming did a brave day's work when he reminded the house of its role and responsibilities to Saskatchewan: "She comes not as a stranger in quest of charity but as an integral part of that great Canadian family. She stands upon her unquestioned right claiming the consideration which is due her. She stands upon her unquestioned right to temporary shelter within that home which she, by her pioneering spirit, has helped to rear."[37]

Not all easterners had grown impatient with Saskatchewan. The Ontario-born journalist Mr. Bruce Hutchinson, for example, harboured hot, deep, steaming ideas about the people of Saskatchewan. Mr. Hutchinson toured the drylands in the 1930s and recalls offering a cigarette to a dust bowl settler who (obviously) took it. But then the over-heated and emotional eastern-born journalist decided to give the man the whole pack of smokes "feeling swinish and mean to own anything when these people, better people than I, the people who had made Canada, were destitute."[38] The smokes were likely appreciated; the Rousseauian condescension less so.

To be fair, there was a great deal of support from every province in confederation for the settlers stricken by drought. When the problem first registered in the minds of Canadians in 1931 and they were told that starvation threatened the plucky pioneers of the south and west plains of Saskatchewan, "a great wave of sympathy broke over the entire country" and 250 carloads of fruit, vegetables, and clothes were sent into the province from points all across Canada.[39]

By 1937, her people had been reduced to beggary. In that year, the entire rural population of Kindersley (about 1,331 people) and 75 per cent of its urban population (likewise about 1,300 at that time) were on relief. Trainload after trainload of vegetables and fruit pulled into Kindersley town loaded with apples, turnips, cabbage, and carrots.[40] In Big Stick, the biggest tally of the thirties flooded the office looking not for relief work or relief seed but food. Six hundred starving people applied for food in early 1937.[41] Christof Adams and his family of ten, for example, got twenty-eight dollars worth of groceries, while the bachelor Ed Brewin, got $5.75 worth. A total of 550 train cars of potatoes were sent into south and west Saskatchewan in 1937.[42] The Rowell-Sirois report calculated that 782 rail cars of food had been shipped into the drylands in the seven years preceding 1937.

The distribution of emergency food shipped into Saskatchewan by train was a matter that required some consideration. With life reordered to its lowest form, and Saskatchewan's people "worse off than the poorest peasants of Europe," one had to take care when handing out carrots or cod from the trains. Historian Fred Wilkes observed that one of the problems was being fair: families knew what other families received because apparently their kids at school talked about how much food they received, how many potatoes they got.[43] And so care and consideration had to go into how many apples were distributed to this or that settler. It seems apparent that, being good and proper Canadians, there were no food riots, but officials did try to keep an eye on the fair distribution of relief food and they did this to avoid conflict.

But food only took care of the immediate problem of starvation. There was still the matter of what to do after one's belly was full. Several dozen Shaunovan settlers, members of the United Farmers of Canada, petitioned for a $3,000 grant per family to relocate to suitable lands in the northern grain belt or to east central Saskatchewan. This request is almost certain to have made Deputy Auld's hair stand on end.[44]

Swift Current council dreamed up an idea to dam the Swift Current Creek to provide irrigation to 35,000 acres of dry land and, more importantly, give relief work to the beaten settlers who remained. It was a desperate Hail-Mary pass because council knew of no other thing it could do, but they reasoned that something must be done "if we are to continue to live in this area."[45]

As horrific as 1937 got, though, Clinworth council did not back away from its pledge to offer a gopher tail bounty in 1937. First place was ten dollars, and place got five dollars, and third place received two and a half dollars. And council reminded the young gun-toting prairie lads who featured largely in these competitions that gopher tails "must be tied in bunches of 100."[46]

And so the trains rolled into the south plains and brought carload after carload of food into rural Saskatchewan. Just as often, the trains rolled in the opposite direction, with carload after carload of people fleeing the drylands. 1937 was a very busy year for re-settlement. There are two black untitled ledger books in Regina that detail the number of settlers who, with government assistance, fled that horrible year. The ledger contains their names, what they took with them, where they were coming from, where they were going, and why. Mr. A.J. Reimer, for example, fled Wymark south of Swift Current for Manitoba; he left with two horses and six cows. He chose Manitoba because it was basking in the warm and pleasing glow of a quite successful crop year. A reporter from Saskatchewan, incredulous over hearing that there were in fact whole regions in western Canada that had *not* been knee-capped by drought, visited Manitoba and found to his great envy that "binders were humming and golden stooks dot the landscape."[47]

The reasons that the settlers gave for leaving the south plains for points elsewhere read as a laundry list of destitution and hopelessness: "Abandoned," "abandoning," "giving it up," "foreclosed," "sold to mortgage company," "leaving idle." One settler, in what may be the best example of restraint during the crisis, told the agent he was "no longer interested." And one man who can have felt no love for his progeny explained to the agent taking the information that he "may rent to his son."

In a preamble to the ledger books, there is a very short, unsigned and undated essay that attempts to bring some sort of form to the formless and order to the chaos. While the writer does not give exact numbers of evacuees for 1937, he writes that many settlers, unable to get assistance, simply "piled their belongings in a hay-rack and moved." The writer concludes that, between 1936 and 1941, the population in Saskatchewan dropped by 51,000 people. And in addition to the ledger, which records the movement of 1,200 families approximating some 6,000 people assisted under an unnamed program in 1937, the Unemployment and Agricultural Assistance Act also records the removal, at a cost of half a million dollars, of another 3,018 families approximating some 10,000 people.[48] Thus, as many as 16,000 people fled in 1937 alone. So, of a total 70,000 settlers who fled the south and west plains between 1914 and 1938, 23 per cent left in 1937.

Families like the Brotens of Coronach provide us with an average example of the settler who fled. Halvar and Laura had come to the south plains from Norway in the summer of 1910, just a few years after their country achieved independence from the much-reduced and anaemic Swedish Empire in 1905. In 1937, they left for Yorkton, where there were trees and lakes, and where it rained with alarming regularity. Most of the household supplies were shipped by train, but Gudrun's father and brothers took much of their belongings by wagon, and that included eight horses and the Brotens' machinery. The journey from Coronach to Yorkton took six days.[49]

Historian James Gray has crafted a memorable portrait of abandonment:

> [Abandonment] went on without rhyme or reason. They moved in single families, in pairs or in groups. They moved in one, two or five wagon outfits. They moved in dire necessity or with some of the comforts of home. They moved almost cheerfully with signs like "Meadow Lake or Bust" and "Melfort or Bust" crudely painted on the sides of the wagons. Or they moved quietly, almost in the hope that no one would see them pass.[50]

It seems that the desire to paint one's wagon with a cheerful, spirit-leavening slogan was something of a universal impulse if one happened to be on the sharp end of drought. A slogan was something at which one might grimly smile whilst one's world fell apart. Call it 'Prairie Irony.' Like our south plains settlers, Kansas settlers were famous for their slogan of the 1930s: "In God we trusted, in Kansas we busted."[51] Even from a distance of seventy years, it still has the charming pathos and rhythmically pleasing power to make one smile and that smile suggests that, for all that was bad, there remained in many settlers a quiet sense of humour, even though at the end of 1937 two in three people in rural Saskatchewan were destitute.[52]

In the middle of this evacuation, the editors of the Swift Current *Sun* chased after the departing trains and shouted glad tidings. Writing in the entirely inappropriate past tense while the event was still unfolding, the editors, as though narrating a Greek tragedy for the benefit of an audience while the play was still being performed, wrote that many settlers "could see no hope for the future" and so "a number of them pulled up stakes" for greener fields but, in September 1937, they insisted that "there was a gradual return of confidence."[53] Cue the train full of settlers rolling slowly past.

The editors apparently chose not to see what was happening. It was not only the settlers in the rural areas who were leaving but "the small towns were being emptied as the people began to desert them."[54] Those who remained did not have an easy go of it: they "shivered or sweltered in shack houses with paper thin walls ... comatosely holding to a fading hope that next year would be better and for seven years each next year had been worse than the one before."[55]

Settling on the south plains was never supposed to be easy. No one ever in their wildest imaginings could have guessed how hard it actually was. Had Mankota settlers ever thought that, penniless and starving, they would have to march across thirty miles of open prairie under the grim, unhappy skies of a cold and unforgiving October and sleep in a ditch near the mouth of a third-rate coal mine to get fuel with which to heat their shacks during the winter, many probably would have thought twice about the promise of the Last Best West and return to the Dakotas and their jobs as teachers and bank clerks.

The bad year of 1937, though, was also the last year. After fumbling and bumbling and failing for close on to twenty-five years, 1937 was the watershed point. There was only one direction the situation could go and that was up; it could not possibly get worse. Even though our federal agriculture minister donned the colourful robes of braggadocio with talk of "tilting a triple-tipped lance at drought," salvation was somewhat more dull and benign and therefore more pleasingly Canadian.[56] It came in the form of a curious mixture of settlers, scientists, "professors of soils," and government men assembled into a group and this organization, the Prairie Farm

Rehabilitation Administration, is known to history by its cheerless, awe-deflating initials: the PFRA.

The PFRA was officially formed in 1935 and became a permanent body after 1937. The very existence of the organization represented something far greater than at first might be thought. The creation of the PFRA was not only a step toward developing practical solutions for dryland agriculture; it also represented a fundamental change in thinking, in perception. Borrowed money, loaned money and guaranteed loans would no longer be thrown out the window in the terrifyingly ridiculous cycle of crop-failure/relief-aid/crop-failure/relief-aid. Money that might have gone to aid relief instead was spent on fixing the problem because, by 1937, quite a few people had figured out not only how not to farm but also how to farm in a dry land.[57]

The PFRA was a proactive organization, not reactive, and as such it represented an enormous step forward in the mentality surrounding south-plains agriculture: this is why it is such an important part of western Canadian history. There would never again be the same sense of dreamy theatricality associated with agriculture as one finds in the words of the government official who, upon observing the crop failure of 1914, said, if in one year a crop failed, "[summer-fallow ensured] the next years results may be safely relied upon." It was an intellectual revolution.

That the PFRA represented a revolution of the mind is the south plains equivalent of an idea developed by historian and critic Mr. Paul Fussell. In his work, *The Great War and Modern Memory*, Fussell suggested that nineteenth-century Victorian sentiments such as heroic honour, courage, and bravery did not survive the trenches of World War I. The cataclysm of war destroyed those grand Victorian ideals; the war made heroism, valour, and honour seem absurd, ridiculous. These lofty Victorian ideals were often expressed using what Fussell calls "High Diction," that grand, over-blown, over-heated poetry one finds, for example, in Rupert Brooke; High Diction too, also died in the trenches. The war was such a savage experience that it made those sentiments ridiculous, out of date, moronic. Something similar occurred on the south plains during the 1930s.

Consider the sentiment that accompanied settlement: the south plains were judged flat, treeless, open, and "therefore" a region uniformly fit for agriculture.[58] It was mentioned earlier that the government of Canada used this kind of logic in suggesting that the steel of the rail tracks will disrupt electrical currents "thereby" causing rain. Other examples of this kind of thinking abound: crop failures were "due entirely to good or bad farming";

if there was a failure in one year, summer-fallow would ensure that the results of the following year "can be safely relied upon"; "honest labour can overcome drought and poor crop conditions." The 1930s represented the death of this kind of silly, hopeless logic.

All of these ideas were rooted in a sense of blind optimism, a propensity for wishful thinking, a kind of misplaced and unquestioned faith in the ability of man to overcome nature. Historian David Jones wrote about this creed and its "overweening faith in the power of man." The modern or rather "post-modern" mind has difficulty following in the mental tracks laid down by those who came before us because their way of thinking is so very foreign. Our own mind is, regrettably, in many ways, permanently tuned to irony and cynicism. We have difficulty conjuring a mental world in which "therefore" was wielded with such ridiculous aplomb as it was throughout the dry years. This mental habit did not survive the Dirty Thirties. Nuance and subtlety replaced ill-considered, ill-thought generalizations, wishful, hopeful thinking. In the Great War, just as in the Dirty Thirties, a great cataclysm wrought tremendous intellectual change.

These new revolutionary transformations and the associated technical skills that grew out of them were cumulative, coming as they did after a twenty-five-year struggle against the desert. They were ideas that had been incubating and struggling to find their proper place and time. As James Gray observes, by the time 1937 rolled around, more knowledge about dryland farming had been gained than "mankind had acquired in twenty centuries."[59] 1914 had been dismissed as a freak; 1917–24 created an increasing concern in many quarters and prompted a number of men to seriously question and challenge the old worn-out orthodoxies of W.R. Motherwell and Angus McKay; the 1930s lit a fire under all concerned and results, finally, were achieved.

The first steps toward rational farming on the south plains were simple (so simple in fact that it leaves one asking why they were not developed long before). The matter of dugouts, for example, provides an illustration of a simple solution that would have gone a great distance toward solving the problem of stock-watering during a drought. Oftentimes, cattle were shipped north to greener pastures so that they might feed. And while many settlers did in fact have dugouts, the idea was not a common one. Either for want of information or communication, the idea was not, in fact, general. Designed as a water reservoir that would trap spring run-off and thus provide water for stock, gardens, and household use, dugouts were not common on the plains until the PFRA men got the idea out and circulating and provided the funds for their development. In 1935 there were only a very few dugouts, but by 1936 there were 1,014. In addition there were 668 stock watering dams and 141 irrigation schemes either developed or in development.[60]

The biggest advancements made by the PFRA, though, came where it was needed most and that was in the area of ploughing. For thousands of years prior to the entrance of the settler onto the south plains, short-grass prairie regions up and down the length of North America had thrived and survived even in seasons of drought. These regions provided a comfortable home for the buffalo and then later for cattle. As long as the short-grass was stitched to the land, these regions flourished.[61] The short-grass was "the perfect fit" for the sandy loam of the drylands because it could hold moisture a foot or more below the surface.[62] But when the settler arrived and tore out the sod, the land was left exposed, "empty, dead and transient." The roots of the grass were gone, the soil became unbound, and it was in this scenario that the settlers arrived with their equipment and the injunction to plough deep and hard to conserve moisture and never mind pulverizing and granulating the soil.

When one sees pictures of soil drifting like snow against a south-plains fence line, it was merely the practical result of this process of summer-fallowing. Settlers, as the Englishman A.G. Street correctly observed, attacked the land, ripped up the grass, unbound the soil, and then beat it with a plough. In dry years, the disintegration of the soil was exacerbated by the heat and so we are faced with the sad and inevitable conclusion drawn by Mr. Gray: "it was those who followed the best scientific methods ... who were the chief fashioners of the disaster." Another of the unnamed settlers in Broadfoot's collection of stories on the 1930s agreed: "you mistreat the land, take away its essential goodness, and this [soil drift/soil exhaustion] will happen."[63]

There was a creeping sense of discomfort with summer-fallow in the 1920s, but since there were no other alternatives, its use remained openly advocated even though such an approach was "as wrong for that area as [it] possibly could have been." And when the dry years came and the wind blew (there is the old joke in Saskatchewan that "if the wind ever stopped blowing we'd all fall over" – the wind blows *all* the time), it took the soil with it, cutting off the life blood of the wheat at the root. The problem grew worse when the settler decided to leave.

The settlers, as has been observed, did not wait around for advancements in agricultural methods but instead "found their own solution in the manner farmers have solved their problems since history began" and simply walked away. They likely didn't know that by leaving they were in fact contributing to the problem.[64] When settlers walked away, the land lay there unused. It is one thing to own land, quite another to care for the land, and thus the soil was allowed to continue drifting and weeds were allowed to keep growing, and this usually meant that the neighbour's field would soon be covered with weeds and drift from the adjacent land.

Alberta had long been an active practitioner of penalizing farmers who allowed their soil to drift and Pinto Creek council tried to follow suit. In an action replicated by RMs across the south plains during the entire 1914 to 1937 period, council passed a motion that levied "penalties where, because of poor farming and neglect, soil is allowed to drift."[65] During the entire 1914–37 period, municipal councils even dispatched roving gangs of school kids to act as weed spotters and, even in the 1930s, they were paid the handsome sum of fifty cents for reporting the location of heretofore unknown patches of Russian, Canada, and Sow thistle.[66] The drought, like a creeping fungus, slowly slithered across the hills and valleys of the plains, turning the soil into a putrescent heap of lifeless dirt. And since no one was legally obliged to do anything, no one did.[67] Over two million acres of land had been abandoned by 1936.

The tragedy is that summer-fallow methods were used by settlers with great success in regions where there was adequate rainfall. Summer-fallow was perfectly acceptable in the northern grain-belt but not on the south plains: it was the wrong tool for the wrong job in the wrong place at the wrong time – everything about it was wrong. Using summer-fallow in a region notorious for drought is like using a sledgehammer to pound in a nail. Dryland farming required the settler then and the farmer today to finesse the land, not bludgeon it. All of this talk about a settler's responsibility for the land is not meant to downplay the drought for that was the chief ingredient that made all of the other elements active. Without drought, as 1915, 1916, and 1928 proved, there was no problem. With drought came miseries untold.

The principal problem, then, lay in how to work the land. The Noble Blade, as James Gray observes, was one of the more successful creatures of the PFRA efforts. Originally used as an implement on fruit farms in California, C.S. Noble adapted the blade for use on the arid south plains. The chief selling feature was its light touch. It did not plough deep, as farmers had been instructed to do for decades; it tilled the soil lightly and it cut more than it ploughed.

And then there was "trash-farming." Most farmers then (and today) bristle at the thought of leaving weeds on their land. "Indian summer-fallow" is the pejorative term to describe a field left to weeds. Just as settlers up north chopped down every tree they could get their calloused hands on, settlers also seemed to think that that land must be clear of all weeds before seeding. But Asael "Ace" Palmer had other ideas.

Palmer advocated a method in which light surface tilling left weeds and stubble on the surface and this replicated the natural conditions of the soil in the region before the settler came. While not "stitched to the land" as such, the weeds and stubble provided a sort of covering net for the soil and this net held the soil in place and arrested, reduced, or eliminated soil drift. Palmer spoke so often and so fondly of this method that his convivial office mates stopped calling him "Ace" Palmer and instead took to calling him "Trash-Cover" Palmer.[68]

Solving soil-drift was important. It was one of the elements of the crisis years between 1914 and 1937 that contributed in no small measure to the larger problems created by drought, and by addressing it the men of the PFRA actually chopped off at the root one of the biggest problems that had plagued agriculture in the drylands for decades. It was recognized as a problem by Angus McKay and others as far back as 1908, but, in keeping with the simple beliefs of the day, McKay argued that soil drift, eventually, "will disappear" though he never explained exactly how.

For all these advancements though, there were still those who wanted to commit the south and west plains to the junk heap. Canada's barrel-chested prime minister Mackenzie King ("Rex" as his friends called him) was one of them. After seeing the wreckage of the plains and the detritus of broken lives that littered it in the form of abandoned farms and abandoned towns, he confided thusly in his journal: "I don't think it [Palliser's Triangle] will be of any real use again."[69] And so Agriculture Minister James Gardiner deserves some extra praise for prying from King's reluctant fingers the $5 million necessary to develop the PFRA.

Some of the beleaguered RMs, whacked stupid by the "unholy mess" of the drought, were babbling incoherent nonsense in 1937. Some of them put up a misguided fight to resist plans of the PFRA. The PFRA ordered the municipalities to sign over title to all land they had received at tax sales and land which had been declared unusable for agriculture. But they resisted because they felt that the more land they signed over, the smaller their tax base would be. When a disbelieving provincial agriculture minister, J.G. Taggart, reminded them that in most cases they hadn't seen a cent of tax money off these lands in some cases for twenty-five years, the stupefied municipalities fell in step.[70] (Rural municipalities in Saskatchewan have a profound and deeply rooted resistance to the imperative – if they are told to do something, they will not. If they are given an option, then they will do it, but only to the extent that they see fit. Alberta by distinct contrast favours the imperative and uses it quite regularly. One can see evidence of this in weed control legislation. In Alberta, rural municipalities *must* deal with weeds: it is required by law. In Saskatchewan, it is only suggested that rural municipalities *may* want to deal with weeds: it is not required by law).[71]

These lands signed over by the RMs were to be used as community grazing pastures. The PFRA included this operational element to its mandate in 1937, also the same year in which it was made a permanent organization. At the end of that year, there were sixteen pastures that had been emptied of settlers, fenced off, and re-grassed. By the end of 1938, there were twenty-eight pastures covering 380,000 acres.[72] And by 1940, 837,940 acres of land had been turned back to prairie and of those acres, 700,000 were on the south and west plains. An additional 411,200 acres were re-grassed the following year.[73] Thus, over one million acres of land were taken out of production in just two or three years following the catastrophe of 1937.

For all of the destructiveness of 1937, the year came to a close dragging behind it some small successes. Land was re-grassed, some settlers were removed, and the first positive steps toward rational agriculture had been taken. As 1937 finished and made way for 1938, hope once again fought aside despair and its handmaidens and made its way back onto the south and west Saskatchewan plains. And this time there was some justification because 1938 was a better year than many had seen in a long, long time, and it proved the scribes of the Swift Current *Sun* right: it did rain in south-west Saskatchewan. And the rain was not just a "frustrating dribble," as Pierre Berton called it, but a real and genuine downpour, and at the right time, too.[74] Deputy Auld said the crop outlook of 1938 was "very encouraging in most districts" and that, on balance, "the outlook of the province was bright."[75] In 1939, Saskatchewan experienced a harvest that was called "one of the best in history" (although $7,500,000 in aid relief was distributed to settlers on the south and west plains).[76]

It is not that things all of a sudden stopped being bad after 1937, but rather the continual and frantic downward spiral in which settlers were helplessly trapped from 1914 onward came to a thudding stop in 1937 – mostly because it was simply impossible for the problem to get worse. In the truest sense of the phrase, there was nowhere left to go but up and that, ultimately, is what 1937 represents: the utter and absolute nadir of south and west plains agriculture during the dry years.

The situation got better but only incrementally, over time, gradually. The eleven RMs whose municipal minutes form the structural foundation of the present work, for example, had tax arrears totalling $1.1 million at the start of 1937 in addition to having roughly $250,000 in tax sale holdings. By the start of 1939, though, tax arrears had fallen to just $500,000 and tax sale holdings had plummeted to levels that had not been seen in the drylands since before the 1920s: $66,740.31. Tax sale holdings in the seventeen years between 1922 and 1939 had *never* been that low. (The records for tax sale holdings only go as far back as the early 1920s.) The tax sale holdings figure for these eleven RMs peaked at almost $250,000 in the twenties; it dropped to $100,000 in 1928 before spiking to just under $300,000 in the 1930s. But by the time 1939 rolled around, the tax sale holdings figure had fallen to levels that many administrators, reeves, and councillors had never seen before. Indeed, it was at a level that they probably thought was not even possible.

1939 allowed everyone some time to stretch. The drought lifted and made room for time to complete what the droughts did not. The depopulation of the south plains would continue over time but that would occur slowly, gradually, and with less of the tragic brutality of the dry years; it continues down to today.

The reprieve, though, would be brief. In 1946, the province again had to come to the aid of the south plains because it seemed that, despite improvements in agricultural methods, if the rain didn't fall the crop wouldn't grow. 1947 was as bad as 1937 for Zygment Burnat, who had settled at Iddelsleigh, in the Alberta portion of the drylands. 1947 was so dry that the family's crop yield from a half section of land, 320 acres, was less than 400 bushels – that works out to 1.25 bushels per acre. The daughter of Mr. Burnat recalls "gathering dandelions to supplement our food supply." This may have the appearance of grim desperation but she wistfully recalls that "they made a tasty salad."[77]

As the droughts of 1946 and 1947 suggest, there were worse droughts than 1937. The droughts of 1961 and 2002 were comparable in scope and severity to the drought of 1914, and indeed these droughts are reckoned as some of the worst droughts of the twentieth century, worse even than 1937.[78] The droughts between 1986 and 1988 wiped out and bankrupted thousands of south and west plains farmers. It was not unusual in those years to hear stories on the nightly news about farmers lying dead in their half-tons next to a shotgun. Professor E.C. Hope had not exaggerated: suicide was a not-infrequent response to drought (and statistics show a marked preference for firearms in the execution of the act). And west plains pride was further humbled in 2001–2002 when cattlemen in the drylands were forced to rely on hay shipments from their eastern Canadian counterparts in what was called the Hay West Campaign, a moniker that has a touch of the gallant to it.

Dr. David Sauchyn is a pioneer in the study of the drought and climate on the western plains and he skippers the Prairie Adaptation Research Collaborative. He observes that the big difference between the droughts of the thirties and those of later years is that prairie people have learned to adapt to living and farming in a dry land.[79] The PFRA played a leading role in that agricultural adaptation. Government too came to recognize that a repeat of the shambolic and chaotic social and economic disasters of the Dirty Thirties was not desirable and so it passed the Prairie Farm Assistance Act in 1939. This act guaranteed settlers a certain level of income when their crops failed and, most importantly, repayment was not necessary. This not only ensured a basic (though still meagre) standard of living for settlers on the south and west plains, but in one fell swoop the PFAA abruptly ended municipal indebtedness brought on by the necessity of local governments providing relief aid; hard labour road-gangs likewise disappeared and so too did absurdity. These elements are entirely absent from later droughts: no one worked on road gangs to feed their families in the devastating drought of 1961 because the state assumed some of the responsibility in the event of a crop failure. Indeed, a Department of Agriculture mandarin noted that direct relief in Saskatchewan all but disappeared in 1939 because of the PFAA and thus so too did all of those elements that characterized life on the south and west plains during the droughts between 1914 and 1937.[80]

Science continually reveals more (or rather reaffirms in better detail what has long been known) about the region in which these settlers were trapped. Dr. Sauchyn observes that the prairies have the most variable climate in Canada, adding, somewhat sardonically, that the south and west plains in particular are the only areas in the country that are defined by the amount of rain they do not get, by their dryness. Sauchyn observes that "we don't get average years on the prairies" but instead we waffle between wet years or dry years with little moderation in between. Of the Medicine Hat region, in particular, and the extreme wet-dry cycle of weather by which it is characterized, Dr. Sauchyn notes that "few places on earth have this kind of variability."[81]

So, there is no end to the story; it only changes. If farmers today want to sell their land and move away to Victoria, they can do so, unlike their forbearers in 1914 who were told they would not be able to cancel their homesteads. The trip to Victoria can now be accomplished in a few hours and comes complete with a comfortable and scenic ferry ride. One no longer has to ride in a stinking cattle car for a week taking care of stock to get to the green valleys of British Columbia.

Road gangs have been replaced by the somehow less dignified cash subsidy programs. Farmers no longer go to the local RM office or the local rail siding for by-the-pound handouts of apples, potatoes or cod, nor is a quarter section of land traded for a box of apples, nor do farmers apply to the local RM administrator for relief aid. Rural councillors no longer have to accept relief aid applications from their rate payers. Starvation today usually happens only in the Third World, and one is reasonably sure that it has been some years since anyone in the Mantario district has eaten porcupine stew. Local rural councils no longer "clamour for aid" to prevent starvation; they clamour for government infrastructure programs to save their roads from disintegration, a direct consequence of rail and elevator consolidation.

Absurdity has been replaced with sophisticated apathy. Naiveté has been replaced with irony, credulity with cynicism. The split between rural and urban has grown wider to the point where it is very easy and in fact common for someone in Saskatoon to completely forget that he or she lives in Saskatchewan.

It has been many years since someone has had to light a lamp at noon so as to be able to see. It has been many years since a mother has had to place wet cloths over the faces of her children "so that they might be able to breathe," and it has likewise been many years since a teacher has had to wait "a year or two" to get paid.

But the droughts haven't stopped.

They never will.

Conclusion: Oblivion (redux)

Historians are like deaf people who go on answering questions that no one asked them. – *Leo Tolstoy*

The principal reason for this work has been to examine and explain the nature, origin, and course of the Dirty Thirties and to do so without making reference to the Great Depression. In doing this, the entire crisis of the dry years between 1914 and 1937 is finally allowed room to breathe, whereas previously it had been shut up in a dark room all but eclipsed by the much grander tale of the global economic collapse. We must remember that in the most recent and updated history of Saskatchewan, Dr. W.A. Waiser told us that "the real challenge" in the Thirties "was not growing enough grain but getting a decent price for it." Obviously, Dr. Waiser cannot and does not ignore the droughts, but his emphasis on economics as the principal problem acts as a shield that keeps the dry years from view.

By prying apart the drought from the economic collapse, we are able to see a separate, clear, and distinct history take shape. We are able to see the development of new and exciting patterns of history in which relief aid, road gangs, and land abandonment form the basic nature and trajectory of life on the south plains between 1914 and 1937. We are able to see that the Dirty Thirties has its very own peculiar history, its own trajectory, its own nature, origin, and course, which is entirely separate from the Great Depression, that the thirties were not, in fact, exceptional. They were indeed hard and severe, but, in function and character, they were little different from the years that preceded them. We are also able to see that there was not just one period of western settlement that stretched in a continuous unbroken line from Clifford Sifton in the late nineteenth century through Frank Oliver in the twentieth, but rather there are two entirely separate and distinct periods of settlement, during which two distinctly and uniquely different areas of the province were settled: the first settlement phase was successful, the second, less so.

The mildly shocking absence of understanding about the history of the many droughts in Saskatchewan, their continuity, their *connectedness* has helped to create and give form to the idea that the Dirty Thirties were exceptional years: they were not. They were merely a part of a continual cycle of drought that stretches back for as long as anyone can remember and even beyond that. Dr. Sauchyn's studies reveal that droughts on the south and west plains are absolutely unexceptional and stretch back hundreds of years. Some of these droughts, he notes, have lasted fifty years and more.

The history of the Dirty Thirties, as we have seen, can be told without reference to the Great Depression. The droughts and the relief aid and the work crews and the tax sales, and the evacuations and land abandonment: these are all special and unique creatures of the drought, not the depression. The drought created its own problems, has its own history, and ran its own course with remarkable continuity for twenty-three years from 1914 down to 1937. Indeed, the argument for continuity between these years can in some ways be entirely supported by the presence or absence of the road-gangs in rural Saskatchewan: when there was drought, road-gangs sprang up all over the plains. Road-gangs were entirely unique to the droughts of the south plains. Rain was to wheat what drought was to road-gangs.

Measuring the enormity of the crisis is a difficult task and one that cannot be fully addressed in any conclusion. It can be considered or summed up in any number of ways: the amount of human suffering, the acres of land sold at tax sales, the number of people who fled, the volume of relief allotments, the number of illegitimate children, the number of people who killed themselves, the amount of cod fish consumed, the number of children who died from malnutrition, or any combination thereof.

The Rowell-Sirois Commission studied the economics of the droughts in detail and this is what they came up with: $738,188 was spent by the provincial and Dominion governments in relief expenditures in 1929; $3,031,957 in 1930; $20,682,744 in 1931; $13,249,178 in 1932; $12,705,455 in 1933; $21,747,248 in 1934; $19,617,989 in 1935; $18,784,879 in 1936. It is probably fortunate that they put together this report in the early spring of 1937 before the failure became evident because the $47,816,010 spent on relief that year might have skewed their averages and their view of things.[1]

In keeping with our economic theme, we can also view the dry years using conditional subsidies as our frame of reference. Conditional subsidies were grants given by the Dominion government on the condition that the province perform a stipulated action, which quite often took the form of spending a certain amount of money in a specific area. Apparently, "leading examples" of the programs funded by this kind of conditional grant included "a grant in support of the treatment of venereal diseases" during the Roaring Twenties.[2]

At any rate, the records of conditional subsidies made to the province stretch all the way back to 1912, and these subsidies exactly parallel the arc of drought: there was, for example, a $27,000 grant made in 1913, but a $61,000 grant in 1914. The 1915 grant was $34,000, but the 1919 grant was $167,000. Grants provided during the drought years of the 1920s stay over $1.1 million until 1926, when they fell back to $124,000.[3] And when the Thirties hit in 1929, those subsidies instantly breach the $2 million mark and remain there for much of the decade.

The frustrating war fought by rural municipalities over relief aid and tax arrears was also highlighted in the Rowell-Sirois Report, and, again, the record of RM borrowing exactly parallels the years of drought. As an effort to offset the decline in revenues by the non-payment of taxes, RMs took $432,000 in general bank loans in 1916, but, by 1921, RMs had taken out general loans in the amount of $3.7 million.[4] This figure drops to $366,000 in 1926 and then rockets to $4.5 million in 1931.

Relief bank loans are also included in the summary of spending by RMs. There was no relief supplied by RMs in 1916, but $1.2 million by 1921; there was only $302,000 in relief aid distributed by RMs in 1926, but again when the dry years hit that figure spikes to $4.8 million in 1931, dropping slightly to $4.5 million in 1935. These figures, too, exactly parallel the droughts and crop failures between 1914 and 1937.[5]

There are also other barometers by which the size and enormity of the cost of drought can be measured, like debt adjustment, mediation, and moratoriums. Debt mediation was introduced in 1914 because of the crop failures in south and west Saskatchewan. Saskatchewan's Agriculture Minister Mr. Hamilton visited the drylands of southern Alberta in August 1922 and examined the workings of its Drought Area Relief Act (which later evolved into the Debt Adjustment Act). Mr. Hamilton returned home and promptly installed a similar program in Saskatchewan. By the end of that year, some six thousand cases had been handled by the board.[6] Closely aligned to the Debt Adjustment Act was the Farm Loans Board, which, by 1922, had doled out $8 million.[7] The RMs were likewise bent over the proverbial barrel: by 1920, the province had guaranteed just under $3 million in relief loans taken by RMs to provide aid to their settlers.[8]

Between 1928 and 1938, the Debt Adjustment Board "adjusted," that is to say reduced or mediated, $82 million in debt, and this included relief aid and tax arrears.[9] The Farm Creditors Arrangement Act operated on similar principles. The committee that oversaw implementation of this act would make mutually agreeable arrangements for repayment between a debtor and a creditor. In some typical examples, a debt of $21,000 was rationalized downward to $7,714; one of $29,293 was finally paid out at $11,290.[10] Recall that the same kind of thing happened in Mankota when rural councils stopped trying to get what they were owed and instead adjusted themselves to taking what they could reasonably expect to get. The FCAA board handled cases totalling $43 million and reduced a total of $14 million in debt. There was also a moratorium on debt in the 1930s.

So here, then, is a kind of rough balance sheet: just under a quarter *billion* dollars in relief aid was supplied to rural Saskatchewan in the 1930s by the Dominion and provincial governments. Millions of dollars in additional relief aid were also spent by rural municipalities.

A total of $10 million was spent on relief road work in the 1930s, during which time forty thousand men went to work on these road crews, primarily in the drought area. During a single year in the 1920s, just under two thousand men laboured on road-gangs, *only* in the drought area. In the crop failure of 1914, seven hundred men from the Maple Creek area alone volunteered for work on road-gangs, on which work the province spent $750,000.

As of 1936, 782 rail car loads of food had been shipped into Saskatchewan. Another 550 followed in 1937.

Hundreds of rail cars full of clothing and fancy hats were sent into Saskatchewan through Red Cross appeals and other relief agencies throughout the dry years.

Just under $3 million in relief loans had been guaranteed by the province in south-west and west-central Saskatchewan RMs between 1918 and 1920.

$8 million in aid was dumped into the drylands in 1914.

Between 1914 and 1937, an estimated 70,000 men, women, and children fled the south and west plains with their lives and spiritual state temporarily in tatters, giving rise to historian Chester Martin's observation that the settlement of the south plains "came at a terrible cost in human suffering."

Oliver's 1908 amendment to the Dominion Lands Act was not an inexpensive proposition.

This is the economic balance sheet, but, mercifully, and contrary to what many university professors will tell their students, there is more to history than economics. Mr. Martin's observation about the terrible cost of human suffering leads us to a question that has not yet been explored in the fullness that it deserves and which was only touched on briefly earlier in this work: what effect did the droughts have on the people who settled the south and west plains?

Saskatchewan people are all very familiar with the well-worn idea that the Dirty Thirties resulted in the people of Saskatchewan drifting toward the heavy state interventions of Mr. Tommy Douglas and the CCF/NDP. After the droughts, settlers sought security in stronger government as a protection and a guarantee against future repetitions of the utter and absolute poverty, devastation, and hurt of the Dirty Thirties: this well-worn track of Saskatchewan historiography. It might be better called a rut because there is more to the Dirty Thirties than just political economy.

The popular and frequent observation is that, during the crises of the dry years, men went to great lengths to work on road-gangs in order to stay off the relief rolls, to avoid having to ask their local council for underwear. The common belief is that the story ends there; that these men remained unchanged. This view of the Thirties emphasizes the bold, plucky, resourceful settler who overcame the odds with a smile, a swagger, and a lot of hard work. This view is celebrated widely all across rural Saskatchewan, but, generally speaking, that is not the case, mostly because it *cannot* be the case.

First and most obviously, we must understand and treat as unexceptional the idea that soul-withering drought, decadal crop failures, and excruciatingly humiliating relief aid had a warping effect on the spirit of the settlers, and then we must follow that unexceptional observation wherever it might lead.

As suggested earlier, the more a man received aid, the more he came to rely on it: this is a simple, basic human truth that received an extensive application in the 1920s and 1930s. The RMs actively and frequently complained about having to carry farmers, which resulted, finally, in their refusal to do so. Settlers were a burden to the municipality. As historian David Jones observes, "settlers had been handfed for several years and had come to expect it."[11]

The taking or non-taking of aid was an intensely moral proposition. Aid was viewed as "repugnant" to "self-respecting men," and so the issue was all tied up in values concerning the strength of one's character. The taking or non-taking of relief aid was a reflection, an expression, of who a person was on the inside and up to a certain point relief aid was in fact resisted, as legend has it, but that changed in the dry years.

In his report to the House of Commons in 1938, E.W. Stapleford, whose job it was to give MPs a sense of what had just happened on the south plains, wrote of how relief changed the spirit of the men who received it. There were three stages: "first, after a desperate struggle to stay off relief, [there was] very reluctant application for assistance. Second [there was] an attitude of passive acceptance of relief as inevitable and, finally, a tendency to demand all that they think they should have."[12]

Settlers in Saskatchewan drifted away from the highly moral ideal of pulling themselves up by their socks and toward a reliance on state aid, and thus the droughts appear to have broken something in the spirit of those who settled south and west Saskatchewan; something was forever altered, forever changed. "Can we wonder," asks Stapleford, "that with year after year of such experiences, human endurance sometimes reaches its limit and something snaps?" That "something" was the belief that a man could and should be able to make his own way without help from the state or other authorities.

Stapleford sent out a questionnaire to settlers, which probed and explored these kinds of questions and ideas, and he concluded that the results reveal "a sad commentary on the devastating effect of [these] adverse conditions on the morale both of individuals and the community."[13] Stapleford found that there was a wide variety of opinion on the effects of year after year of drought, but the one common theme was spiritual capitulation, or, in other words, the loss of hope. Stapleford said there was a "definite tendency to discouragement and loss of ambition" for many people. Two years of drought can be borne, he suggested, perhaps even three, but after ten years and in many regions twenty, he found that "discouragement replaces hope and an attitude of apathy develops ... and this seems to be what happened to a great many people under the stress of drought."

A part of the spirit that created and developed Saskatchewan died in the droughts and dust storms between 1914 and 1937. The death of that particular element of the Saskatchewan spirit seems to have been replaced with apathy, a desire for greater securities and assurances, perhaps even the desire for a greater level of government involvement in daily life. Stapleford wrote that "a very large number of those who replied to the questionnaire expressed the opinion that 'the state owes us a living.'"[14] Anecdotal evidence supports this: Alberta today is full of Saskatchewan refugees who argue that they have fled from the province precisely because of this apathy, this belief that Saskatchewan is full of people who persist in accepting the idea that government should do for us what we should be able to do for ourselves. This is a culturally pervasive spiritual habit that developed in the dust storms and soil drift of the dry years.

J. Isabel Winterstein was on the ground in 1937 and claimed to have been a witness to the development of that apathy. As a representative of the United Farmers of Canada, she delivered an address 1937 in which she argued that children and young adults had "adopted a defeatist psychology" because they felt there were "no opportunities for [the] realization of ambitions" in Saskatchewan.[15] It might have been an original and thought-provoking idea in 1937 but not so much today. Her words are a terribly familiar refrain for thousands of Saskatchewanians and the highway to Calgary is clogged with people who claim the very same thing.

But the point to note is that this "defeatist psychology," this sense that our province "has nothing to offer" (Stapleford's "apathy"), is another unique creature of the dry years. It may seem as though this "apathy" has been around forever, but that is just not the case. These ideas did not simply exist in the air and ether of our province; it is not "the way things have always been" – it got that way, it was caused by something. This defeatism and the sense that our province has nothing to offer is an ugly, unlovely child of the dry years, and it is a regrettable stain on the spirit of Saskatchewan.

In addition to these ideas of apathy, there was the development of another much deeper, critical spiritual crisis on south plains in the 1930s. Mrs. Winterstein claimed that the "moral code" of young people had been abandoned and that people had "come to regard ordinary moral standards with impunity" with "fatal results." Mr. Stapleford noticed this thing too. He argued that young people had been "thwarted in the normal desire to marry [which] create[d] a serious social problem." We can safely assume here that the issue to which both Stapleford and Winterstein were referring was the matter of the over 5,000 illegitimate births, which occurred predominantly in the rural areas of Saskatchewan between 1931 and 1938.

Saskatchewan underwent a small "*r*" social revolution during the 1930s. Sexual mores were held in abeyance for over a decade, suicide was rampant, murders frequent, more women than men were having illicit affairs, and divorce rates skyrocketed. One physician who answered Stapleford's questionnaire was fairly clear on this point: the drought was "conducive to a lowering of the morale of many individuals" and, he added, "the character of some of them has deteriorated."[16] Stapleford recalled one pioneer who answered: "My boy was five years old when the drought began. I am very thankful he was not fifteen years of age at the time."[17] Historian Fred Wilkes says that the dry years "mocked the dignity of man, betrayed his best judgement, and struck at his faith in God."[18] This is another way of saying man was debased and defiled, made to look foolish, he had his spirit humbled and his faith rocked. It is only natural then that there should have been a response to this.

A settler by the name of T.L. Duncan lived in Alberta's half of the dry-lands in the Tilley area near Medicine Hat, and he watched lives and spirits crumble. Mr. Duncan observed the effects of drought and isolation on three bachelors who lived up the road and who had been engaged in starvation farming. Living alone, miles away from anyone, and under some very extreme forms of stress, Mr. Duncan drew the fairly obvious conclusion that "the mental state of these settlers is certain to deteriorate under these conditions."[19] And while Mr. Duncan was drawing attention primarily to the loneliness and isolation of their existence, if we also add drought, starvation, relief aid, and continual, repetitive, monotonous failure, one does not need to jump too far to reach the same conclusion as Mr. Duncan: that this kind of life "does not lead to normal existences."[20] And indeed it did not.

In some ways, the broad and basic contours of Saskatchewan history itself support this idea that the Dirty Thirties carved out broad, deep, and profound change in the social landscape of Saskatchewan. There are two *distinct* periods in Saskatchewan history: pre- and post-1939, or, more pointedly, before and after the droughts. Each of these eras has a markedly different feel, as though neither period knows quite what to make of the other. The pre-1930s period has its settlers and homesteads and frontiers, its brothels, port liquor, oxen, and $1.25 wheat. The post-1930s period has electrification, mechanization, rationalization, organization, consolidation and $1.25 wheat. The general sense that these two periods are separate and worlds apart in nature is striking and distinct. The people and the values of the post-1939 world seem so very far apart from those of the pre-1939 world, as though they are different worlds entirely, and, if this is the case, if they are different worlds, then something in the pre-1930s era had to die, corrode, fade, or crumble and ultimately be replaced.

American historian Mr. Frederick Jackson Turner famously wrote of the closing of the frontier in the United States. But no one has ever considered the closing of the frontier in Canada; no one has wrote about the ending of the settlement era, what happened and what it means, what changed. That the settlement era ended or died in the droughts is obvious, but the question remains: "What occurred within the social fabric of rural Saskatchewan during the dying days of the frontier?" Very little attention has been paid to the dry years and absolutely none to the social and moral dislocations that necessarily accompanied it.

Alongside the intriguing social questions related to the dry years, the political questions also need to be addressed. Untangling the political knots and questions to the dry years can result in a debate with no end. Was Frank Oliver's decision to open the south plains to settlement correct? Was it a good decision? Was it an informed decision? If not, then why? Were settlers the responsibility of the government? To what degree? Was the province responsible? Was Auld correct in approaching the crises as he did? Did he help or harm rural Saskatchewan? The questions quickly pile up.

Frank Oliver's decision to open the drylands was both wrong and ill-informed. Haste and impatience made it wrong; ignoring all the conventional wisdom of the day likewise made it wrong. With both pistols blazing he blasted his way onto the pages of history and at the end of the day the toll in human misery simply cannot uphold the view that his amendment was wise and good. The Rowell-Sirois Commission explicitly recognized this: "Rapid exploitation made mistakes in land utilization inevitable. Regulation and control were foreign to the immigration and homestead policies of the Dominion government and to the spirit of the agrarian frontier ... no particular blame is being attached to anyone in that regard, but the fact does remain that very little attention was paid to the suitability of land for agricultural purposes."[21] By 1940, a total of 958,460 acres of land had been taken over by the Land Utilization Board and signed over to the Prairie Farm Rehabilitation Administration who turned the land back to grass; by 1945, the figure was at just over 1.2 million acres or about 7,500 quarter sections of land.[22] The RM of Mantario, the area in which the Huelskamp family had tried to farm, was singled out by the LUB as being particularly notable for the amount of abandoned land the RM had in its possession: by 1945, the RM still held title to 208 quarters of land, or just a little over 33,000 acres.[23]

Wrong or not, however, the amendment created the conditions under which a good portion of the south plains were settled. Had it not been for the amendment, Saskatchewan and Alberta would look very different today. But does that make Oliver's decision any better? To suggest 'yes' would be to suggest that the end justifies the means, which is dangerous territory because that puts the goal ahead of the process to achieve the goal and that breaks open onto messy moral ground (the "gotta break a few eggs to make an omelette" theory).

If, by 1914, settlement was an accomplished fact (and it was), one can cease questioning the right-wrong nature of the amendment (such questions lead nowhere) and the inquiry then turns on issues of responsibility, but this too is equally perplexing because it requires one to measure culpability and responsibility. In the Canadian context, making this measurement is often as simple as saying the government was, is, and forever shall be responsible. But it is not that easy, still less so when one struggles today in this post-modern world to find any appropriate, publicly acceptable benchmarks against which to measure responsibility.

Assuming it was the government's responsibility to assist settlers, and that is not entirely unreasonable to suggest, the question becomes one of degree. To what extent should the government assist? For its role in creating the mess, the Dominion government showed remarkable elasticity in accommodating the settlers and their demands. The Dominion government went so far in the 1920s as to encourage settlers to declare bankruptcy and get out of the drylands: all would be forgiven.

But the province, as we have seen, moved in a different direction. Even into the 1930s, the Saskatchewan government would not embrace evacuation or removal as policy in the same way that Alberta did in the 1920s. True, the Land Utilization Board removed settlers to other areas of the province, but that was only ever a *by-product* of the primary policy goal of classifying and assessing lands as fit or unfit for agriculture: the settler, for all intents and purposes, was incidental. The Saskatchewan government decreed a policy of non-evacuation, and, even though the LUB removed settlers, it successfully operated within the confines of the policy of non-evacuation.

The settlers and the provincial government had different goals. The Saskatchewan government was building a province within a nation and all matters refracted through the prism of that goal. The settlers, for their part, came to Canada for freedom, for opportunity, to escape tenant farming in Old Europe or the United States, to be "masterless men" in D.H. Lawrence's famous phrase. These goals and purposes are continually at odds through the entire twenty-five-year history of drought in the early years of settlement on the south plains.

The province's policy direction was steered in large measure by Deputy Auld, a career bureaucrat who held immense power within the Ministry of Agriculture. Mr. Auld was the man principally responsible for shaping agricultural policy in Saskatchewan during the dry years, and his thoughts, words, and opinions cry out for judgment.

Auld is an easy target. His own words and ideas run at antagonizing, not to say hostile variance with, those of the settler. He denied the existence of a region prone to drought, he denied the government had any responsibility to act on it – in the end, he suggested that settlers should provide themselves with relief aid. The tone of his correspondence with settlers was frequently condescending, and he seemed to enjoy parading his erudition before the settlers, as was the case when he quoted Shakespeare to a grizzled, haggard, burned-out settler. Deputy Auld is not a historical figure who is easy to like.

But, on his watch and during his tenure, the south and west plains survived the catastrophic years of 1914–37. Where the rural areas of east-central and south-east Alberta were gutted of almost all human life (gutted to the point where, in certain areas, one can drive three hours on a Sunday morning and not see another human soul), south Saskatchewan was put on life support. Evacuation never became policy and the region survived to become the healthy area it remains today. If we take as our barometer of success the ultimate salvation and survival of the south plains, then the Deputy is to be commended for his actions. (This approach reads history backward.) If we take as our barometer of success the effectiveness of the efforts to care for the settlers who were placed in a do-or-die situation in what can be accurately called one of the grossest policy miscalculations in Canadian history, then the conclusions regarding Auld will be correspondingly different. (This approach views history how it was at the time.)

Even though the province steered course away from responsibility, the Dominion government recognized its culpability for its policy failure with the passage of the 1939 Prairie Farm Assistance Act. This act, according to historian John Archer, "indicated some responsibility for farmers placed on land which should not have been settled."[24] The act assured farmers that the next time their crop production fell below five bushels an acre, the government would provide unconditional support, thus ending the absurd cycle of crop failure–relief aid–road-gangs.

As time moves on and we separate ourselves from the past, we continually learn more and more about the monster the settlers were dealing with on the south plains in the early years. One is surprised to learn, for example, that the twentieth century on the south plains is today considered by many scientists to have been a wet century.

University of Regina Professor Dr. David Sauchyn and the Prairie Adaptation Research Collaborative have studied this region of south

Saskatchewan. Dr. Sauchyn was among the first scientists studying the prairie region to examine tree rings, which unintentionally reveal information about drought, its length and frequency. His conclusions indicate that in addition to the twentieth century being wet, the droughts of previous centuries were longer and more severe, and he notes that, in a few instances, droughts on the south plains have lasted at times for a century.[25] Dr. Sauchyn's ideas are supported by the conclusions of Dr. B.R. Bonsal, a climate scientist who has traced the footprint of the Great Sand Hills. He has concluded that two hundred years ago the south-west plains region had a greater resemblance to the Sahara desert.[26] Traces of this desert were certainly evident to Mr. Gust Mutter, who grimly remembers that "the land was dry and sandy and nothing much grew except Russian thistle."[27] For Mr. Mutter, it was the winters that mattered – Chinooks frequently rolled through the south and west plains and this, he concludes, was "the only thing good about that country."[28]

As mentioned, drought is not just a lack of water but a prolonged absence of water. And one of the elements that make the south plains different from other regions is not just the absence of rain but the rate at which moisture evaporates and the periods during which it falls. On the one hand, we have rain's absence: Dr. Bonsal observes that, during the drought of 1961, for example, the south plains received about four and a half inches of rain, which is roughly 50 per cent of normal growing season precipitation.[29] 1961 was even more destructive than 1937.

The "temporal distribution" of rain also matters. In the drought of 1988, rainfall during May and June was well below normal, while July and August had ample rainfall. But the fatally dry conditions during the most critical part of the growing season resulted in one of the worst crop yields of the twentieth century.[30] And here we reach a crowning absurdity: even when it rains in the drylands, there is still a drought.

Timing and quantity are important, but so too are evaporation rates. If the rain dries before it sinks into the soil, it will not be of much value, and this is a common problem on the south plains. Dr. Sauchyn has pointed out that high winds, Chinooks, and incredibly strong winds during the summer result in a higher level of moisture loss on the south plains and this is to say nothing of the lighter soils common to the region. It is characteristic of lighter soils that they have less ability to retain water.[31] Of course, the question remains: would Frank Oliver have settled the drylands if he had known all of this? The answer is probably "yes."

A municipal councillor from one of the most devastated areas on the south plains was at a meeting during the worst years of the 1930s and he recalled a story in which one settler said that he was "prepared to stay with this ship until she sank." An oldtimer responded that "if we get no more rain than we've had in the last few years, she'll be a long time sinking."[32]

Laughter was in short supply during the dry years, but it never quite disappeared. Laughter never really does. It is one of those elements of the human spirit that persist. A smile or a laugh is something that cannot be resisted, like a sneeze. The settler who painted "Meadow Lake or Bust" or even "In God we trusted, in Kansas we busted" on his wagon did so because it was the only way he could find a smile in the midst of so much that was wrong and hurtful. A man will rummage through even the greatest of tragedies in order to find a smile or a laugh and so retain just a little trace of what it should feel like to be human.

It wasn't just laughter that people found, but beauty also. Those struck down by dust storms, or grasshoppers, or whatever calamity was on for that day still managed to see in the destruction a kind of sublime, almost entrancing aesthetic. We recall the tales of lighting lamps at noon or of fearfully watching a dust storm approach and those images conjure negative colours – shadings of how bad things were. But, even to the people who were on the sharp end of this nature gone mad, they still saw beauty in it. The desolate and isolated lunar misery through which the Mankota settlers trudged to get coal was likely offset more than once by a second, or a minute, or a morning of wonderment at the desolate, stark, and forsaken beauty that surrounded them. Certainly this was not the rule, but it happened and the fact that it did says wonderful things about the human spirit. It also adds another dimension to the crises of the dry years – one cannot view these years as uniformly bad all of the time. Our initial inclination might be to see the dry years in this way, but that would be a mistake.

There is an old Taoist parable that is frequently told in China. A farmer has had a run of bad luck for many years. One day his horse runs away. The neighbours hear this and commiserate with the old farmer. They say what a terrible misfortune it was. But the old farmer only said "we'll see." Later, the horse returns with three other wild horses trailing behind. The neighbours exclaimed what wonderful news it was. But the old farmer only said "we'll see." The next day, the farmer's son was riding one of the wild horses. The horse bucked the young lad and his leg was broken. The neighbours exclaimed how awful it was. The old farmer only said "we'll see." A week later, the emperor's troops rode through the village recruiting all able-bodied men for war, but the farmer's son couldn't go because of the broken leg. The neighbours excitedly shared round this wonderful news. But the old farmer only said "we'll see."

Everything that happens, good or bad, is provisional, contingent upon what happens next. All states of existence are temporary, fleeting. Grinding through those hard, dry, desperate years, many settlers could only hold on for dear life, bumping and dragging along behind a power entirely out of their control. But they held on desperately waiting for what would happen next.

The Konschuh family fled the drylands after almost ten years of crop failure. They were virtually penniless and had signed on to work the lands of Western Stock Ranches in return for food, clothing, and shelter. Reflecting the old Taoist parable, they even lost many of their horses on the way. The neighbours would have agreed it was terrible news. But this was not the end.

The Konschuhs eventually purchased Western Stock Ranches directly from Mr. Honens, the man to whom they were indebted for years after 1923. Peter Konschuh, son the patriarch Phillip, bought it in 1942 and over the course of eighteen years expanded the ranch before leaving farming in the 1960s. Peter always referred to it as "a swell place to live."[33]

Adam, son of Phillip, was a young man in his mid-twenties when the family fled. The world must have seemed like it was coming apart. He went to Cluny, married, had a large and handsome brood of children, and eventually got his own place all around which he defiantly planted trees as protection from the brutal prairie winds. His daughter recalls that their homestead was one of the prettiest in the region due in large part to the fact that their hill-top homestead "was one of the few with trees around it."[34] Adam also developed extensive irrigation works on his farm, and here one must conclude that he was motivated, at least in part, by his experiences in west Saskatchewan.

The Konschuhs also committed another small act of defiance. When they were fleeing the drylands, the family took their barn with them. It was "dismantled board by board" and reconstructed at Cluny.[35]

Adam, his daughter recalls, was a good singer with a deep voice, and, like many Germans, he "loved philosophical discussion." He moved to Calgary in 1957, where he eventually passed away. Jake, Adam's brother, the Konschuh who wiled away his hours studying "steam engineering," moved to Cluny, coached hockey, and was a trustee on the local school board. Phillip, the patriarch, the German shoemaker from Saratov Russia, left farming in 1928. He passed away in Cluny surrounded by his family. One of the Konschuh grandchildren still farms the family lands at Cluny, and it was an area in which the family must have taken at least some happiness and pleasure because there are approximately fifteen entries for different branches of this family in the local Cluny history book. Like many thousands of settlers, the Konschuhs embarked on a long, dark ride in 1913 and experienced a kind of rebirth on the other side. This was not uncommon.

The family of Anthony Huelskamp was also able to enjoy some measure of peace after the savage droughts. Anthony's daughter, little Polly, who was just a child at that time, recalls arriving on the bare west plains likely having little idea that she and her family would spend the next six or seven years of their lives living on the knife's sharp edge, although the scene that greeted them might have given them pause as a kind of ominous talisman – they arrived only to find an empty "ship-lapped tar-roofed shack" and nothing else. For as soul-shaking as the prospect of living in a ship-lapped tar-roof shack might have been, the Huelskamp house was actually pretty standard for that time and place. Housing on the south and west plains was rated to be some of the worst in the Dominion, not least because early settler dwellings were characterized by the least room-space per person in the entire country. Houses on the south plains were usually "small, unpainted, dreary wooden shacks inadequate in size and warmth" and whose furnishings were characteristically "utilitarian," absent living room furniture, rugs, books, pictures, and "other furnishings of a modest urban home."[36] It goes without saying that there were no trees, and this contributed to the pathetic nature of most early south and west plains homes. (Settlers in the north and east could at least build homes out of wood.)

During their time at Masonville, Polly recalls that they kept lights in the windows of their house as an aid for people who might become lost during the ferocious winter blizzards. The Huelskamps, though, fled the west plains and lit out for points further west, with branches of the family eventually spreading to Calgary and Vancouver, a long way away from the two-room shack and the starvation of Alsask in the dry years, and where Polly was "enjoying a peaceful old age."[37]

The Lomow's, that hardy tribe of Russians who sang and danced and fought their way across the stormy North Atlantic only to see their farm crumble to dust in the 1930s, likewise fled west. They would have stayed, Alex recalls, "but every year kept getting worse."[38] From Kamsack, the family left to Medicine Hat and Calgary, where Alex wrote with not a little sadness about the failure of so much that had seemed possible, that "it's the turn of future generations to take up the challenge of the land and forge ahead with hope and courage." These are not the words of someone who did not have an appreciation of farming and its possibilities. They are the words of a man who had grown attached to the land he farmed.

There is no single way to view or remember the Dirty Thirties. They cannot be remembered only as universally bad. Some stories have happy endings, some don't, and there are myriad combinations between those two extremes. Even the histories of the little dryland communities reflect this idea.

The writers of *Val Echo*, that history of the area done in 1955 by the teachers and students of Val Marie High School, wrote of the 1930s that "a few settlers left" but added that "most stayed in this almost desert … and built a progressive community."[39] This goal of building a "progressive community," indeed the *ideal* of Progress, exerts an enormously powerful almost talismanic draw on the people of the little communities of Saskatchewan. References to it are everywhere: the history of the RM of Wilton is subtitled "Fifty Years of Progress," the subtitle for the earliest history of Kindersley is subtitled, "Fifty Years of Progress," the subtitle for the first history of the Saskatchewan Association of Rural Municipalities is "Sixty Years of Progress," the slogan for the town of Leader is "Where Progress is Unlimited." And, as the reader by now may have guessed, there is in fact an RM of Progress.

There is a deeply rooted impulse in Saskatchewan to glorify progress – forward-looking prosperity is seen as an end in itself, as a necessary and self-evident good. This deification of progress likely has its roots in the undignified and brutal struggles of the early settlement years, and this impulse to glorify progress is reflected in the Val Marie history: "And so the undaunted resourceful pioneers carved their homes from the wilderness. Courage and cooperation were the factors that made the wild and woolly west beautiful and prosperous."[40] *Ad infinitum*. Of the Dirty Thirties, the writers of the Val Marie history are laconic: the government gave "some relief" and also "some relief was given in the form of vegetables."

Next door to Val Marie is (was) a strange, curious, exotic little town called Aneroid whose name suggests anti-inflammatory ointments but which actually refers to the brand name of a barometer lost by a member of a survey crew (hence the title of their history "The Rising Barometer," a clever enough play on words but somewhat incorrect because there is not much left of the town – a more accurate title would have been "The Falling Barometer").

Aneroid sits amongst Assiniboia, Shaunovan and Swift Current ("it is approximately sixty miles from all of these places"). In the 1920s, Aneroid had a doctor, a bank, a drug store, a general store, a Masonic Lodge, a hotel, and four restaurants ("they all sold bread"). There was even a newspaper called the Aneroid *Magnet* and an amateur radio station, which was run by Mr. Wallace Orr ("until he was stopped by federal authorities"). In addition, there was a local branch of the Ku Klux Klan ("there were people here who publicly questioned the Klan's teachings") and a soap factory ("which failed as housewives thought powdered soap was extravagant.").[41]

Aneroid incurred deep scars in the Thirties and those wounds were clearly and distinctly felt even fifty years later in 1980 when the editors of the community history wrote their introduction: "No words can describe the devastation which the drought wrought in this vast area. Nature destroyed the years of back-breaking work in a short space of time and worse, broke the spirit of many who felt the country to be doomed."[42] One's heart aches at the failure of so much that had been possible in Aneroid.

Even at the individual level, there are stories with wildly different trajectories. Mr. William Dale's family originally came from Ireland and settled in Quebec in the 1830s. His wife, Amanda Chamberlain, was born in Quebec and was descended from one of the first white families to settle the Ottawa valley who in turn came up from New England in 1800 likely as Loyalists. They had originally emigrated from Scotland in 1600.

They moved west in the early years and raised their family. They had six children. Along with being a farmer, Mr. Dale and his wife also raised horses, including Clydesdales, Percherons, and Belgiums. Over time they acquired thirty head, which could be sold for $300 per animal. Then the droughts came: "the 1920s saw many crop failures," a family member recalls, and "when the thirties got worse" and dust storms rolled in, the Dale's rolled out. They moved to Victoria, just about as far west of Saskatchewan as one can get and still remain in Canada. Here Mr. Dale's son Bill trained in track and field and participated in the 1938 British Empire Games in Australia and later served with his brother in the RCAF during World War II.[43] Thus the family's trek took them, quite literally, from one side of Canada to the other. The most painful stop was on the south plains.

On the other side of the coin, we have this: an anonymous government clerk circulated an order in 1945 indicating that interest payments on all relief debts accrued between 1931 and 1944 would be cancelled.[44] This effort was specifically directed at the thousands of settlers who had fled the drylands for the northern grain belt, oftentimes ending up in settlement camps.

It was directed at these people because, as it turned out, these settlers in 1945 "have in many cases reached old age" and the stock and implements they had shipped up north in the 1930s has "either died or is now obsolete." This is how the Thirties ended for some settlers – with a pathetic little whimper – an obscure government official caring for people who had grown old and had criminally wasted their lives trapped in a futile and hopeless cycle of absurdity.

The Konschuhs, and the Dales, and the Huelskamps, and the Lomows provide us with remarkable examples of the Taoist belief that all is not lost, that all is contingent, that life is provisional and entirely dependent upon what happens next. Echoing the substance of that Taoist parable is Prime Minister John A. MacDonald, who was fond of saying "the long game is the true one." In the short term, the lives of many thousands of people were put on hold – they were "lost years" as Mr. James Gray rightfully remembers them. Mr. Walter Anderson, who settled in Carlstadt/Alderson ("The Star of the Prairie") in Alberta remembers the Dirty Thirties as "a waste of life."[45]

But even still, in many cases they were not "last years." The Konschuhs and the Dales provide the proof of what can and likely often did happen next, after the droughts. They offer a proof that it was (and is) possible to make something out of nothing and thus their story is not one of defeat but rather one of victory and it was a story replayed in a thousand different ways up and down the length of the south plains.

And what of the south plains? Whither the drylands? The government-sanctioned clearances that occurred in Alberta in the 1920s are without parallel in Canadian history. The massive population haemorrhages and abandonments in Saskatchewan are likewise without parallel and in numbers exceed Alberta's in both the 1920s and the 1930s. The south and west plains supported life, but they also took life. So how does one make sense of this region?

Pulitzer Prize-winning novelist Wallace Stegner grew up in Eastend. Eastend is located just a little west of Aneroid. Stegner remains extremely divided about the value of this region. His father was one of thousands who came, tried and fled, but that is not the reason for his complex feelings about this region. In the mid-1950s Mr. Stegner returned to Eastend. He analyzed it thusly: "a dull dull little town where nothing passes but the wind, a town so starved for excitement that a man's misfortune in losing his false teeth in the river can enliven a whole winter's pool-room and hardware-store conversation."[46]

Mr. Stegner is critical of south plains settlement and refers to it as a "brief improbable dream" that has faded.[47] It was improbable because of the nature of the region that was being settled. Mr. Stegner argues that the "iron inflexibilities" of high winds, low rainfall, short growing season, monotonous landscape, and wide extremes of temperature must necessarily "limit the number of people who can settle, and limit the prosperity and contentment of the ones who manage to stick."[48] With tongue firmly in cheek, Mr. J.R. "Bud" Thompson calls the Alsask region "the driest, coldest, hottest, windiest place you have ever been at, or ever may go to."[49] Mr. Stegner's statement, then, and even to a lesser extent Mr. Thompson's, tends to suggest that the population dislocations of the south plains were necessary, inevitable, foreordained. It had to happen.

Of settlement, generally, of the mass transplanting of people into a wilderness, Mr. Stegner is likewise critical because he feels there is so much good that is lost in the process. "Conventions suffered decay and disintegration ... and the amenities suffered even worse than the conventions." The matter of sewage and public rest-rooms might be highlighted here: Mr. Stegner noted in 1955 that in all of Eastend, "there is not a service station with a toilet to which a woman from the country can take a desperate child."[50] Indeed, public sewage was a substantial sign of progress. When a public sewage system arrived in Aneroid in 1963, "it was like a dream come true."[51]

More specifically, though, Mr. Stegner was speaking of culture when he spoke of the elements of life that are lost in the process of settlement. Mr. Stegner unfairly and somewhat cynically observes that what developed in Saskatchewan was not culture but instead "a whole baggage of habits, customs, tendencies, leanings, memories, political and religious affiliations, codes of conduct, educational practices," and it is this that he sees as the great failing of settlement. Even the once vibrant local pride in which settlers revelled in the early years seems dead to Mr. Stegner. He notes that in Eastend there is no longer a town baseball team "to play for the town's honour against Shaunovan" (although that vibrant local pride persisted down the road in Aneroid where, in 1975, the local ball club was so good that it "carried the village name" all across "the south half" of the province).[52]

There is much anecdotal evidence to support the observation that, despite a brief flirtation with the possible, an inevitable cultural withering occurred, a withering of that unique and particular Saskatchewan culture (it did develop, contrary to what Mr. Stegner claims) that continues down to today: there are no more annual sports days followed by evening dances;

.22 rifles are illegal without the necessary permits thus impairing gopher hunts; rabbit culls are frowned upon; harvest parades are rare; pool halls and barber shops have disappeared; rural schools and churches once the site of festivals and plays and Christmas pageants are gone; compelling political ideologies have all vanished.

And what of the Dirty Thirties? What of the dry years? What of the memory of this period in Saskatchewan history? Even when the droughts occurred, there was a distinct lack of awareness amongst Canadians as to what was going on. Mr. James Gray notes that the development of the PFRA is unknown to 99 out of 100 Canadians and known "only vaguely at best" by 99 out of 100 people living in the south and plains.[53] Even at the time of the national Red Cross appeal for relief in 1931, "nobody outside the Palliser's Triangle was told much or knew about what was going on inside."[54] The crises of the dry years were unknown at the time and have faded since.

Of course, people were and are generally aware of the Dirty Thirties, but, beyond that, of its nature and tragic course, of its own peculiar history, there lay nothing. This is not helped at all by the absence of historical work on the subject. James Gray's *Men Against the Desert* remains the standard work on the Dirty Thirties, and it was published forty years ago. The PFRA no longer exists. It was replaced in 2009 with the Agriculture Environment Services Board, whose acronym is the decidedly clunky, rhythmically impaired "AESB." There are no schools of thought or recent works or challenges to Saskatchewan's settlement history. There is only emptiness.

Even some individual family entries in local community histories bypass not only the 1920s but also the 1930s. Mr. Jake Bassendowski wrote a fine and compelling personal history in the RM of Shamrock history book, but when it came to the Dirty Thirties, he merely notes: "the years of relief in Saskatchewan is quite a story in itself." He stops there. Mr. Keith France remembered that 1928 was a good year and "our next good crop was in 1942, with the Dirty Thirties in between."[55] Like Bassendowki, he stops there. Mr. Ole Carlson's daughter Edna Russell remembers that "there were good crops in 1915 and 1916 and again in 1927 but many failures in between."[56] She likewise stops there. The memory of the dry years is a hit and miss affair. There is more missing than hitting. Mr. Stegner recalled arriving in Canada and remembers that he and his friends had the distinct impression that Saskatchewan, and indeed Canada, was "a new country and a new country has no history." Even though he was writing about a period a hundred years ago, that general sense still remains: Saskatchewan has no history.

Many administrators with whom the present writer spoke during the course of research for this work knew very little of what had occurred in their own RMs during either the twenties or the thirties. Many of the communities that sprung up in the early rush, communities like Aneroid, had newspapers but not a trace of those papers from the early settlement years can be found. There are, for example, only three months of Aneroid newspapers from the early settlement years. Coverage resumes in the 1940s and 1950s, but there is nothing prior to that. There is no newspaper record from Leader that predates 1948. The Alsask newspaper, as Mr. Thompson informed the present writer, was established in 1911 by a Mr. A.G. Holmos, and yet the earliest newspaper record we have of Alsask begins sometime in the 1940s. (Mr. Thompson has two copies of the Alsask paper – one from 1935 and one from 1974, and they were used as part of the remembrances of the history of Alsask at its 100th anniversary in August 2010.) In between, though, there is nothing. The newspapers from all those little communities that sprung up in those heady early days of settlement have vanished. They were stuffed into walls as insulation, buried in the basement of a house that burned down or perhaps simply thrown into the garbage as waste, embarrassing evidence of a bad memory, proof of the collapse of the possible, a mocking reminder of the failure of a grand promise.

In fairness, though, drought, like PFRA history, is not very sexy. Mr. Gray is certainly clever enough to recognize that his subject is not really exciting "unless 50,000 farmers planting crested wheat grass on five acre plots is exciting."[57] Those years, and despite Mr. Gray's momentous literary efforts to combat it, have drifted into a formless, shapeless blob, which attracts very little attention from scholars and even less interest from the public. The world is so very different today from that of the dry years. It is sophisticated and "post-modern" and very far removed from the frontier world. Indeed, many cities and towns in Saskatchewan have tried desperately to rid themselves of their agricultural settlement past.

Both Regina and Saskatoon have enthusiastically abandoned the historically pungent names of their annual summer fairs, Buffalo Days and Pioneer Days. Today Regina has its "Exhibition" while Saskatoon has "The Ex". These cities discarded the particular, the unique, the historic, the colourful, in favour of the bland, the generic, and the vacuous.

Saskatoon has also rid itself of the Louis Riel Relay and Riel Days. A downtown park that had been named Gabriel Dumont Park was renamed "Friendship Park" and in that park there is the statue of a man on a horse with a gun, which one can only presume is Gabriel Dumont because all signage that would have indicated who he was has been removed.

The memorial to Immigration Hall in Saskatoon, the hall in which thousands upon thousands of settlers stayed prior to venturing out to their homesteads, was torn down and not replaced. The memorial itself was only ever a small plaque hidden by bushes and nailed to a building on a little-used intersection. The only way one could view it was by getting out of one's car and moving some tree branches.

The very word "pioneer" today elicits mild embarrassment while the word "settler" is rarely used, and in the meanings of these very words, but especially "pioneer," one might find a reason for the utter lack of attention to the dry years, specifically, and Saskatchewan settlement history, generally. The word "pioneer" in Saskatchewan is forever and irredeemably linked with our grandparents, with senior citizens, with oldtimers. When the word "pioneer" is used, the Saskatchewan mind automatically conjures up an oldtimer in overalls driving a John Deere D down Main Street in the annual harvest parade that used to be held in small Saskatchewan towns but which fell out of fashion sometime shortly after the 1980s. The Saskatchewan mind simply does not make the necessary connection that this man might have lived through one of the greatest spiritual struggles in Canadian history. He is just an oldtimer, as natural and ubiquitous as PFRA pastures, barbed wire fences, rock piles, and weather-beaten saddle-backed barns – and these things Saskatchewan people have come to regard as unexceptional. They go unnoticed and if they go unnoticed, so too does our past. The oldtimer does not attract attention; neither does the history through which he lived. The story of settlement is something quaint and archaic, it is the story of our grandparents and great grandparents.

Local community histories have played a valiant role in keeping the memories of those years alive, but the readership of these works is very small. Instead, reflecting a broader and more general cultural fever that af-flicted minds in the 1990s, many small communities have splashed colour-ful murals all over the sides of buildings and bus stations depicting the settlement years. This is horribly inadequate. It is short-course quickie-hist-ory designed not only to educate visitors but also to remind residents of the history of their own towns. That Saskatchewan people need to be reminded of their past indicates just how far in esteem the history of Saskatchewan has fallen at the general cultural level.

The small communities in the drylands are simply not keen on their past, perhaps in part because they themselves remain unaware. Perhaps they simply don't find anything of interest in it. Swift Current has adopted the slogan: "Swift Current: where life makes sense." Veering wildly away from its past and its grand, tragic-victorious history, the city fathers have chosen to emphasize lifestyle amenities. The community of Leader offers "Where progress is unlimited," and Kindersley has "Experience our energy!" a punning reference to the prodigious amounts of oil-well drilling in the area but a step up from its previous "The town with a future" – but apparently no past.

Maple Creek is one of the few communities to embrace its history with the town slogan: "Where the Past is Present." But then again, folks down Maple Creek way have always been a little different.

The slogans get more banal, feeble, and wimpish as one moves away from the small towns. Saskatchewan celebrates "The Land of Living Skies" on its licence plates and "Saskatchewan Naturally" on signs welcoming people to our province. Saskatoon has "Saskatoon Shines," Moose Jaw has "Moose Jaw: Surprisingly," and Regina recently adopted "Regina: Infinite Horizons." *Anything* would be better than that, even the memorable, back-handed one-liner offered by Mr. Gray: "No prairie community ever went farther with less going for it than Regina."[58] Picture it in neon.

What these slogans actually mean is anybody's guess. Reflecting yet another insipid general cultural trend, perhaps the designers of the slogans wanted each person who read them to come up with their own special idea of what they mean. But it is quite apparent that there has been a profound rush to embrace the vacuous, the generic, the meaningless, the non-particular, the non-specific, the moronic.

There are no public memorials to the people who settled the region, and indeed there is no indication that one is entering a special area when one drives through the south and west plains, aside from the innocuous PFRA pastures that dot the countryside. The only thing that remains from our settlement period is forlorn detritus, and even the detritus is being removed. Mr. J.R. "Bud" Thompson is fond of touring through the remote areas of the west plains. In the course of these tours, he sees "pasture land with rock piles and maybe a caved in cellar hole, long over grown by buckbrush with perhaps the remnants of old farm equipment half buried in blow dirt."[59] These are the only monuments we have to the settlement years, and, when that is gone, there will not be much left.

There has been no Canadian writer like America's John Steinbeck (author of *The Grapes of Wrath*), who succeeded in permanently etching the dry years into the collective Canadian consciousness. There nothing on film and very little on the printed page; aside from James Gray, there are no histories of it. Talk is local, myth is common, tall tales accepted as true. The history of the Dirty Thirties is one of the strangest stories in all of Canadian history, one of the most bizarre and tragic and ridiculous, and it has drifted into nothingness. Mr. Ralph Mutter recalled that he did not ask very many questions about the family past when he was growing up. As he put it, "I was ten years old and didn't care where Hatton was."[60] The present writer grew up with that very same historical sensibility, as did thousands of people in Saskatchewan. It is here, in this neglect that we shower upon our past that we see the proof of the truth in what Stegner wrote in the 1950s: "this is a new country and a new country has no history."

We began our story with Hatton and we shall end with Hatton. The death of Hatton was a long-drawn-out affair that began in 1921. Hatton might have survived the crisis of the dry years but only if there was a period of stabilization. Historian David Jones observed that, for the dryland-ers, there really was no transition period at all: it went straight from bad to worse. Everyone, notes Laura Phaff, suffered greatly during those years, "which resulted in many pulling up stakes, loading their possessions into a CPR box car and heading for greener pastures." But it took a long time for Hatton to shrivel up and atrophy. There was, according to Mrs. Phaff, "a nucleus who had faith to believe" and those few remained in the district in the years after fire and municipal dissolution.[61] Mrs. Phaff remembers a time when, driving north along that grim back road, all one could see anymore was a school and a church, and "a few rundown weather beaten shacks." Even though gas was discovered in 1950, even though a well was built in 1954, and even though a compressor station was erected in 1960, it was a case of too little too late. The church closed in 1950, the school fol-lowed suit in 1966. Today there is nothing.

Hatton is not so very far from the community of Estuary. In 1921, Estuary proudly opened the grand Palace Hotel and the name and its decor reflected a very sharp appreciation in those early settlement years for the opulent, the refined, the tasteful, even out in the middle of nowhere.

According to the reporter who was dispatched by the Medicine Hat *News* in 1921 to review the promise and glory of the hotel, the Palace fea-tured large oak and leather upholstered chairs, eighteen four-chair tables ("for a seating capacity of seventy two"). There were eleven wide and spa-cious windows off the dining room that looked into the beautiful valley in which Estuary was located. There were twenty-four rooms on the second floor and each came complete with a "Brussels Rug." The Estuary Hotel allows us a glimpse into the refined and stately accommodations that could have been expected in the Hatton's Hotel Forres.

Both hotels burned to the ground.

Both communities died in the droughts.

There were seven streets in Hatton: Cummings, McTavish, Main, Hamilton, Kincorth, Wilson, and Stephens. There were three avenues: Prairie, Pacific, and, of course, Railway Avenue. These are the streets up and down which Mr. Rayton repeatedly drove his fancy motor car at excessive speeds. This is how Mr. Rayton is known to history.

Allie Auger owned the general store and the lumber yard. William Watson ran the post office. Norm Robson was the proprietor of the hotel, and "Happy" Nicholas ran a blacksmith shop up the street. There was a theatre in which Hatton people were entertained by "travelling live shows." Dan Hanton and Hugh MacLeod policed the town. Fred Meier ran the disreputable pool hall. Yee Lung fled China, crossed half the world, and somehow ended up in the middle of nowhere cooking food for "barbarians" as white men are frequently (hopefully affectionately) called by Asian men. The Reverend Mr. Krug taught the Germans.

The history of the community of Hatton was written by Mrs. Laura Phaff, a relative of Mr. Gottlieb Pfaff. She wrote her conclusion to the brief history of Hatton as prose. It works just as well as poetry:

> What used to be streets
> Which at one time were even named
> Are overgrown with weeds.
> It's hard to realize that many cars, trucks, or wagons
>   drove there
> Or people walked there.
> The old wooden sidewalks
> Were torn up and used for firewood many years ago.
> The old school bell that tolled four times per day
> To beckon students to their classes
> Is forever silent.
> The voices of happy children
> At the school playgrounds
> Are heard no more.

Population Losses: An Overview

Key to RMs (with principal communities) whose municipal minutes are cited in this work:

- 45 Mankota (Mankota)
- 49 White Valley (Eastend)
- 51 Reno (Consul)
- 75 Pinto Creek (Kincaid)
- 111 Maple Creek
- 137 Swift Current
- 141 Big Stick (Golden Prairie)
- 230 Clinworth (Sceptre)
- 232 Deer Forks (Burstall)
- 262 Mantario, amalgamated with Chesterfield, 1968 (Mantario)

There were 90 south and west plains RMs that received relief aid during the early years of the drought between 1917 and 1924. These RMs lost 22 per cent, or 10,959, of their "*resident farmers*": their numbers declined from 48,537 to 37,578. See Table A3.

Note: Prior to the early 1920s, the Saskatchewan Government only monitored the number of "resident farmers" in each RM.

Table A1: Number of "Resident Farmers" who abandoned their lands, 1917–23.

RM	1917	1923	Gain/loss (%)
45	425	525	+19
49	675	400	−40
51	550	325	−40
75	700	500	−28
111	350	286	−18
137	604	600	−0.6
141	450	254	−43
230	750	435	−42
232	400	325	−18
262	650	305	−53
Totals	5,554	3,955	−29

Between 1923 and 1939, these 90 south and west plains RMs lost 10 per cent of their "general population." The number of people fell from 139,577 to 126,176, for a total loss of 13,401 people. See Table A4.

Table A2: Population change, 1923–39.

RM	1923	1939	Gain/loss (%)
45	1,211	1,650	+36
49	1,218	950	–22%
51	884	800	–9%
75	1,751	1,350	–22%
111	1,019	800	–21%
137	2,923	2,590	–11%
141	998	970	–2%
230	1,993	1,600	–19%
232	1,623	1,280	–21%
262	1,240	864	–30%
Totals	14,860	12,854	–13%

In the Dirty Thirties, the drought spread to RMs in central and southeast Saskatchewan.

There were 91 RMs heretofore unaffected by the drought but from which 14 per cent of the general population fled between 1929 and 1939: the population in these RMs declined from 175,187 to 149, 875, for a total loss of 25,312. See Table A5.

The total general population losses from these 181 RMs affected by drought in the dry years areas amounts to 38,713. This figure does *not* include the 10,959 resident farmers and their families who fled. All figures cited refer *only* to rural Saskatchewan: the figures excludes all hamlets, villages, towns, and cities.

Table A3: Number of "resident farmers" in RMs that received relief aid during the early years of the drought, 1917 to 1924.

Note: Since the Department of Municipal Affairs did not begin recording the general population numbers in each RM until the 1920s, we have to rely on the number of "Resident Farmers" in each RM during the middle phase of the crisis.

RM	1917	1924	% Gain/Loss
2	275	290	+5.1
5	325	320	−1
6	300	280	−6
7	402	290	−27
8	500	352	−29
9	316	250	−20
10	345	350	+1
11	590	335	−43
18	500	300	−40
19	350	250	−28
35	280	400	+42
36	260	250	−3
37	400	325	−18
38	695	380	−45
39	1,200	700	−41
40	800	370	−53
44	425	525	+19
45	400	400	0
46	400	257	−35
49	675	400	−40

RM	1917	1924	% Gain/Loss
51	550	325	−40
64	310	300	−3
65	450	420	−6
66	375	300	−20
67	436	325	−25
68	230	200	−13
69	480	436	−9
71	870	866	−0.5
73	775	830	+7
75	700	500	−28
76	600	500	−16
77	625	375	−40
78	450	450	0
79	550	350	−36
97	260	280	+7
104	1,820	700	−61
106	650	400	−38
107	1,200	450	−62
108	725	700	−3
109	350	350	0
110	600	250	−58
111	350	286	−18
132	350	192	−45
134	470	400	−14
135	530	537	+1
136	500	375	−25

RM	1917	1924	% Gain/Loss
137	604	600	−0.6
138	800	750	−6
139	550	450	−18
141	450	254	−43
142	250	320	+21
163	375	235	−37
164	545	400	−26
165	629	590	−6
166	1,500	580	−61
167	452	220	−51
168	804	872	+8
169	500	625	+25
171	580	550	−5
172	435	394	−9
193	400	401	+0.25
195	250	247	−1
224	500	345	−31
225	345	350	+1.4
228	500	510	+2
229	780	556	28
230	750	435	−42
231	800	1,000	+25

RM	1917	1924	% Gain/Loss
232	400	325	−18
255	500	600	+20
256	400	305	−23
257	450	300	−33
258	500	750	+50
261	500	300	−40
262	650	305	−53
284	450	450	0
285	1,200	688	−42
286	450	500	+11
288	480	480	0
314	450	325	−27
315	450	350	−22
316	700	550	−21
317	222	470	+111
318	500	573	+14
319	500	450	−10
321	250	212	−15
322	442	300	−32
347	1,000	540	−46
Total:	**48,537**	**37,578**	**−22**

Source: Saskatchewan, Department of Municipal Affairs, Annual Reports, see relevant year.

Table A4: Population losses between 1923 and 1939 in those RMs that received relief aid during the early years of the drought.

RM	1923	1939	% Gain/loss
2	1,437	1,200	−16
5	1,864	1,400	−24
6	1,448	1,300	−10
7	1,704	1,650	−3
8	1,760	1,000	−43
9	748	1,050	+40
10	610	750	+6
11	1,340	1,300	−3
18	970	970	0
19	775	775	0
35	1,601	1,762	+10
36	1,100	1,250	+13
37	1,325	1,200	−9
38	2,100	1,450	−30
39	2,000	1,380	−31
40	1,421	1,500	+5
44	1,700	1,500	−11
45	1,211	1,650	+36
46	762	750	−1.5
49	1,218	950	−22
51	884	800	−9
64	1,350	1,150	−14
65	1,680	1,220	−27

Table A4: Continued

RM	1923	1939	% Gain/loss
66	1,454	1,350	−7
67	1,892	1,740	−8
68	1,000	1,160	+16
69	2,280	1,520	−33
71	2,278	2,500	+9
73	2,431	2,575	+5
75	1,751	1,350	−22
76	1,888	1,400	−25
77	1,257	1,175	−6
78	1,044	1,125	+7
79	1,448	1,315	−9
97	1,375	1,425	+3
104	2,275	2,000	−12
106	1,952	1,530	−21
107	1,968	1,780	−9
108	1,938	1,720	−11
109	1,474	1,400	−5
110	1,086	900	−17
111	1,019	800	−21
134	1,472	1,500	+2
135	2,268	1,990	−12
136	1,500	2,490	+66
137	2,923	2,590	−11
138	2,340	1,650	−29
139	1,395	1,040	−25
141	998	970	−2

Table A4: Continued

RM	1923	1939	% Gain/loss
142	350	672	+92
163	1,100	1,010	−8
164	1,363	1,307	−4
165	2,036	1,600	−21
166	3,100	2,900	−6
167	800	1,250	+56
168	2,459	2,200	−10
169	1,815	1,200	−33
171	2,163	2,012	−7
172	1,342	1,370	+2
193	2,167	1,300	−40
195	1,197	1,250	+4
224	1,708	1,150	−32
225	1,550	870	−43
226	1,380	1,300	−5
228	2,520	1,990	−21
229	2,143	1,840	−14
230	1,993	1,600	−19
231	4,478	3,500	−21
232	1,623	1,280	−21
255	1,670	1,475	−11

Table A4: Continued

RM	1923	1939	% Gain/loss
256	950	1,250	+31
257	747	1,200	+60
258	1,500	1,200	−20
261	1,162	1,170	+0.7
262	1,240	864	−30
284	1,713	1,450	−15
285	2,276	2,104	−7
286	1,481	1,400	−5
288	1,800	1,370	−23
314	1,126	1,500	+33
315	1,200	1,150	−4
316	1,485	1,300	−12
317	1,300	1,480	+13
318	2,208	1,500	−32
319	1,360	1,600	+17
321	631	720	+14
322	852	740	−13
347	2,255	2,150	−4
Total:	139,577	126,176	−9.6

Source: Saskatchewan, Department of Municipal Affairs, Annual Report; see relevant year.

Note: Statistics are not available for RMs 13, 14, 15, 16, 17, 20, 21, 22, 43, 48, 50, 52, 80, 81, 82, 140, 170, and 227.

Table A5: Population losses between 1929 and 1939 in central and southeast Saskatchewan RMs that received $200,000 or more in relief aid during the Dirty Thirties.

RM	1929	1939	% Gain/loss
1	1,030	1,000	−2
3	1,489	1,400	−6
4	1,792	1,800	+0.4
12	1,093	1,300	+18
31	1,137	1,250	+9
32	1,206	1,275	+5
33	1,548	1,300	−16
34	1,474	1,630	+10
42	2,629	2,415	−8
70	2,143	2,225	+3
72	1,861	1,430	−23
74	2,143	1,800	−16
94	1,550	1,485	−4
95	1,540	983	−36
96	1,525	1,230	−19
98	2,347	1,750	−25
99	1,545	1,150	−25
100	2,200	2,025	−7
101	1,600	1,590	−0.6
102	1,500	1,080	−28
103	1,889	1,800	−4
105	2,345	1,800	−23
125	1,767	1,520	−13

Table A5: Continued

RM	1929	1939	% Gain/loss
126	2,400	2,400	0
127	3,000	2,690	−10
128	2,575	1,927	−25
129	2,200	1,365	−37
130	2,036	1,600	−21
131	1,900	1,400	−26
132	615	470	−23
133	919	995	+8
155	1,950	1,920	−1.5
156	1,900	1,350	−28
157	2,485	2,600	+4
158	2,750	2,600	−5
159	3,200	1,550	−51
160	2,200	1,675	−23
161	2,225	1,800	−19
162	1,330	1,020	−23
189	2,000	1,700	−15
190	2,150	1,735	−19
191	1,700	1,388	−18
194	2,725	1,420	−47
217	2,400	2,200	−8
218	3,150	2,800	−11
219	2,850	2,560	−10
220	1,960	1,700	−13
221	2,300	2,000	−13

Table A5: Continued

RM	1929	1939	% Gain/loss
222	1,901	1,200	−36
223	1,482	860	−41
249	2,000	1,850	−7
250	1,775	1,360	−23
251	1,725	1,225	−30
252	1,354	1,275	−5
253	1,350	900	−33
254	2,574	1,500	−41
259	1,646	1,800	+9
260	1,495	1,200	−19
281	1,775	1,450	−18
282	1,890	1,800	−4
283	1,900	1,350	−28
287	1,680	1,600	−4
289	1,300	950	−26
290	850	750	−11
291	900	685	−23
292	1,127	685	−39
312	2,150	1,800	−16
313	1,280	1,100	−14
320	2,000	1,000	−50
341	2,600	2,250	−13

Table A5: Continued

RM	1929	1939	% Gain/loss
342	2,063	1,675	−18
343	2,025	1,775	−12
344	2,625	2,600	−0.9
345	2,400	2,100	−12
349	1,575	1,360	−13
350	1,585	1,280	−19
351	1,600	1,492	−6
352	1,481	1,450	−2
371	3,234	3,000	−7
372	2,425	2,000	−17
373	2,800	2,750	−1.7
378	1,142	1,100	−3
381	2,425	2,300	−5
382	2,690	2,500	−7
403	4,050	4,050	0
404	2,950	2,950	0
405	2,225	2,200	−2
410	1,625	1,400	−13
434	3,240	3,200	−1
Total:	175,187	149,875	−14

Source: Saskatchewan, Department of Municipal Affairs, Annual Reports; see relevant year.

Note: RMs in east-central, north-east, north-central, and north-west Saskatchewan received, on average, between $50,000 and $200,000 in relief aid during the 1930s, which is far below the average for other RMs. See: Saskatchewan Department of Agriculture, Annual Report, 1943, Index; Map: Relief Aid.

Population Increases: An overview

Table A6: Population increases in RMs located along the North Saskatchewan River between Saskatoon and North Battleford between 1924 and 1939.

RM	1924	1939	% increase
226	226	1,300	575
346	500	1,950	390
348	270	830	307
374	589	5,000	849
375	450	2,100	467
376	570	2,400	421
377	470	2,400	511
Total:	3,075	15,980	520

Note: The RM of Victory No. 226 is an exception to the rule that settlers fled north. Located in the heart of the drylands, the RM of Victory is located right next to the South Saskatchewan River where settlers could find wood and water.

Table A7: Population increases in northwest Saskatchewan.

RM	1929	1939	% increase
61	650	1,500	231
63	384	1,600	417
379	750	1,800	240
380	600	1,827	305
402	560	3,100	554
406	400	1,860	465
408	286	1,950	682
409	350	1,900	543
435	900	4,400	489
436	600	3,000	500
437	410	2,600	634
438	406	1,600	394
466	540	2,900	537
467	520	2,250	433
Total:	7,356	32,287	439

Note: RMs No. 61 and 63 are also interesting exceptions to the rule that settlers fled north during the droughts: settlers fled to any region that had wood and water, no matter where it was. RMs No. 61 and 63 are located on the south-east plains near what is known today as Moose Mountain Provincial Park but which, in the 1930s, was still just a large lake surrounded by many trees.

Source: Saskatchewan, Department of Municipal Affairs, *Annual Reports*, see relevant year.

Table A8: Tax arrears and tax sale holdings for select RMs that received relief aid in the droughts of the 1920s and the 1930s.

Tax Arrears = the amount of money settlers owed to the RM in back taxes.
Tax Sale Holdings = the dollar value of the amount of land the RM owned
as a result of property seizure.

	1922		1924	
RM	Tax Arrears	Tax Sale Holdings	Tax Arrears	Tax Sale Holdings
45	$43,866	$19,533	$32,131	$13,281
49	45,287	12,750	30,935	18,563
51	46,341	18,392	44,692	24,824
75	42,116	11,177	29,779	5,398
111	29,914	23,828	37,000	23,761
137	49,801	51,881	48,232	22,131
141	31,181	26,288	29,305	23,611
230	65,109	19,429	50,404	14,712
232	24,345	17,195	29,910	6,563
261	40,489	12,203	18,277	5,013
262	66,867	13,277	72,905	13,293
Total:	**$485,316**	**$225,953**	**$423,570**	**$171,150**

Table A8: Continued

	1928		1932	
RM	Tax Arrears	Tax Sale Holdings	Tax Arrears	Tax Sale Holdings
45	$19,777	$4,229	$150,510	$1,804
49	24,120	3,626	51,072	15,512
51	22,435	11,219	40,641	17,510
75	18,920	392	77,989	121,915
111	10,268	19,591	24,484	11,895
137	35,780	21,673	75,469	41,689
141	10,481	12,985	18,340	15,341
230	33,696	12,815	75,949	22,297
232	6,694	7,024	20,879	6,499
261	15,614	3,451	29,353	15,221
262	54,031	9,283	93,038	12,681
Total:	**$251,816**	**$106,288**	**$657,724**	**$282,364**

Table A8: Continued

	1934			1936	
RM	Tax Arrears	Tax Sale Holdings		Tax Arrears	Tax Sale Holdings
45	$216,843	$1,812		$250,362	$1,799
49	75,309	11,583		77,394	25,920
51	62,797	14,570		75,075	15,127
75	135,697	113,972		172,467	111,360
111	34,431	11,895		56,316	11,895
137	95,036	42,686		106,110	39,396
141	30,690	13,793		43,068	13,427
230	109,863	18,400		114,944	16,721
232	39,893	6,736		48,829	6,368
261	58,956	8,081		72,707	6,962
262	128,904	8,243		152,181	8,162
Total:	**$988,419**	**$251,771**		**$1,169,453**	**$257,137**

Table A8: Continued

	1939		1942	
RM	Tax Arrears	Tax Sale Holdings	Tax Arrears	Tax Sale Holdings
45	$115,397	n.a.	$139,518	n.a.
49	46,524	$183	39,070	$3,523
51	35,009	3,253	43,644	3,002
75	112,546	6,468	135,176	4,988
111	24,842	7,867	25,798	6,380
137	57,422	27,383	84,321	15,425
141	18,881	4,547	12,543	3,334
230	26,771	8,709	16,328	8,939
232	25,400	4,391	10,776	4,596
261	40,787	3,939	32,908	4,426
262	47,589	n.a.	54,464	192
Total:	$551,168	$66,740	$594,546	$54,805

Source: Saskatchewan, Department of Municipal Affairs, *Annual Reports*: RM Assets and liabilities; see relevant years.

Table A9: Municipal relief debt and provincial loans, 1934–38.

	1934		1935	
RM	Relief Debt	Provincial Seed/ Relief Loans	Relief Debt	Provincial Seed/ Relief Loans
45	$436,988	$87,088	$552,941	$215,685
49	40,747	11,839	104,964	67,908
51	85,206	11,434	141,080	59,897
75	404,359	109,469	531,429	223,844
111	8,393	4,395	18,348	12,961
137	126,037	32,040	168,685	65,629
141	56,565	10,299	109,685	53,172
230	68,636	12,963	162,179	74,357
232	87,952	19,799	165,314	101,384
261	44,522	12,613	109,581	26,565
262	23,046	6,004	70,613	277,843
	$1,382,451	**$317,943**	**$2,134,819**	**$1,179,245**

Table A9: Continued

RM	1936		1937	
	Relief Debt	Provincial Seed/ Relief Loans	Relief Debt	Provincial Seed/ Relief Loans
45	$621,420	$231,216	$771,745	$227,815
49	136,563	70,111	231,288	65,196
51	190,102	65,177	189,194	65,190
75	631,848	253,978	775,569	254,443
111	35,358	15,889	85,119	16,461
137	266,664	120,663	449,340	117,805
141	147,741	62,069	231,148	60,881
230	217,408	95,270	286,122	93,348
232	215,025	120,552	328,581	114,866
261	157,609	40,772	232,871	42,991
262	101,022	33,477	160,889	32,131
	$2,720,760	**$1,109,174**	**$3,741,866**	**$1,091,127**

Table A9: Continued

	1938	
RM	Relief Debt	Provincial Seed/ Relief Loans
45	$879,615	$238,497
49	247,746	62,688
51	250,696	55,498
75	896,700	277,123
111	128,263	15,460
137	563,516	81,434
141	212,898	44,362
230	351,736	86,870
232	309,886	85,203
261	243,438	32,543
262	171,067	20,303
	$4,255,561	**$999,981**

Total Relief Debt (1934–38) = $14,235,457.
Total Provincial Seed/Relief Loans (1934–38) = $4,697,470.
Source: Department of Municipal Affairs, *Annual Reports*, see relevant year.

Notes

Introduction

1   *Prairie Echoes of Hatton: A Story of Hatton and Surrounding Area* (n.p., 1983), 1–3.

2   *Saskatchewan Archives Board* (hereafter *SAB*) MA, 11(a) Papers of the Department of Municipal Affairs, Disorganized Village Records, Village of Hatton: Council Minutes, 1922–1934, 3 May 1922, 10 June 1922.

3   Ibid., 4 November 1922.

4   William Wardill, *Sand Castles: A Story of Dryland Settlement* (Eatonia, SK: Seagrass Specialties, 1996), p. 69.

5   *Prairie Echoes*, p. 38.

6   Village Records, 23 October 1924. Hatton was settled in large measure by Russians and German-speaking Russians. According to writer Timothy Egan, "they liked to sing and kept the floors of their houses clean enough to dine on." In fact, Egan observes of these immigrants, "Dust inside the house was something they would not tolerate." See Timothy Egan, *The Worst Hard Time* (New York: Mariner Books, 2006), p. 60.

7   David Jones, *Empire of Dust: Settling and Abandoning the Prairie Drybelt*

(Edmonton: University of Alberta Press, 1987), p. 281, see note 63.

8   Ibid., 21 April 1925.

9   *Prairie Echoes*, p. 3.

10   Village Records, 10 June 1922. Outside Regina city hall, there is a memorial to those pioneers who settled the early west, including Chinese people. The memorial provides a fascinating glimpse into the reasons why some Chinese fled their home country and the freedom they found in Canada. The memorial retells the story of a Chinese man who cut off his queue, or top-knot, a traditional sign of obedience to China's foreign Manchurian rulers. The man's friend was aghast and said, "they [court officials] will come and slice off your head." But the man replied, "let them come and find me."

11   *Prairie Echoes*, pp. 4–7. The figure of 800 people is an estimate provided by former resident Mrs. Laura Phaff and likely represents the population of not only the town but also the immediate surrounding area. Estimates from the Department of Municipal Affairs place the town's population at somewhere around 200 people.

12   Golden Prairie, *History of the Golden Prairie Community*, (Medicine Hat, AB: Val Marshall Printing, 1983), p. 83.

13   *Richmound's Heritage: A History of Richmound and District, 1910–1978* (Richmound: Richmound Historical Society, 1978), p. 305.

14   Village Records, 8 January 1929.

15   Ibid., October 1932.

16   Ibid., January 1932.

17   Ibid., 1 June 1933.

18   Margaret Munro, "Geologists Discover 'footsteps' of Dunes," Regina *Leader-Post*, Thursday, 5 November 2009, p. B-5.

19   *Captured Memories: A History of Alsask and Surrounding School District* (Altona, MB.: Friesen, 1983), p. v.

20   Curtis McManus, "Happyland: the agricultural crisis in Saskatchewan's drybelt, 1917–27," University of Saskatchewan, MA thesis, 2004 (unpublished).

21   E. Wheaton et al., "Agricultural Adaptation to Drought (ADA) in Canada: the case of 2001 to 2002," Saskatchewan Research Council, May 2007, p. iii.

22   Curt McManus, "History, Public Memory and the Land Abandonment Crisis of the 1920's," *Prairie Forum* 33, no. 2 (2008): 257–74.

23   R.L. Carefoot, *History of Golden Prairie*, p. 16.

24   David Jones, *Empire of Dust: Settling and Abandoning the Prairie Drybelt* (Edmonton: University of Alberta Press, 1987).

1: The Descent

1   Canada, *House of Commons Debates*, 23 June 1908, 11143–11144.

2   David C. Jones, *Empire of Dust: Settling and Abandoning the Prairie Drybelt* (Edmonton: University of Alberta Press, 1987), 10, 21.

3   Ibid., 10.

4   Lewis G. Thomas, *The Prairie West to 1905: A Canadian Sourcebook* (Toronto: Oxford University Press, 1975), 224.

5   Ibid., 224.

6   Ibid., 225.

7   Pierre Berton, *The Promised Land: Settling the West, 1896–1914* (Toronto: McClelland & Stewart, 1984), 206.

8   Ibid., 207.

9   Thomas et al., *The Prairie West to 1905*, 226.

10   David Breen, *The Canadian Prairie West and the Ranching Frontier, 1874–1924* (Toronto: University of Toronto Press, 1983), 51–52, 168.

11   Thanks to University of Saskatchewan history professor Dr. Brett Fairbairn for making this suggestion.

12   Breen, *The Canadian Prairie West*, p. 58. Breen adds that this allegiance "remained an enduring characteristic of the region's political structure until well after the turn of the century." One could add that it is still very true today.

13   Thomas et al., *The Prairie West to 1905*, 226.

14   W.A. Waiser, *The New Northwest: The Photographs of the Frank Crean Expeditions, 1908–1909* (Saskatoon: Fifth House, 1993), 1, 9–11, 47–50.

15   Sarah Carter, *Lost Harvests: Prairie Indian Reserve Farmers and Government Policy* (Montreal: McGill-Queen's University Press, 1990), 237, 245.

16   Ibid., 245.

17   Ibid., 245, 249.

18   Ibid., 245.

19   Barry Potyondi, In *Pallier's Triangle: Living in the Grasslands, 1850–1930* (Saskatoon: Purich Publishing, 1995), p. 67.

20 Bill Waiser, *Saskatchewan: A New History* (Calgary: Fifth House, 2004), p. 56.

21 Wallace Stegner, *Wolf Willow* (New York: Penguin, 1992), p. 221.

22 *Prairie Crucible: The Roads of History* [Bingville, Jenner] (Altona, MB: Friesen, 1991), p. 377.

23 Debates, 14 March 1907, 4690, see also Martin, 'Dominion Lands', 162–64.

24 Ibid., 23 June 1908, 11142.

25 Martin, 'Dominion Lands', 162–64. The Kincaid Act would be followed by other legislation after 1910 that encouraged the development of stock-raising homesteads, in effect, turning much Nebraska land back to a cattle preserve.

26 Jones, *Empire of Dust*, 134–35.

27 Ibid., 135.

28 Angus MacKay, "Preparing Land for Grain Crops in Saskatchewan." Pamphlet #3, Experimental Farm for Southern Saskatchewan, 1910, p. 2.

29 W.R. Motherwell, "Dryland Farming in Saskatchewan," excerpt of an Address Delivered at the Fifth Annual Dryfarming Congress, 5 October 1910, p. 2.

30 As cited in Jones, *Empire of Dust*, p. 138.

31 *Saskatchewan Archives Board* (hereafter *SAB*), GR-44, R-5-2, Papers of F.H. Auld, A.F. Mantle, "Progress in Western Agriculture," 1911.

32 MacKay, "Preparing Land," p. 2.

33 Motherwell, "Dryland Farming," p. 2.

34 MacKay, "Preparing Land," p. 2.

35 Gordon Barnhart, *Peace, Progress, and Prosperity: A Biography of Saskatchewan's First Premier, T. Walter Scott* (Regina: Canadian Plains Research Center, 2000), p. 24.

36 See Martin, 'Dominion Lands', pp. 164–65.

37 *Debates*, 14 March 1907, p. 4699.

38 Ibid., p. 4715.

39 Ibid., p. 4727.

40 Ibid., 23 June 1908, p. 11145.

41 Saskatchewan, Department of Agriculture, *Annual Report*, 1908, 75–80.

42 Ibid., p. 78.

43 Ibid.

44 E.W. Stapleford, "Report on Rural Relief Due to Drought Conditions and Crop Failures in Western Canada," Canada, Department of Agriculture, 1938, p. 31.

45 Canada, Department of Interior, *Annual Report*, 1908 (Ottawa: C.H. Parlemee, 1909), p. xiv.

46 *Captured Memories: A History of Alsask and Surrounding School District* (Altona, MB: Friesen, 1983), p. v.

47 Saskatchewan, Department of Agriculture, *Annual Report*, 1908, p. 93.

48 Canada, Sessional Papers, Department of Interior, *Annual Report*, 1908, vol. XLIV, No. 10, "Report of the Dominion Lands Agent," p. 33.

49 Ibid., p. 4.

50 Randy Widdis, *With Scarcely a Ripple: Anglo-Canadian Migration into the United States and Western Canada, 1880–1920* (Montreal: McGill-Queen's University Press, 1998), p. 294.

51 Ibid., p. 295.

52 Canada, Sessional Papers, 25, vol. XLV, no. 16, 1911, xx.

53 Ibid., xx. Delaware was the first state admitted to the Union. Its motto is "Liberty and Independence"; the state motto for Alabama is the historically pungent "We Dare Defend Our Rights." Saskatchewan has "Land of Living Skies."

54 Karel Bicha, *The American Farmer and the Canadian West, 1896–1914* (Lawrence, KS: Coronado Press, 1968), 88.

55　Canada, *Sessional Papers*, 25, vol. XLV, no. 16, 1911, xxix.

56　Ibid., 25, vol. XCLVII, no. 18, 1913, xx.

57　Ibid., xxii.

58　Ibid., 25, part 1, vol. XLVIII, no 19, 1914, xxiv; see also 25, part 1, no. 19, 1915, xxiv.

59　*Prairie Crucible*, pp. 153–54.

60　Canada, Sessional Papers, 25, part 1, vol. XLVIII, no. 19, 1914, xi. We shall return to this idea of "Progress" at a later stage in the book.

61　Saskatchewan, Department of Agriculture, *Annual Report*, 1907, p. 116.

62　Ibid., 1908, 76.

63　Ibid., 1909, 78.

64　*Aneroid: The Rising Barometer, 1905–1980* (Altona, MB: Friesen, 1980), p. 196.

65　Fred Wilkes, *They Rose from the Dust* (Saskatoon: Modern Press, 1958), p. 97.

66　This story was communicated to the author during a telephone conversation, 5 March 2010.

67　Communicated to the author during an interview with Mr. Ralph Mutter, Wednesday, September 1 2010.

68　*Richmound's Heritage: A History of Richmound and District, 1910–1978* (Richmound Historical Society, 1978), p. 225.

69　Ibid., p. 225.

70　*Coronach from the Turning of the Sod: The Story of the Early Settlers in the RM of Hart Butte No. 11* (Winnipeg: Intercollegiate Press, 1980), p. 229.

71　Ibid., p. 258.

72　*Coronach*, p. 296.

73　*Richmound*, p. 305.

74　*Coronach*, p. 296.

75　*Aneroid*, p. 92.

76　Wilkes, *They Rose from the Dust*, p. 97.

77　James Gray, *Red Lights on the Prairies* (Calgary: Fifth House, 1995), pp. 7–15, 199–204.

78　Ibid., p. 12.

79　*Richmound*, p. 270.

80　*Coronach*, p. 258.

81　*Richmound*, pp. 257, 272.

82　Interview with Mr. Ralph Mutter, September 1, 2010.

83　*Aneroid*, p. 196.

84　Canada, *Sessional Papers*, 25, part 1, vol. XLVIII, No. 19, 1914, viv–x.

85　Saskatchewan, Department of Agriculture, *Annual Report*, 1909, p. 75.

86　Ibid., p. 73.

87　Alberta, Department of Agriculture, *Annual Report*, 1909, p. 45.

88　Ibid., p. 69.

89　Saskatchewan, Department of Agriculture, *Annual Report*, 1909, p. 94.

90　"Mossback" and "Sodbuster" were (and perhaps still are) pejorative terms applied to the settler by cattle ranchers.

91　Saskatchewan, Department of Agriculture, *Annual Report*, 1909, p. 91.

92　*Val Echo: A History of Val Marie* (Val Marie: Val Echo Publishing, 1955), p. 16. This short book was written by the teachers and pupils of the school at Val Marie.

93　Saskatchewan, Department of Agriculture, *Annual Report*, 1910, 68.

94　Ibid., 68.

95　Alberta, Department of Agriculture, *Annual Report*, 1910, 42.

96　Ibid., 42.

97　Ibid. See also Bicha *The American Farmer*, 96. Bicha notes that during the eighteen-year period of his study, 1910 was the year when the American exodus out of the dry lands was highest. Of course this does not

98 take into account the number of Americans who fled after 1917.

98 Alberta, Department of Agriculture, *Annual Report*, 1910, 229–30. It is of more than passing interest to note that Saskatchewan did not maintain a publicity commissioner similar to Alberta. Interesting because it is one more way that the differences between the two provinces is revealed in addition to how each government would handle the same circumstances during the coming droughts of the 1920s.

99 Canada, *Sessional Papers*, vol. XLVI, no. 17, 1912, p. 51–53.

100 Ibid., 23–25.

101 Canada, *Sessional Papers*, vol. XLVII, no. 18, 1913, p. 32.

102 The percentage figures are based on the number of homestead applications being filed versus the number of cancellations being filed in each year.

103 Canada, *Sessional Papers*, vol. VL, no.19, 1915, 45–47.

104 Ibid., pp. 44–46.

105 Ibid., p. 45.

106 Ibid., p. 31.

107 Canada, *Sessional Papers*, vol. XLVI, no. 17, 1912, 18; Canada, *Sessional Papers*, vol. XLVII, no. 18, 1913, 16.

108 Saskatchewan, Department of Agriculture, *Annual Reports*, 1914, 106.

109 Ibid., p. 113. This average was calculated using the yield returns of all crop districts except districts three and six.

110 Ibid., p. 113.

111 Ibid., p. 111.

112 Saskatchewan, Department of Agriculture, *Annual Report*, 1914, pp. 106, 108. Auld was soon to replace Mr. Mantle as deputy. Mr. Mantle signed on as Major in the 68th Battalion of the Canadian Expeditionary Force. He would die in the war.

113 Golden Prairie, *History of the Golden Prairie Community* (Medicine Hat, AB: Val Marshall Publishing, 1968), p. 16.

114 *Harvest of Memories: RM 134 and Shamrock* (Regina: Focus Publishing, 1990), p. 337. The Bassendowski's trek from the Old World was, like many other pioneers, a long and interesting one which, one must reluctantly admit, seemed to have a descending arc: Germany–New York–Montreal–Winnipeg–Regina–Moose Jaw–Herbert–Shamrock.

115 *History of Golden Prairie*, p. 83.

116 "Wheat in Shot-Blade" *Kindersley Clarion*, 25 June 1914, p. 1.

117 Medicine Hat *News*, 20 July 1914, p. 1.

118 "If You Want Work," Kindersley *Clarion*, 30 July 1914, p. 1.

119 "Additional Relief Work to be Done by Government," Saskatoon *Star-Phoenix*, 2 October 1914, p. 1.

120 Medicine Hat *News*, 2 June 1914, p. 1.

121 Ibid., "Homesteaders to Get Work in Harvest," Medicine Hat *News*, 23 July 1914, p. 1.

122 Ibid., 4 August 1914, p. 1.

123 Ibid., "Provincial Government Will Assist the Homesteaders," Medicine Hat *News*, 1 August 1914, p. 1.

124 Ibid., p. 2.

125 Interview with Mr. Ralph Mutter, September 1, 2010. There is a prodigious amount of natural gas exploration in the Hatton area these days. Thanks to Mr. Kelly Mutter for suggesting that nearby Bitter Lake may in fact have been so named because of the amount of gas in the water-table.

126 *Aneroid*, p. 205.

127 Saskatchewan, Department of Agriculture, *Annual Report*, 1914, p. 9.

128 Ibid., p. 111.

129 "Premier Scott Comes to Aid of Farmers," Kindersley *Clarion*, 27 August 1914, 1.

130 Ibid., p. 1.

131 "Help for Settlers," Maple Creek *News*, 27 August 1914, p. 2

132 *History of the Golden Prairie Community*, p. 1.

133 "Comes to Aid of Farmers," Kindersley *Clarion*, p. 1.

134 "Too Much Heat, Not Enough Rain," Maple Creek *News*, 23 July 1914, p. 1.

135 Barnhart, *Peace, Progress and Prosperity*, 89.

136 Ibid., 74.

137 Ibid., 77. Thanks to University of Saskatchewan history professor Bill Waiser for explaining Scott's beliefs about the connectedness of agriculture and the future of Saskatchewan.

138 Conservative Party of Canada, "Relief for the Western Settler" (Ottawa: Federal Press Agency, 1914), 2.

139 "No Cancellations to be Accepted," Kindersley *Clarion*, 13 August 1914, p. 1.

140 "Relief for the Western Settler," p. 2.

141 The figure for 1914 relief aid given by the province was $8,655,698. See Saskatchewan, Department of Agriculture, *Annual Reports*, 1943, p. 160

142 E.W. Stapleford, "Report on Rural Relief Due to Drought Conditions and Crop Failures in Western Canada," Canada, Department of Agriculture, 1938, p. 31.

143 "Relief for the Western Settler," 1. Italics in the original.

144 Ibid., p. 2. The RNWMP needed to purchase at least one thousand horses in 1914.

145 "Action Necessary to Help Settlers," Maple Creek *News*, 23 July 1914, p. 1.

146 "Help for Settlers," Maple Creek *News*, 27 August 1914, p. 1.

147 "Relief for the Western Settler," p. 2.

148 "Help for Settlers," Maple Creek *News*, 27 August 1914, p. 2.

149 See Jones, *Empire of Dust*, for an exploration of this story. Suffield, near Medicine Hat, is still used as a training ground for the British Army. Prince Harry trained in the Suffield block.

150 "Report of the Ranching and Grazing Investigation Commission" (Ottawa: Department of Interior, 1913), pp. 1–3.

151 Ibid., p. 4

152 Ibid., p. 6.

153 Martin, 'Dominion Lands', pp. 179–80.

154 Breen, *The Canadian West*, pp. 188–91.

155 James Gray, *Men against the Desert* (Saskatoon: Western Producer Prairie Books), p. 12.

2: "In the Thrill Zone of the Onrushing Calamity"

1 Saskatchewan, Department of Agriculture, *Annual Report*, 1916, 10. Auld replaced A.F. Mantle, who perished while fighting in the Great War. Major Mantle fought with the 68th Battalion of the Canadian Expeditionary Force.

2 Ibid., 120.

3 Saskatchewan, Department of Agriculture, *Annual Reports*, 1918, 111; 1919, 104.

4 The Teachers and Pupils of Val Marie High School, *Val Echo: A History of Val Marie* (Val Marie: Val Echo, 1955), p. 25.

5 Saskatchewan, Department of Agriculture, *Annual Report*, 1920, n.p. See introduction.

6 Alberta, Department of Agriculture, *Annual Report*, 1918, 128. While Saskatchewan established a royal

commission in 1920, the Alberta government established aid offices at Lethbridge, Medicine Hat, and Youngstown to provide settlers with the "necessities of life." See Alberta, Department of Agriculture, *Annual Report*, 1919, p. 10.

7   Carl Anderson, "'Dominion Lands' Policy, Drought, and Saskatchewan's Better Farming Commission," *Saskatchewan History* 61, no. 1 (2009): 4.

8   *Saskatchewan Archives Board* (hereafter *SAB*), R-261, 23-1-3, "Papers of the Deputy Minister," J.H. Veitch to Charles Dunning, 18 February, 1920.

9   Ibid., L.J. Harvey to Charles Hamilton, 19 July 1920, p. 1.

10 Ibid., p. 1.

11 *SAB*, Ag. 2-7, Papers of Department of Agriculture, "Correspondence re: Movement of settlers, 1922-1925," CNR Freight Agent E.A. Field to F.H. Auld, 25 July 1923.

12 *SAB*, "Report of the Sub-Committee," 2.

13 Ibid., 5.

14 *SAB*, R-261, 23-1-3, Vietch to Dunning. pp. 1–2.

15 Ibid., "Copy of Resolutions of the Better Farming Conference," p. 167.

16 Saskatchewan Archives Board, "Report of the Royal Commission of Inquiry into Farming Conditions, 1920," pp. 10–11. This statement by Mr. Spence was not true. Summer-fallow was not "forced" on anyone. Soil exhaustion had been long known as one of the disadvantages to summer-fallow. Mr. Motherwell and Mr. MacKay both knew of it at least as far back as 1910, likely much earlier.

17 Ibid., 10–11. That the province also had to be forcibly frog-marched into financing some form of experimental research is suggested when the dithering Premier Dunning explained to the Legislative Assembly in 1919 that "it does not appear that the provincial government should undertake the establishment of experimental farms in competition with the federal government." See Journals and Sessional Papers, Legislative Assembly of the Province of Saskatchewan, Session 1919–1920 (Regina: J. W. Reid, 1920), 18 December 1919, p. 55.

18 Report of the Royal Commission, p. 16. Spence was borne in Scotland, one of many Scots who contributed to the formation and development of not only Canada but also Saskatchewan. He held many senior Ministerial positions in the provincial government before ultimately finishing his career as first director of the Prairie Farm Rehabilitation administration. He is a member of the *Saskatchewan Agricultural Hall of Fame*

19 Ibid., p. 44.

20 Ibid., p. 11.

21 Anderson, "Saskatchewan's Better Farming Commission," p. 17.

22 John Bracken, *Dryland Farming in Western Canada* (Winnipeg: Grain Growers Publications, 1921), 2. Bracken would later become the premier of Manitoba.

23 Ibid., p. 174.

24 Ibid., 301.

25 *SAB*, R-261, F23-1-1, Keelor to Department of Agriculture, 23 May, 1921.

26 Ibid.

27 *Richmound's Heritage: A History of Richmound and District, 1910–1978* (Richmound: Richmound Historical Society, 1978), p. 165.

28 SAB, R-261, f23-1-1, Keelor to Auld, 22 July 1921.

29 Ibid.

30 Ibid., Auld to Keelor, 27 May 1921.

31 Ibid.

32 Alberta, Department of Agriculture, *Annual Report*, 1922, "Report of Mr. James Murray," p. 18.

33 SAB, R-261, f 22.15, "Drought-General."

34 "Agricultural Trains Not To Run This Year," Regina *Morning Leader*, 17 May 1923, p. 3.

35 Saskatchewan, Journals and Sessional Papers, Legislative Assembly of the Province of Saskatchewan, Session 1919–1920 (Regina: J.W. Reid, 1920), 18 December, 1919, p. 55.

36 Saskatchewan, *Journals*, 1921–1922 (Regina: J.W. Reid, 1922), 24 January 1922, p. 69.

37 "Agricultural Trains Not To Run This Year," p. 3.

38 *RM of Big Stick Archives*, (Golden Prairie), "Minutes of RM Meetings, 1920–1984," 5 August 1922. This particular problem would be solved in part by the now-ubiquitous three-strand barbed wire fence found throughout the south plains of rural Saskatchewan.

39 *RM of Maple Creek Archives* (Maple Creek), "Minutes of Council Meetings, 1921–1972," 25 February 1923.

40 *RM of Clinworth Archives* (Sceptre), "Minutes of RM Meetings, 1912–1981," 3 June 1922.

41 Ibid., 4 February 1922.

42 Ibid.

43 *SAB*, R-261, F23-1-1, Keelor to Premier Martin, 27 July 1921.

44 David C. Jones, *Empire of Dust: Settling and Abandoning the Prairie Drybelt* (Edmonton: University of Alberta Press, 1987), 130.

45 *SAB-R*, R-261, F23-1-1, Martin to Auld, April 1921.

46 Henry Nash Smith, *Virgin Land: The American West as Symbol and Myth* (Cambridge, MA: Harvard University Press, 1950), 211.

47 Ibid., 211.

48 Regina *Leader*, 4 May 1886, p. 1; Jones, *Empire of Dust*, 24. See also Jones, *Empire of Dust*, 21, for the Department of Interior pamphlet that reflected the belief that rain followed the plough; the pamphlet reads, in part: "Magician's wand never produced more striking effect than did the placing of a pair of steel rails over the stretch of the prairies southwest from Saskatoon."

49 Jones, *Empire of Dust*, pp. 21, 24.

50 "Schuler Column," Medicine Hat *News*, 16 July 1921, p. 3.

51 William Wardill, *Sand Castles: A Story of Dryland Settlement* (Eatonia: Seagrass Publications, 1996), p. 70.

52 *SAB*, R-261, 23-1-1, Sargeant to Auld, 14 July 1921.

53 Ibid.

54 Ibid., Harvey to Auld, 11 August 1921.

55 Ibid.

56 Ibid.

57 See, "Relief for Dried out Farmers," Kindersley *Clarion*, August 28, 3; "I.O.D.E. Form Committee to Help Needy," Kindersley *Clarion*, September, 1924.

58 *RM of Clinworth Minutes*, 3 February 1923.

59 Jones, *Empire of Dust*, p. 113.

60 *SAB*, R-261, 23-1-1, Auld to Harder, 9 August 1921.

61 Ibid.

62 "Fall Rye," Medicine Hat *News*, 19 August 1921, p. 2.

63 *SAB*, R-261, 23-1-1, Murphy to Hamilton, 10 July 1926.

64 Ibid., Hamilton to Herzu, 1926.

65 Ibid.

66 *SAB*, Ag. 2-7, Honens to the Department of Agriculture, 26 March 1923.

67 The Konschuhs fled Russia in 1902, just a few years before small-scale revolt prompted Tsar Nicholas to

introduce a kind of parliament to Russia for the first time in 1905. The revolution of 1917 would be more thorough-going and far-reaching. The quote on the Bolsheviks can be found in J.F.C. Wright, *Saskatchewan: The History of a Province* (Toronto: McClelland & Stewart, 1955), p. 212. Wright also offers the not-entirely-un-truthful observation that "some militant leaders in the Saskatchewan agrarian movement mouth[ed] Marxist phrases fed them by dedicated members of the Communist Party of Canada, most of whom would see Bolshevik Russia only in books and illustrated propaganda pamphlets."

68   *SAB*, Ag. 2-7, "Application for Free Shipment of Settler's Stock and Effects from Points in Dry Area."

69   *Memories of Cluny* (Winnipeg: Inter Collegiate Press, n.d.), pp. 457–59.

70   Ibid., pp. 457–60.

71   Ibid., p. 461.

72   Ibid., p. 465.

73   Ibid., p. 457.

74   Ibid., pp. 458, 463. That the Konschuhs prospered in Cluny is indicated by the fact that there are fully fifteen branches of the Konschuhs in the Cluny history book.

75   *SAB*, R- 261, F23-1-1, Schmidt to the Provincial Government, 16 July 1921.

76   *Tears and Thanksgiving: The RM of Benson No. 35* (Altona, MB: Friesen, 1981), p. 307.

77   Ibid., p. 869.

78   SAB, R-261, F-23-1-1, Auld to Thomas Lannan, 22 July 1921.

79   Ibid.

80   Saskatchewan Archives Board, R-261, f22.15, "Drought-General," Memo for Auld, 24 November 1919.

81   *Captured Memories: a History of Alsask and Surrounding School District* (Altona MB: Friesen, 1983), pp. 304–5.

82   *SAB*, M-13 14 f1, Huelskamp to Dunning, 8 July 1922.

83   Ibid., pp. 2–4.

84   Ibid., Dunning to Huelskamp, 14 July 1922.

85   Ibid.

86   Ibid., Memo to Premier Dunning, 28 August 1922.

87   Ibid., pp. 2–4.

88   Ibid., p. 3.

89   Ibid., p. 3. The comment that it was a federal responsibility was not isolated to Smith but was apparently government policy. MLA George Spence (former head of the Royal Commission) asked Agriculture Minister Charles Hamilton in late 1921, a year and a half after the completion of the Better Farming Conference, what Hamilton's government was doing to implement the recommendations of the BFC. In what would become a typical reply, Hamilton explained that most of the recommendations of the commission were a federal responsibility, such as grazing lands, second homesteads, and the withdrawal of certain lands from settlement, etc. This technically correct though very narrow and limited reasoning excused the province from almost anything. Hamilton did not mention anything about evacuating settlers, also a recommendation of the commission. See Journals, First Session of the Fifth Legislative Assembly of the Province of Saskatchewan, Session 1921–1922 (Regina: J.W. Reid, 1922), 15 December 1921, p. 24.

90   Masonville was a postal sub-division that served a dozen families in the Alsask district. Anton had named it in honour of his wife's maiden name: Mason.

91   SAB, M6, Y-0-4, "Drought Areas," Huelskamp to Dunning, 22 April 1923. pp. 2121–2122.

92 Ibid., Auld to Dunning, 28 April 1923, p. 2123.

93 Saskatchewan, Department of Agriculture, *Annual Report*, 1923, p. 13.

94 *SAB*, M6, Y-O-4, Huelskamp to Dunning, 13 May 1923, p. 2125.

95 *SAB*, M-13, 14, f1, Internal Memo, Department of Agriculture, 10 November 1922.

96 Ibid.

97 Ibid.

98 Alberta, Department of Agriculture, *Annual Report*, 1924, pp. 20–21.

99 *SAB*, Ag., 2-7, G.H. Smith to Auld, 6 January 1923.

100 Ibid., Auld to A.E. Hatley, 9 January 1923.

101 Ibid., Smith to Auld, 13 January 1923.

102 Ibid., Hatley to Auld, 23 January 1923.

103 Alberta, Department of Agriculture, *Annual Report*, 1924, p. 21.

104 Jones, *Empire of Dust*, p. 214.

105 Ibid., p. 214.

106 SAB, M-13, 14, f1, Cory to Dunning, 26 January 1923.

107 Ibid., Internal Memo, Auld to Dunning, 31 January 1923.

108 Ibid.

109 Ibid.

110 Ibid., Hamilton to Cory, 29 January 1923.

111 Saskatchewan Archives Board, R-261, f 22.15, "Drought-General," Black to Auld, 13 December 1921.

112 Anderson, "Saskatchewan's Better Farming Commission," p. 17.

113 Saskatchewan, Department of Agriculture, *Annual Report*, 1923, pp. 13–14.

114 *SAB*, M-13, 14, Stewart to Dunning, 29 April 1924.

115 Ibid.

116 *SAB*, M-13, 14, Stewart to Dunning, 29 April 1924.

117 Ibid., 2.

118 Ibid., Auld to Stewart, 31 May 1924.

119 Saskatchewan, Department of Agriculture, *Annual Reports*, 1925, p. 238; 1926, p. 250; 1927, pp. 259–60.

120 Anderson, "Saskatchewan's Better Farming Commission," p. 17.

121 Jones, *Empire of Dust*, p. 117.

122 Ibid., p. 117.

123 Department of Agriculture, Annual Reports, 1925, p. 12.

124 Jones, *Empire of Dust*, p. 33.

125 Ibid., 13.

126 *SAB*, R-261, F23-1-1, Stonehouse to Auld, 27 March 1922.

127 Jones, *Empire of Dust*, p. 204.

128 *Prairie Crucible: The Roads of History* (Altona, MB: Friesen, 1991), p. 154.

129 John Archer, *Saskatchewan: A History* (Saskatoon: Western Producer Books, 1980), p. 153.

130 Ibid., p. 153.

131 Bylaws for Rural Municipalities in the Province of Saskatchewan (Saskatoon: Western Municipal News, 1910), pp. 23, 76, 96–97.

132 Ibid., 4.

133 Alexis de Tocqueville, *Democracy in America* [translated by George Lawrence] (New York: Harper-Perennial, 1968), p. 62.

134 Ibid.

135 Saskatchewan, Department of Municipal Affairs, *Annual Report*, 1918, p. 8.

136 Ibid., 8.

137 Jones *Empire of Dust*, p. 121.

138 Saskatchewan, Department of Municipal Affairs, *Annual Report*, 1921, p. 5.

139 *The Story of Rural Municipal Government in Alberta: 1909–1969* (n.p., n.d.), p. 51.

140 Ibid.

141 *RM of Clinworth Archives* (Sceptre, Saskatchewan) "Minutes of RM Meetings, 1912–1981" (hereafter Clinworth Minutes) December 1921; see also *RM of White Valley Archives*, "Minute Book for RM of White Valley #49 from March 1916–December 1921" (hereafter White Valley Minutes #1), 5 January 1920, p. 178.

142 White Valley Minutes #1, 5 January 1920, p. 178.

143 Clinworth Minutes, 1 February 1919.

144 Ibid., 6 March 1920.

145 Saskatchewan Archives Board, R-261, f 22.15, "Drought-General," Memo to Dunning, 19 January 1920.

146 Clinworth Minutes, 6 March 1920.

147 Sceptre, *The Past to the Present: 70 Years, 1909 to 1979* (Sceptre-Lemsford Historical Association, 1979); see entry under "Lawton, William."

148 Ibid., 14 January 1922.

149 Ibid., 18 March 1922.

150 Jones, *Empire of Dust*, p. 101.

151 White Valley Minutes #1, 5 March 1921, p. 264.

152 *RM of Reno Archives* (the trailer behind the RM office, Consul, Saskatchewan) "Transfer Ledger, 1918–1923"; see relief notes under Tab 'R.'

153 Ibid., "Transfer Ledger, 1924–1932," Relief notes under Tab 'R.'

154 *RM of Big Stick Archives* (Golden Prairie, Saskatchewan), "Seed Grain Advances Register, 1919–1920," 2–23.

155 White Valley Minutes #1, pp. 174–75

156 Ibid., 24 January 1920, 181–83.

157 Ibid., 21 February 1920, 193.

158 Ibid., 197.

159 Saskatchewan, Department of Municipal Affairs, *Annual Report*, 1921, p. 8; 1922, p. 5. See also Saskatchewan, Department of Agriculture, Annual Report, 1943, p. 169. The total value of relief aid supplied in 1920 was $356,215.00, a decrease from the $2.2 million spent in 1919. See ibid.

160 "Pay your Taxes," Kindersley *Clarion*, 5 October 1922, p. 3.

161 Ibid., 3.

162 Ibid., 3.

163 Jones, *Empire of Dust*, p. 155.

164 Ibid., p. 155.

165 White Valley Minutes #1, 7 August 1920, 233.

166 Ibid., 3 April 1920, p. 210.

167 Ibid., 4 February 1921.

168 Saskatchewan, Department of Municipal Affairs, Annual Report, 1921, p. 6.

169 *RM of Big Stick Archives* (Golden Prairie, Saskatchewan) "Minutes of RM Meetings, 1920–1923" (hereafter Big Stick Minutes), 4 February 1922.

170 Ibid., 6 May 1922.

171 Big Stick Minutes, 5 August 1922.

172 Ibid.

173 Ibid., 3 February 1923.

174 Ibid., 8 July 1922.

175 Ibid., 5 July 1922.

176 White Valley Minutes #1, p. 288.

177 *RM of Maple Creek Archives* (Maple Creek, Saskatchewan) "Minutes of the RM Meetings" (hereafter Maple Creek Minutes), 7 February 1925.

178 Ibid., 31 July 1922.

179 *Rural Municipal Government in Alberta*, p. 82.

180 Clinworth Minutes, 5 February 1921.

181 Jones, *Empire of Dust*, p. 157.

182 Ibid., p. 157.

183 Clinworth Minutes, 16 September 1924. Councillor Ducie's brothers were Barnardo Boys; see *The Past to the Present*, "Ducie, William."

184 Ibid.

185 Big Stick Minutes, 23 March 1923.

186 Ibid., 3 October 1925.

187 Ibid., 5 January 1924.

188 *RM of White Valley Archives,* "Minutes Book for RM of White Valley from January 1922–1936" (hereafter White Valley Minutes #2), 3 January 1922, p. 8.

189 Clinworth Minutes, 4 February 1922.

190 Ibid., 1 April 1922.

191 "Coleville Grain Growers After Another Bank," Kindersley *Clarion,* 24 August 1922, p. 1.

192 Ibid., p. 1.

193 Clinworth Minutes, November 1920.

194 David C. Jones, "Schools and School Disintegration in the Alberta Dry Belt of the Twenties," *Prairie Forum* 3, no. 1 (Spring 1978): 4.

195 Reno Minutes, Letter – Insert to Minutes, 23 February 1922.

196 Ibid.

197 Jones, *Empire of Dust,* p. 183.

198 Reno Minutes, Letter – Insert to Minutes, 23 February 1923

199 Ibid.

200 SAB, MA, 11(a), Disorganized Records of the Village of Hatton, 1922–1934, February, also October 1924.

201 Jones, *Empire of Dust,* p. 185.

202 Big Stick Minutes, 2 April 1921.

203 Big Stick Minutes, 2 February 1926.

204 Maple Creek Minutes, 25 November 1922.

205 Ibid., 27 March 1922.

206 Ibid.

207 Clinworth Minutes, 2 August 1924.

208 Jones, *Empire of Dust,* p. 188.

209 Clinworth, 3 January 1922.

210 Ibid., 24 April 1924.

211 Reno Minutes, 3 December 1921.

212 "Provincial Government Arranges for Reopening of Schools in Drought Areas," Medicine Hat *News,* 19 August 1921, p. 1.

213 Jones, *Empire of Dust,* p. 197.

214 Ibid., p. 197.

215 Ibid., p. 196.

216 Big Stick Minutes, 4 March 1922.

217 Saskatchewan Archives Board, R-261, f 22.15 "Drought-General," memo to Premier Martin, 12 April 1921.

218 Big Stick Minutes, 4 March 1922. See also Clinworth Minutes, 5 November 1921.

219 Ibid., 4 March 1922.

220 Ibid.

221 Reno Minutes, Insert, 22 July 1921.

222 Ibid., 3 December 1921.

223 White Valley Minutes #2, 286.

224 Ibid., 286.

225 *Rural Municipal Government in Alberta,* p. 52.

226 Ibid.

227 Clinworth Minutes, December 1921.

228 Big Stick Minutes, 2 July 1921.

229 *SAB,* R-261, F23-1-1, Auld to G.R. Murdoch, 14 November 1921.

230 *RM of Reno Archives,* "Tax Sale and Redemption Record, 1921–1925," (missing front cover and bearing no identifying marks) the 419 figure derives from a calculation of the total tax sale entries in this log.

231 *SAB,* MA-3, Records of the Department of Municipal Affairs, "Seed Feed and Relief: 1921–1924," J.J. Smith to E. Erikson, 12 October 1921. The government assumed responsibility for debt collection only after the RM had failed in that regard. In other words, the loans were guaranteed.

232 Ibid., Erickson to Smith, 17 October 1921.

233 Ibid.

234 Ibid.

235 Ibid., MacDonald to Smith, 29 October 1922.

236 SAB, Ag., 2.7, Papers of the Department of Agriculture, "Correspondence re: Movement of Settlers, 1922–1925," Eastfield to Auld, 25 July 1923.

237 *Town of Maple Creek Archives* (Maple Creek, SK) "Tax Sale and Redemption Record, 1915–1925" (hereafter MC Tax Records), pp. 1–3.

238 Ibid., 12–21.

239 Saskatchewan, Department of Municipal Affairs, Annual Reports, 192, pp. 26–33; 1926, pp. 26–39. Historian Barry Potyondi notes that the Maple Creek district experienced a 62 per cent homestead failure rate, with 32 per cent abandoning their farms between 1920 and 1930. *In Palliser's Triangle: Living in the Grasslands, 1850–1930* (Saskatoon: Purich Publishing, 1995), 93. The tax-sale records for the RM of Maple Creek were unavailable.

240 See, for example, White Valley Minutes #1, 5 June 1920, 230–32.

241 Big Stick Minutes, 2 October 1926; 2 April 1927.

242 *RM of Chesterfield Archives* (Eatonia, Saskatchewan) "RM of Royal Canadian: Lands Sold and Redemption Record, 1924 to 1932," pp. 1–20.

243 Ibid.; see "Purchaser" columns.

244 Saskatchewan, Department of Municipal Affairs, *Annual Reports*, 1920, pp. 26–37; 1926, pp. 26–33.

245 Clinworth Minutes, 1 November 1926.

246 *Prairie Echoes of Hatton: A Story of Hatton Saskatchewan and Surrounding Area* (n.p., 1983), p. 3. This is one of the very few references made to the land abandonment crisis of the 1920s in local community history books. Often, what seems to happen is that people assumed that the land abandonment problem in their RM affected only their RM.

There have never been any wider connections made.

247 Clinworth Minutes, 16 September 1924.

248 Ibid.

249 SAB, R-5-9, Papers of F.H. Auld, "An Agricultural Policy for Saskatchewan," Radio Address, 22 November 1926, p. 3.

250 Ibid., pp. 1, 4.

251 Ibid., p. 10.

252 Ibid., p. 10.

253 Ibid., "The Mixed Farming Committee Report," 14 February 1925, pp. 2–8.

254 Ibid., "Some Problems Relating to the Use of Sub-Marginal Lands," Public Address, 1934, p. 2.

255 Ibid., 1.

256 Saskatchewan Archives Board, R-261, f22.15, "Drought-General," C.P. Wright to F.H. Auld, 3 April 1925.

INTERLUDE: A COLLECTION OF ABSURDITIES

1 Saskatchewan Archives Board, Papers of Charles Dunning, M6, Y-O-4, "Drought Areas," p. 2133.

2 Saskatchewan Archives Board, Department of Agriculture, Field crops branch, Ag.3, f112, Relief, 1929–1936.

3 "South Country Farmer Insane," Swift Current *Sun*, 26 May 1914, p. 1.

4 "Suicide of [_____]," Swift Current *Sun*, 7 July 1914, p. 1.

5 "Prominent Glidden Farmer Commits Suicide on Dominion Day," Kindersley *Clarion*, 8 July 1937.

6 "A Cure for Drunkenness" advertisement, *Maple Creek News* 17 May 1914, p. 5.

7 Pinto Creek Minutes, 22 June 1937.

8   Saskatchewan Archives Board, Papers of Charles Dunning, M6, Y-105-1(a), "Canadian Railway Branch-lines: General, September 1922 to January 1926" Pim to Dunning 32784, 1922, p. 1. The letter is riddled with, and hobbled by, exclamation points.

9   *Report of the Royal Commission on Dominion-Provincial Relations–Saskatchewan*, 1937, p. 295.

10   Saskatchewan Archives Board, R-261, Deputy Minister's Files, Royal Commissions and Committees of Inquiry, f23-1-1, Kirk to Dunning, 13 October 1921.

11   Ibid. Thanks to Bill Waiser for pointing out that Kirk may not have been delusional but may have very well seen in his dream a vision of the South Saskatchewan Dam project of the 1960s.

12   Deer Forks, *Minutes of RM Meetings*, 2 January 1935.

13   Ibid.

14   Swift Current *Minutes of RM Meetings*, 3 February 1937.

15   Saskatoon *Star Phoenix*, "Relief Office of Government Here Closed as Saving," 1 September 1934, p. 1.

16   *Richmounds Heritage: A History of Richmound and District, 1910–1978* (Richmound: Richmound Historical Society, 1980), p. 273.

17   David Jones, *Empire of Dust: Settling and Abandoning the Prairie Drybelt* (Edmonton: University of Alberta Press, 1987), p. 53.

18   *Richmounds Heritage*, p. 273.

19   Ibid., 274.

20   *Aneroid: the Rising Barometer 1905–1980* (Altona, MB: Friesen, 1980), p. 171.

21   Toil, Tears and Thanksgiving: the RM of Benson No. 35 (Altona, MB: Friesen, 1981), p. 868.

3: Hard Times

1   Bruce Hutchinson, *The Unknown Country: Canada and Her People* (Toronto: Longmans, Green and Co., 1943), p. 294.

2   John Archer, *Saskatchewan: A History* (Saskatoon: Western Producer Prairie Books, 1980), p. 226.

3   Gerald Friesen, *The Canadian Prairies* (Toronto: University of Toronto Press, 1997), p. 386.

4   James Gray, *Men against the Desert* (Saskatoon: Western Producer Prairie Books, 1968), p. 45.

5   Archer, *Saskatchewan*, p. 228.

6   Bill Waiser, *Saskatchewan: A New History* (Calgary: Fifth House, 2004), p. 294.

7   Saskatchewan Archives Board, Agricultural Statistics Branch, R-266, I-Relief Files, 1 Relief Statistics for Rural Municipalities and Local Improvement Districts, 1919–1946, file-a, see file for RM #75.

8   Ibid.; see file for RM #231.

9   Gregory Marchildon and Carl Anderson, "Forgotten Farmer-Minister in R.B. Bennett's Depression Era Cabinet," *Prairie Forum* 33, no. 1 (2008): p. 80.

10   SAB, R-266, I-1. See file for RM #273 and RM #183.

11   Saskatchewan, Department of Agriculture, *Annual Report*, p. 96.

12   Friesen, *The Canadian Prairies*, p. 389.

13   *Prairie Echoes: A Story of Hatton Saskatchewan and Surrounding Area* (n.p., 1983), p. v.

14   E.W. Stapleford, "Report on Rural Relief Due to Drought Conditions and Crop Failures in Western Canada," Canada, Department of Agriculture, 1938, p. 86.

15   Barry Broadfoot, *Ten Lost Years: Memories of Canadians Who Survived*

the Great Depression (Toronto: Doubleday, 1971), p. 37.

16   Harvest of Memories: RM 134 and Shamrock (Regina: Focus Publishing, 1990), p. 295.

17   Aneroid: The Rising Barometer (Altona, MB: Friesen, 1980), p. 377.

18   Ibid., p. 154.

19   Ibid., p. 116.

20   Fred Wilkes, They Rose from the Dust (Saskatoon: Modern Press, 1958), p. 179.

21   Broadfoot, Ten Lost Years, p. 41.

22   Canada, House of Commons Debates, 1938, vol. 1, p. 319.

23   Ibid., p. 319.

24   Ibid., p. 319. Central Canadian farmers did not, as a general rule, use summer-fallow.

25   Archer, Saskatchewan, p. 215.

26   Saskatchewan, Department of Agriculture, Annual Reports, year ending April 1929, p. 9.

27   Timothy Egan, The Worst Hard Time (New York: Mariner Books, 2006), p. 87.

28   Friesen, The Canadian Prairies, p. 384.

29   Hutchinson, The Unknown Country, pp. 294–95.

30   Friesen, The Canadian Prairies, p. 387.

31   Saskatchewan, Department of Agriculture, Annual Report, 1931, p. 9.

32   Ibid., p. 9.

33   Ibid., 1932, p. 8.

34   Archer, Saskatchewan, p. 220.

35   Waiser, Saskatchewan, p. 293.

36   Report of the Royal Commission on Dominion-Provincial Relations – Saskatchewan (Ottawa: 1937), hereafter called the Rowell-Sirois Report, p. 291. As the Commissioners point out, the SRC likely thought that fruits and vegetables would be supplied through other relief agencies and so they felt no need to supply duplicate services. As it

was, if you were on SRC relief, this is what you would receive: potatoes, beef, pork, fish, butter sugar, rolled oats, salt, tea, coffee, jam or honey, beans, pot barley, corn meal, yeast, baking powder, pepper, soap, coal oil, matches, "epsom salts and saltpetre." See ibid. p. 291.

37   Ibid., p. 291.

38   Ibid.

39   Saskatchewan, Department of Public Health, Annual Reports, 1938, pp. 218–19.

40   See H. Blair Neatby, "The Saskatchewan Relief Commission, 1913–1934," Saskatchewan History 3, no. 2, (1950): 41-51.

41   Saskatchewan Archives Board, Agricultural Statistics Branch, R-266, "Reestablishment Assistance," f10, 3 and 4, "Tables of Relief Services Advances."

42   Neatby, "The Saskatchewan Relief Commission," p. 41.

43   Ibid., p. 42.

44   E.W. Stapleford, "Report on Rural Relief Due to Drought Conditions and Crop Failures in Western Canada," Canada, Department of Agriculture, pp. 33–34.

45   Neatby, "The Saskatchewan Relief Commission," p. 43.

46   Deer Forks, Minutes of RM Meetings, 2 July 1930.

47   Ibid., February, 1933.

48   Archer, Saskatchewan, p. 221.

49   Deer Forks Minutes, February, 1933.

50   Burstall, Treasured Memories: A History of Burstall and District, (Burstall: Burstall History Book Committee, 1983), pp. 13–17. Messr's Alex and Peter Lomow, brothers of Leon, wrote this fascinating tale for the Burstall Community History book. The exceptional prose of the story is remarkable because English was their second language. The Burstall-Hatton-Leader district

attracted a huge influx of not only Russian settlers, but German-speaking Russians who had settled in Russia during the seventeenth and eighteenth centuries.

51 Deer Forks Minutes, 2 April 1933.

52 SAB, Ag. 3, f112, "Revised Maximum Credits for Petrol Products," 1935.

53 Deer Forks Minutes, 5 August 1937. Permission was required in those days to cut wood in certain areas.

54 Mankota, *Minutes of RM Meetings* (hereafter Mankota Minutes), 7 October 1933. According to Mr. Mike Sherven, the administrator for the RM of Mankota, the coal mines (there were three of them) were abandoned and shut down in the 1940s. Few traces remain and to gain access one must traverse a rigorously bumpy section of trail that runs through a PFRA pasture.

55 Gray, *Men against the Desert*, p. 60.

56 *Memories of Cluny* (Winnipeg: Intercollegiate Press of Canada, n.d.), p. 458.

57 "Darcy Hande, Saskatchewan Merchants in the Great Depression: regionalism and the crusade again Big Business," *Saskatchewan History* 43, no. 1 (1991): 21.

58 Ibid., p. 22.

59 Pinto Creek, *Minutes of RM Meetings*, 5 September 1931.

60 Mankota Minutes, 2 December 1933.

61 Advertisement, Kindersley *Clarion*, 30 September 1937, p. 4.

62 Hande, "Saskatchewan Merchants," p. 23.

63 Saskatoon *Star-Phoenix*, "Moral Standards Collapse Under Depression Strain," 7 July 1937, p. 5.

64 Pinto Creek, Minutes, 5 October 1929.

65 E.W. Stapleford, "Report on Rural Relief Due to Drought Conditions and Crop Failures in Western Canada," Canada Department of Agriculture, 1938, p. 87.

66 Rowell-Sirois, p. 292. Under the SRC, settlers were allowed a maximum $9.00 a year for clothes for an adult, $6.25 for a boy, $5.25 for as girl. By 1937, the annual allotment had increased to $14.00 to a maximum of $140.00 for "a family of 20."

67 L.M. Grayson and Michael Bliss, *The Wretched of Canada* (Toronto: University of Toronto Press, 1971), p. 33.

68 *Harvest of Memories: RM 134 and Shamrock* (Regina: Focus Publishing, 1990), p. 453.

69 *Aneroid: The Rising Barometer*, p. 127.

70 *Coronach from the Turning of the Sod: The Story of the Early Settlers in the RM of Hart Butte No. 11* (Winnipeg: Inter Collegiate Press, 1980), p. 243.

71 Ibid., p. 243.

72 Hutchinson, *The Unknown Country*, p. 293.

73 Ibid., pp. 293–94.

74 Saskatoon *Star-Phoenix*, "Moral Standards Collapse Under Depression Strain," 7 July 1937, p. 5.

75 Stapleford, "Report on Relief," p. 87.

76 Saskatchewan, Department of Public Health, *Annual Report*, 1921, p. 76.

77 Ibid., 1924,p. 96.

78 Ibid., 1929, p. 81; 1932, p. 92; 1934, p. 96.

79 Ibid., 1938, p. 114.

80 Ibid., 1929, p. 81. See also ibid., p. 76. Of the 680 illegitimate children born in 1932, 353 were born in the rural areas. See ibid., 1932, p. 93.

81 Ibid., 1929, p. 81. In examining the ages at which young women got married in the 1930s, it was found that there was a continual back-and-forth between two demographic groups with the highest instances of marriage. For women, it vacillated between young girls in the 15 to 19 age group, and young women in the 20- to 24-year-old age group. For men, alas, there was only consistency: the

24-year-old age group was always and consistently the demographic from amongst which the highest number of men were married each year.

82   In 1932, there were seven illegitimate children born to girls under fifteen and young German girls mothered three, the highest number of any one single ethnic group. There were 233 illegitimate children born to young girls between the ages of 15 and 19 and again the Germans had the most at forty-two; there were 259 illegitimate children born to young women in the 20–24 age group, with the Germans again producing the most at fifty-four. See ibid., 1932, p. 93.

83   Ibid., 1921, p. 87.

84   Ibid., 1929 p. 98.

85   Ibid., 1932, p. 115; 1938, p. 133.

86   Ibid., 1924, p. 80; 1938, p. 133.

87   Stapleford, "Report on Rural Relief," p. 87.

88   *Prairie Echoes: A Story of Hatton and Surrounding Area* (n.p., 1983), p. 71.

89   Saskatchewan Archives Board, Department of Agriculture, R-261, Drought-General, f22.15, W.H. March to F.H. Auld, 2 May, 1932.

90   Swift Current, *Minutes of RM Meetings*, 2 September 1933.

91   SAB, MA, f5, Special File, Memo, Department of Municipal Affairs.

92   Pinto Creek Minutes, 18 February 1933.

93   *Coronach*, p. 244.

94   *Harvest of Memories*, p. 455.

95   Ibid., p. 455.

96   Ibid., p. 55.

97   Saskatchewan, Department of Public Health, *Annual Report*, 1938, pp. 218–19.

98   Ibid. See also ibid., 1936, p. 196.

99   SAB, R-261, f22-15, Deputy Minister Innes to Deputy Minister Auld, 28 July 1931.

100   James Gray, *Men against the Desert*, p. 19.

101   Saskatchewan, Department of Public Health, *Annual Report*, 1938, pp. 220–21. In 1929, eighty-five males killed themselves, as compared to ten females. Amongst the victims, there were eight boys and one girl under fifteen; twenty-four single men between the ages of 25 and 44; twenty-four married men and three married women between the ages of 45 and 64. The most common form of self-execution for men was death by firearms (29) and for women, the majority (3) preferred self-strangulation.

102   Rowell-Sirois Commission, p. 291.

103   *Harvest of Memories*, p. 435.

104   *Richmound's Heritage: A History of Richmound and District* (Richmound: Richmound Historical Society, 1978), p. 271. The three exclamation points are in the original.

105   Ibid., p. 166.

106   *Coronach*, p. 243.

107   Ibid., p. 243.

108   Gray, *Men against the Desert*, pp. 48–49.

109   *Harvest of Memories*, p. 512.

110   *Aneroid*, p. 144.

111   *Coronach*, p. 112.

112   Ibid., p. 112–13.

113   Bret Quiring, *Saskatchewan Politicians: Lives Past and Present* (Regina: Canadian Plains Research Center, 2004), p. 190.

114   Norman Ward and David Smith, *Jimmy Gardiner: Relentless Liberal* (Toronto: University of Toronto Press, 1990), pp. 174–75.

115   *Coronach*, p. 197.

116   *Aneroid*, p. 165.

117   Ibid., p. 190.

118   Swift Current Minutes, 16 March 1935.

119 Neatby, "The Relief Commission," p. 56.

120 Saskatoon *Star-Phoenix*, "Few People Moving Out of the Southern Drylands," 19 September 1934, p. 3.

121 Neatby, "The Relief Commission," p. 56.

122 *Harvest of Memories*, p. 55.

123 Ibid., p. 55.

124 Neatby, "The Relief Commission" p. 56.

125 Mankota, *Minutes of RM Meeting*.

126 Swift Current Minutes, 2 May 1936.

127 *Harvest of Memories*, p. 55.

128 Ibid., pp. 55, 57.

129 Ibid., p. 56.

130 Big Stick, *Minutes of RM Meetings*, 3 July 1936.

131 Ibid., 10 October 1934.

132 SAB R-266, I-1 a, "Relief Files," see #141.

133 SAB R-266, I-1 "Relief Files a," see RM #230.

134 Saskatchewan Archives Board, R-266, III Subject Files, f4, Drought Committee, 1946, "Relief Services Advances."

135 Ibid., "Rural Population, Total Relief Feed and Fodder, 1929/30-1938/39."

136 SAB R-266, #10, 3/4 "Synopsis of Expenditures of Agricultural Relief, 1907–1941."

137 Marchildon, and Anderson, "Robert Weir," p. 83.

138 Ibid., p. 83; see also Gray, *Men against the Desert*, p. 133.

139 Archer, *Saskatchewan*, pp. 214–15.

140 Gray, *Men against the Desert*, p. 4.

141 Archer, *Saskatchewan*, 227; Waiser, *Saskatchewan*, p. 296.

142 Big Stick Minutes, Monday, 5 January (or October?), 1931.

143 Neatby, "The Saskatchewan Relief Commission," p. 50.

144 Ibid., p. 50.

145 Clinworth, *Minutes of RM Meetings*, 4 January 1934.

146 Clinworth, 3 September 1935.

147 Ibid., 7 October 1929.

148 Ibid., 7 August 1933.

149 Ibid., 12 August 1935.

150 Deer Forks Minutes, 5 January 1931.

151 Ibid., 6 July, 1932.

152 Ibid., 3 December 1930.

153 Neatby, "The Saskatchewan Relief Commission," p. 45.

154 Deer Forks Minutes, 5 October 1932.

155 Saskatchewan Archives Board, R-261, 22-13-1, "Agricultural Re-Establishment," Statement Issued by T.C. Davis in Connection with Disposition of Crop in Saskatchewan.

156 Ibid.

157 Pinto Creek Minutes, 6 August 1932.

158 Swift Current Minutes, 15 July 1932, 7 September 1935.

159 Deer Forks Minutes, 7 September 1938.

160 Archer, *Saskatchewan*, p. 237. Neatby, "The Saskatchewan Relief Commission," p. 51.

161 Archer, *Saskatchewan*, p. 237.

162 SAB MA, f5, Special File, "Grants, Loans and Estimated Expenditures of School Districts."

163 Swift Current Minutes, 5 April 1930, 5 March 1932; Pinto Creek 16 March, 1929, 14 March 1931.

164 Big Stick Minutes, 6 December 1930.

165 Clinworth Minutes, 3 August 1936.

166 E.W. Stapleford, "Report on Rural Relief Due to Drought Conditions and Crop Failures in Western Canada," Canada, Department of Agriculture, 1938, pp. 55–56.

167 Rowell-Sirois, p. 278.

168 *Aneroid*, p. 376. The Rowell-Sirois Commission determined that "it has become impossible for pupils

in rural districts either to drive to nearby town schools ... or to board in town in order to secure a high school education." See Rowell-Sirois, p. 279. So, Mrs. Schmidt's observation that she was teaching sixteen-year-olds in grade six was likely helped along by the fact that there was simply nowhere else for these kids to go.

169   *The Story of Rural Municipal Government in Alberta: 1909–1969* (n.p., n.d.), p. 162.

170   *Richmound*, p. 352.

171   Ibid., p. 352.

172   Ibid., p. 165.

173   Clinworth Minutes, 5 July 1937.

174   Pinto Creek Minutes, 7 October 1933.

175   Clinworth Minutes, , 5 April 1933.

176   Swift Current Minutes, 26 March 1932.

177   Mankota Minutes, 1 June 1935.

178   Russell, "The Co-operative Government," p. 86.

179   Ibid., p. 87.

180   Big Stick Minutes, 5 December 1931.

181   Ibid., 15 July 1935.

182   Clinworth Minutes, 3 October 1932.

183   Swift Current Minutes, 5 September 1931.

184   Pinto Creek Minutes, 4 June 1932, 2 July 1932.

185   Big Stick Minutes, 5 February 1937. These parcels of land were likely a part of the effort in the 1930s to classify lands as suitable/unsuitable and signed over to the Land Utilization Board, which would then turn the blocks of land into community pasture.

186   Editorial, Swift Current *Sun*, "Be It Resolved," 27 July 1937, p. 4.

187   Big Stick Minutes, 4 November 1935.

188   Russell, "The Co-operative Government," p. 87.

189   Wallace Stegner, *Wolf Willow: A History, a Story, and a Memory of the Last Plains Frontier* (New York: Penguin, 1990), p. 129.

190   Ibid., p. 133.

191   Ibid., pp. 133–36.

192   Saskatchewan Archives Board, Department of Municipal Affairs, "Radio Address Given by Mr. Matte on the Work of the NSRB, January 31 and February 14 1939," MA.3, f-8, p. 5.

193   Deer Forks Minutes, 6 May 1914.

194   SAB, R-266, #10, 3/4, "Copy of a General Letter to Rural Municipalities Advising of the Organization of Relief Camps," 30 August 1930. A "straw boss" is an overseer selected from amongst the men.

195   Saskatchewan, Department of Highways, *Annual Report*,1931/32, p. 8.

196   Ibid., p. 8.

197   *Richmound*, p. 243.

198   Highways, *Annual Report*, 1930/31, pp. 6–10.

199   Swift Current Minutes, 2 November 1929.

200   Mankota Minutes, 5 July 1930.

201   Big Stick Minutes, 2 August 1930; 4 October 1930.

202   Pinto Creek Minutes, 2 December 1933.

203   *The Story of Rural Municipal Government in Alberta, 1909–1969*, p. 10.

204   Swift Current Minutes, 20 September 1930.

205   Pinto Creek Minutes, 2 August 1930.

206   SAB, R-266, "Copy of General Letter."

207   "The way it was: highway work camps," *The Western Producer*, 10 February 1977.

208   Ibid.

209   Big Stick Minutes,. 15 July 1935.

210   Golden Prairie, *A History of the Golden Prairie Community* (Centennial History Group, 1968), p. i.

211 Swift Current Minutes, 1 June 1935.

212 Mankota Minutes, 14 July 1932.

213 Mankota Minutes, 4 August 1934, Pinto Creek 4 June 1932, Clinworth, 1 October 1934, Swift Current, 3 May 1930, and 4 April 1931.

214 Saskatchewan Archives Board, Department of Agriculture, R-370, f1, "Dominion-Provincial Agreements," Road Work, 1937.

215 Neatby, "The Saskatchewan Relief Commission," p. 52.

216 Ibid., p. 52.

217 Department of Highways, *Annual Reports*, 1931/32, p. 9.

4: Exodus

1 I wish to thank my father David for pointing out and exploring with me this idea of consolidation.

2 Medicine Hat *News*, 1 June 1937, p. 1.

3 Barry Potyondi, *In Palliser's Triangle: Living in the Grasslands, 1850–1930* (Saskatoon: Purich Publishing, 1995), p. 6.

4 Bill Waiser, *Saskatchewan: A New History* (Calgary: Fifth House, 2004), p. 299.

5 The figures are contained in the *Canada Census*, quoted in Gerald Friesen, *The Canadian Prairies: A History* (Toronto: University of Toronto Press, 1984), p. 388.

6 T.J.D. Powell, "Northern Settlement, 1929–1935" *Saskatchewan History* 30, no. 3 (1977): p. 93.

7 James Gray, *Men against the Desert* (Saskatoon: Western Producer Books), p. 194.

8 Powell, "Northern Settlement," pp. 87, 89.

9 Ibid., p. 86.

10 Ibid., p. 91.

11 Saskatchewan Archives Board, Department of Agricultural Statistics, R-266, #10, 3, Re-establishment Assistance, "List of Settlers Moved by Department of Agriculture, 1930, 1931, 1932."

12 Saskatchewan, Department of Agriculture, *Annual Report*, 1934, see "Agricultural Relief Services" in introduction to report, n.p.

13 SAB, R-266, Department of Agricultural Statistics, Re-establishment Assistance "Settlers Effects Shipments" Ledger.

14 Ibid., "Movement of Settlers Effects Under Special Rates, January 1, 1930–December 31, 1935."

15 Saskatchewan Archives Board, Department of Municipal Affairs, MA.3, f8, Radio Address Given by Mr. Matte on the Work of the NSRB, 31 January and 14 February 1939, pp. 2–3.

16 Ibid., p. 3.

17 Ibid., f24, "Land Resettlement Agreements," 1935.

18 Gray, *Men against the Desert*, p. 196.

19 Canada, House of Commons *Debates*, 1937, vol. 1, p. 436.

20 "Drought Area Farmers Would be Welcome in the Peace River Country," Medicine Hat *News*, 25 August 1937, p. 1.

21 Saskatchewan Archives Board, Department of Agriculture, R-261, 22.14.1 Agricultural Reestablishment, 1935–1936, J. Mitchell to F.H. Auld, 18 June 1935.

22 Ibid.

23 R-261, 22.13.2 Agricultural Reestablishment – Circulars etc., 1934–1936, Auld to RM Secretaries, 6 April 1935.

24 Ibid., underlined in original.

25 Ibid., Memo, signed by F.H. Auld, 15 October 1934.

26 Ibid., Auld to RM's, 1934, undated.

27 Clinworth, *Minutes of RM Meetings*, 1 May 1933.

28 Big Stick, *Minutes of RM Meetings*, 6 August 1937.

29 Mankota, *Minutes of RM Meetings*, 2 September 1933.

30 Pinto Creek, *Minutes of RM Meetings*, 6 October 1934.

31 SAB, MA.3, f25, "Ottawa Correspondence re: relief settlement, 1936."

32 Swift Current, *Minutes of RM Meetings*, 1 December 1934.

33 Canada, House of Commons *Debates*, vol. 2, 1938, p. 1460, see also vol. 3, p. 2441.

34 Ibid., vol. 3, p. 2441.

35 Ibid., 1938, vol. 3, p. 2441.

36 Barry Broadfoot, *Ten Lost Years: Memories of Canadians Who Survived the Great Depression* (Toronto: Doubleday, 1973), p. 54.

37 *Aneroid: The Rising Barometer, 1905–1980* (Altona, MB: Friesen, 1980), p. 120.

38 Ibid., p. 120.

39 Mankota Minutes, 4 September 1937.

40 T.J.D. Powell, "Northern Settlement, 1929–1935," *Saskatchewan History* 30, no. 3 (1977): 86.

41 Taken from "Milestones and Memories," by "The Stroller," Regina *Leader-Post*, 12 July 1934, as quoted in *The Report of the Royal Commission on Dominion-Provincial Relations – Saskatchewan*, 1937 (hereafter the Rowell-Sirois Report), p. 158.

42 *Canada Census*, "Agriculture, Part 2," p. 43.

43 *Canada Census*, 1936, vol. 1.

44 Saskatchewan Archives Board, R-266, I.1, "Relief Files a"; see RM #243.

45 Ibid.; see RM #244.

46 Ibid.; see RM #1.

47 Gray, *Men against the Desert*, p. 31.

48 Saskatchewan Archives Board, Department of Agriculture, Ag.3, f112, Relief 1929–1936, "Remarks on the Conditions in the Rural Municipality of Chaplin," p. 1.

49 Ibid., "Report on Conditions in the Rural Municipality of Wood River."

50 Saskatchewan, Department of Public Health, *Annual Reports*, pp. 220–21.

51 Saskatchewan Archives Board, Department of Agriculture, R-261, f22.15, Drought General, L. Wilson to F.H. Auld, 6 July, 1931.

52 Timothy Egan, *The Worst Hard Time* (New York: Mariner Books, 2006), p. 47.

53 Saskatchewan Department of Agriculture, *Annual Report*, year ending 1936, pp. 96, 102.

54 Saskatchewan, Department of Agriculture, *Annual Report*, "Report of the Land Utilization Branch of the Department of Agriculture," 1 May 1938, p. 195.

55 SAB, R-261, 22.13.1, Agricultural Reestablishment, "Radio Address, R.W. Neely, CJGK, 7 February 1936." See also Dan Balkwill, *The Prairie Farm Rehabilitation Administration and the Community Pasture Program, 1937–1947*, University of Saskatchewan, MA thesis, p. 41.

56 Saskatchewan, Department of Agriculture, *Annual Report*, "Report of the Land Utilization Branch of the Department of Agriculture," 1 May 1938, p. 195.

57 Ibid.

58 Ibid., p. 196.

59 SAB R-266, III Subject Files, f10 Re-establishment Assistance, "List of Settlers Assisted by the Land Utilization Board to Move to Points in Saskatchewan Not Classified as Northern."

60 Ibid., "List of Settlers Assisted by the Land Utilization Board to Move to Northern Areas."

61 Ibid., "List of Settlers Assisted by the Land Utilization Board Moved to Points Outside Saskatchewan."

62	Clinworth Minutes, 5 April 1937.
63	Swift Current Minutes, 5 June 1937.
64	Big Stick Minutes, 1 February 1935.
65	Ibid., March 1935.
66	SAB, R-261, Auld to Sargeant, 19 September 1935.
67	SAB, R-261.
68	Ibid.
69	Archer, *Saskatchewan*, p. 246.

INTERLUDE: PUBLIC HEALTH

1	Saskatchewan, Department of Public Health, *Annual Reports*, 1938, pp. 218–19.
2	Ibid.
3	Ibid., 1938, pp. 220–21.
4	Ibid.
5	Ibid., 1937, p. 138.
6	Ibid.
7	Ibid., p. 194.
8	Ibid., 1932, p. 208; 1934, p. 186; 1936, p. 204; 1937, p. 190.
9	Ibid., 1938, pp. 220–21.
10	Ibid., 1932, p. 210.
11	Ibid.
12	Ibid., 1929, pp. 175–76.
13	Ibid., 1938, pp. 220–21.
14	Ibid. The year in which most people committed suicide was 1930, the second full year of the drought in which 127 people committed suicide.
15	Ibid., 1934, p. 188.
16	Ibid.
17	Ibid., 1938, p. 220.
18	Ibid., 1938, pp. 220–21.
19	Ibid.
20	Ibid., 1936, p. 204.
21	Ibid., 1938, pp. 218–19.
22	Ibid., 1937; see pp. 182, 188, 192–93.

5: THE WRECK OF '37

1	E.W. Stapleford, "Report on Rural Relief Due to Drought Conditions and Crop Failures in Western Canada," Canada, Department of Agriculture, 1938, p. 37.
2	*Report of the Royal Commission on Dominion-Provincial Relations – Saskatchewan*, 1937, hereafter called the Rowell-Sirois Report, p. 38. This figure does not include the money that RMs spent for relief aid. See also, Saskatchewan, Department of Agriculture, *Annual Report* 1943, pp. 159–62.
3	Stapleford, "Report on Rural Relief," p. 27.
4	*Mankota: The First Fifty Years* (Mankota, SK: Mankota Book Committee, 1980), p. 3.
5	Saskatchewan Archives Board, Department of Agriculture, R-266, I-1, "Relief files, a"; see the respective RM number.
6	"Optimism and Rain," Swift Current *Sun*, 6 April 1937, p. 4
7	"No Abandonment," Medicine Hat *News*, 29 June 1937, p. 3. This lake has been variously called Johnston Lake and Johnstone Lake.
8	*The Story of Rural Municipal Government in Alberta: 1909–1969* (n.p., n.d.), p. 10.
9	Saskatchewan Archives Board, Department of Agriculture, R-261, f22.15, "Drought General," F.H. Auld to J.P. Robinson, 4 May 1937.
10	Saskatoon *Star-Phoenix*, "A Drouth Conference," 3 May 1937, p. 11.
11	"Big Rain" Medicine Hat *News*, 15 July 1937, p. 1.
12	Saskatoon *Star-Phoenix*, A Drouth Conference, p. 11.
13	Ibid.
14	Medicine Hat *News*, 1 June 1937, p. 1.

15 James Gray, *Men against the Desert* (Saskatoon: Western Producer Prairie Books), p. 212.

16 E.W. Stapleford, Report on Rural Relief, Canada, Department of Ag., 1938, p. 57.

17 Saskatoon *Star-Phoenix*, "Big Harvest in America," 28 June 1937. p. 1.

18 Saskatchewan, Department of Agriculture, *Annual Reports*, 1937, pp. 54–55.

19 Ibid., p. 5.

20 Medicine Hat *News*, 22 July 1937, p. 1.

21 Ibid., "Conditions Very Bad in Saskatchewan Say Officials," 29 June 1937, p. 1.

22 Letter to Editor, Medicine Hat *News*, 29 June 1937. p. 3, 5.

23 Saskatoon *Star-Phoenix*,16 August 1937, p. 7.

24 Saskatoon *Star-Phoenix*, "No Crop: Dunblane," 17 August 1937, p. 17.

25 Saskatoon *Star-Phoenix*, "May Invade North," 11 June 1937, p. 4.

26 Barry Broadfoot, *Ten Lost Years: Memories of Canadians Who Survived the Great Depression* (Toronto: Doubleday, 1971), p. 39.

27 *Maple Creek and Area: Where the Past Is Present*, vol. 1 (Altona, MB: Friesen, 2000), p. 272.

28 Ibid., p. 272.

29 *Between and Beyond the Benches: Ravenscrag* (Regina: W.A. Print Works, 1982), p. 349.

30 Broadfoot, *Ten Lost Years*, p. 40.

31 Swift Current *Sun*, "Failure," 7 July 1937, p. 4.

32 Barry Broadfoot, *Ten Lost Years*, p. 8.

33 Medicine Hat *News*, 29 June 1937, p. 1; 22 July 1937, p. 1; see also 4 August 1937, p. 1.

34 Swift Current, *Minutes of RM Meetings*, Minutes, 2 October 1937; 26 June 1937, see also H. Blair Neatby, "The Saskatchewan Relief Commission, 1931–1934," *Saskatchewan History* 3, no. 2 (1950): 50.

35 Stapleford, "Report on Rural Relief," p. 44.

36 Gray, *Men against the Desert*, pp. 34, 99.

37 Canada, House of Commons *Debates*, vol. 1, 1938, pp. 167–68.

38 Bruce Hutchinson, *The Unknown Country: Canada and Her People* (Toronto: Longmans, Green and Co., 1943), p. 295.

39 E.W. Stapleford, "Report on Rural Relief Due to Drought Conditions and Crop Failures in Western Canada," Canada, Department of Agriculture, 1938, p. 52.

40 Kindersley *Clarion*, "Plan Not Confined to Relief Applicants," 21 October 1937, p. 1.

41 Big Stick, *Minutes of RM Meetings*, 5 February 1937.

42 Stapleford, "Report on Rural Relief," p. 37.

43 Fred Wilkes, *They Rose from the Dust* (Saskatoon: Modern Press, 1958), p. 183.

44 Saskatoon *Star-Phoenix*, "Ask for Immediate Aid in Drouth Country," 14 June 1937.

45 Swift Current Minutes, 2 October 1937.

46 Clinworth, *Minutes of RM Meetings*, 4 January 1937.

47 Saskatchewan Archives Board, Department of Agricultural Statistics, R-266, #10, "Reestablishment Assistance." The information is contained in two black ledger books. See also Swift Current *Sun*, "Manitoba Has Crops But We Miss Murder," 31 August 1937, p. 1.

48 Saskatchewan Archives Board, Department of Agriculture, R-370, f1, "Dominion Provincial Agreements."

49 *Coronach from the Turning of the Sod: The Story of the Early Settlers in the*

RM of Hart Butte No. 11 (Winnipeg: Inter Collegiate Press, 1980), p. 168.

50   Gray, *Men against the Desert*, pp. 192–93.

51   I wish to thank Professor Martha Smith-Norris of the University of Saskatchewan for including this little tidbit in one of her lectures on the settlement of the American west.

52   Gerald Friesen, *The Canadian Prairies: A History* (Toronto: University of Toronto Press, 1984), p. 388.

53   Swift Current *Sun*, 21 September 1937, p. 4.

54   Gray, *Men against the Desert*, p. 63.

55   Ibid., p. 2.

56   Medicine Hat *News*, 9 August 1937, p. 1. The "triple-tipped lance" to which the honourable member referred was the creation of pasture land, improved fallow, and dugouts.

57   Grey, *Men against the Desert*, p. 179.

58   Dan Balkwill, *The Prairie Farm Rehabilitation Administration and the Community Pasture Program, 1937–1947*, University of Saskatchewan, MA thesis, p. 21.

59   Gray, *Men against the Desert*, p. 67.

60   Ibid., p. 103.

61   Timothy Egan, *The Worst Hard Time* (New York: Mariner Books, 2006), p. 112.

62   Ibid., p. 112.

63   Broadfoot, *Ten Lost Years*, p. 37.

64   Gray, *Men against the Desert*, pp. 15, 33, 188.

65   Pinto Creek, *Minutes of RM Meetings*, 1 June 1935.

66   Ibid., 6 July 1929.

67   Gray, *Men against the Desert*, p. 188.

68   Ibid., p. 79.

69   W.A. Waiser, *Saskatchewan: A New History* (Calgary: Fifth House, 2005), p. 321.

70   Balkwill, *The P.F.R.A and the Community Pasture Program*, p. 50, see note 42.

71   When the Saskatchewan Association of Rural Municipalities (SARM) was developing a weed control program, it was observed that Alberta requires weed control while Saskatchewan does not. The question was asked of long-serving and highly respected SARM executive director Mr. Ken Engel how to make weed control effective if there was no requirement for it. Understanding the nature of the organization's membership, Mr. Engel replied that it was a problem to work around – weed control was not mandatory for Saskatchewan rural municipalities and any requests to make it so would certainly not come from SARM.

72   Gray, *Men Against the Desert*, p. 177.

73   Saskatchewan, Department of Agriculture, *Annual Report*, year ending 1939, p. 5.

74   Pierre Berton, *The Great Depression: 1929–1939* (Toronto: Random House, 1990), p. 433.

75   Ibid., p. 5.

76   Department of Agriculture, *Annual Report*, year ending 1940, 84–85.

77   *Prairie Crucible: The Roads of History* (Altona, MB: Freisen, 1991), p. 219.

78   E. Wheat et al., "Agricultural Adaptation to Drought (ADA) in Canada: The case of 2001 to 2002," Saskatchewan Research Council, p. 2.

79   Dr. David Sauchyn, address delivered at "The Water Roundtable," Regina Saskatchewan, 16 March 2010, unpublished.

80   Saskatchewan, Department of Agriculture *Annual Report*, 1943, p. 162.

81   Dr. Sauchyn, *Water Roundtable*, 16 March 2010.

Conclusion: Oblivion (redux)

1   *Report of the Royal Commission on Dominion-Provincial Relations – Saskatchewan*, 1937, hereafter the Rowell-Sirois Report, p. 39.

2   Ibid., p. 274.

3   Ibid., p. 275.

4   See Rowell-Sirois Report, Schedule A, Statement No. 12, p. 421.

5   See ibid. Liabilities column.

6   David Jones, *Empire of Dust: Settling and Abandoning the Prairie Drybelt* (Edmonton: University of Alberta Press, 1987), p. 169.

7   Ibid., p. 157.

8   Carl Anderson, "'Dominion Lands' Policy, Drought, and the Better Farming Commission," *Saskatchewan History* 61, no. 1 (2009): 7.

9   E.W. Stapleford, "Report on Rural Relief Due to Drought Conditions and Crop Failures in Western Canada," Canada, Department of Agriculture, 1938, p. 59.

10   Ibid., p. 60.

11   Jones, *Empire of Dust*, pp. 122–23.

12   Stapleford, "Relief," p. 87.

13   Ibid., p. 86.

14   Ibid., p. 86.

15   Saskatoon *Star-Phoenix*, "Moral Standards Collapse Under Depression Strain," 7 July 1937, p. 5

16   Stapleford, "Report on Rural Relief," p. 86.

17   Ibid., p. 87.

18   Fred Wilkes, *They Rose from the Dust* (Saskatoon: Modern Press, 1958), p. 186.

19   David Jones, *Feasting on Misfortune: Journeys of the Human Spirit in Alberta's Past* (Edmonton: University of Alberta Press, 1998), p. 66.

20   Ibid.

21   Rowell-Sirois Report, pp. 137 and 323.

22   Saskatchewan, Department of Agriculture, *Annual Report*, 1940, p. 107; 1945, p. 187. The RM of Big Stick had signed over 50,000 acres to the LUB; Shamrock signed over title to 22,000 acres; the largest parcel of land was signed over by the RM of Lomond located adjacent to the RM of Hart Butte: Councilmen let go of 228 quarter sections of land, or 36,480 acres. See ibid., 1940, p. 108.

23   Ibid., 1945, p. 183.

24   John Archer, *Saskatchewan* (Saskatoon: Western Producer Prairie Books, 1979), 240.

25   This information was provided by Dr. Sauchyn at a meeting concerning agricultural adaptation to drought on the south plains, Saskatoon, 9 February 2010.

26   Margaret Munro, "Geologists Discover 'footsteps' of Dunes," Regina *Leader-Post*, Thursday, 5 November 2009, p. B-5.

27   *Tears, Toil and Thanksgiving: the RM of Benson No. 35* (Altona, MB: Friesen, 1981), p. 869.

28   Ibid.

29   B.R. Bonsal et al., "Canadian Prairie Growing Season Precipitation Variability and Associated Atmospheric Circulation," *Climate Research* 11 (28 April 1999): 191.

30   Ibid., p. 191.

31   See *A Dry Oasis: Institutional Adaptation to Climate on the Canadian Plains*, ed. Gregory Marchildon (Regina: Canadian Plains Research Center, 2009), p. 32.

32   Stapleford, "Report on Rural Relief," p. 89.

33   *Memories of Cluny* (Winnipeg: InterCollegiate Press, n.d.), p. 463.

34   Ibid., p. 459.

35   Ibid., pp. 459, 465.

36   Rowell-Sirois Report, pp. 293–95.

37   *Captured Memories: A History of Alsask and Surrounding School District*, n.d., p. 304.

38   *Treasured Memories* (Burstall History Book Committee, 1983), p. 21.

39   *Val Echo: A History of Val Marie* (Val Marie: Val Echo, 1955), p. 25.

40   Ibid.

41   *Aneroid: The Rising Barometer* (Altona, MB: Friesen, 1980). See introduction.

42   Ibid., p. 3.

43   *Harvest of Memories: RM 134 and Shamrock* (Regina: Focus Publishing, 1990), pp. 404–5.

44   SAB R-370, f1, Dominion Provincial Agreements.

45   *Prairie Crucible: The Roads of History* (Altona, MB: Friesen, 1991), p. 159.

46   Wallace Stegner, *Wolf Willow: A History, a Story, and a Memory of the Last Plains Frontier* (Toronto: Penguin, 1990), p. 297.

47   Ibid., p. 300.

48   Ibid., p. 287.

49   *Captured Memories: A History of Alsask and Surrounding School District* (Altona, MB: Friesen, 1983), p. v.

50   Stegner, *Wolf Willow*, pp. 294, 305.

51   *Aneroid: The Rising Barometer*, p. 5.

52   Ibid.

53   James Gray, *Men against the Desert* (Saskatoon: Western Producer Books, 1968), p. viii.

54   Ibid., p. 19.

55   *Harvest of Memories: RM 134 and Shamrock* (Regina: Focus Publishing, 1991), p. 338. see also entry for Keith France.

56   *Prairie Crucible*, p. 225.

57   Gray, *Men against the Desert*, p. 9.

58   James Gray, *Red Lights on the Prairies* (Calgary: Fifth House, 1995), p. 67.

59   *Captured Memories*, p. v.

60   Interview with Mr. Ralph Mutter, September 1, 2010

61   *Prairie Echoes of Hatton: A Story of Hatton and Surrounding Area* (n.p., 1983), p. v.

Bibliography

Primary Sources

Manuscript Collections: Saskatchewan Archives Board

Saskatchewan. Department of Agriculture.
———. Department of Agricultural Statistics.
———. Department of Municipal Affairs.
———. Papers of Charles Dunning.
———. Papers of Charles Hamilton.
———. Papers of the Deputy Minister.
———. Papers of F.H. Auld.

Government Documents

Alberta. Department of Agriculture, *Annual Reports*.
By-laws for Rural Municipalities in the Province of Saskatchewan. *Western Municipal News*. 1910.
Canada. *House of Commons Debates*, 1906–1908, 1937–1939.
———. House of Commons *Sessional Papers*, 1907–1917.
———. "Relief for Western Settlers." Ottawa: Federal Press Agency, 1914.
———. "Report on Rural Relief Due to Drought Conditions and Crop Failures in Western Canada." Ottawa, 1938.
———. "Report on Dominion-Provincial Relations: Saskatchewan." Ottawa, 1937.

——. "An Economic Classification of Land in the Govenlock-Eastend-Maple Creek Area." Ottawa: Department of Agriculture, 1948.
Saskatchewan. "Preparing Land for Grain Crops in Saskatchewan." Pamphlet no. 3, Experimental Farms for Southern Saskatchewan.
——. "Dryland Farming in Saskatchewan." Address Delivered by W.R. Motherwell at the Fifth Annual Dryfarming Congress. 1910.
——. Department of Agriculture, *Annual Reports*, 1907–1937.
——. Department of Municipal Affairs, *Annual Reports*, 1915–1923.
——. Department of Agriculture, "How Debtors and Creditors May Cooperate." 1914.
——. Department of Highways, *Annual Reports*, 1930–1932.
——. *Journals and Sessional Papers of the Legislative Assembly*, 1919–1922.
——. "The Report of the Royal Commission of Inquiry into Farming Conditions." 1921.

Municipal Archives

RM of Big Stick Archives. *Minutes of Meetings, and Transfer Ledgers, 1920–1940.*
RM of Chesterfield Archives. *RM of Royal Canadian: Lands Sold and Redemption Record, 1924–1932.*
RM of Clinworth. *Minutes of Meetings, 1919–1937.*
RM of Deer Forks Archives. *Minutes of Meetings*, see relevant year.
RM of Mankota Archives. *Minutes of Meetings*, see relevant year.
RM of Maple Creek Archives. *Minutes of Meetings, 1919–1922.*
RM of Pinto Creek Archives. *Minutes of Meetings*, see relevant year.
RM of Reno Archives. *Minutes of Meetings, Transfer Ledgers, 1919–1926.*
RM of Swift Current Archives. *Minutes of Meetings*, see relevant year.
RM of White Valley Archives. *Minutes of Meetings, 1919–1924.*
Town of Maple Creek Archives. *Tax Sales and Redemption Record, 1915–1925.*

Newspapers

Kindersley *Clarion.*
Medicine Hat *News.*
Maple Creek *News.*
Regina Morning *Leader.*
Regina *Leader.*
Saskatoon *Star-Phoenix.*
Swift Current *Sun.*
Western Producer.
Wynyard *Advance Gazette.*

Community Histories

Aneroid: The Rising Barometer, 1905–1980. Altona, MB: Friesen, 1980.
Between and Beyond the Benches: Ravenscrag. Regina: W.A. Print Works, 1982.
Captured Memories: A History of Alsask and Surrounding School District. Altona, MB: Friesen, 1983.

Coronach from the Turning of the Sod: The Story of the Early Settlers in the RM of Hart Buitee No. 11. Winnipeg: Inter Collegiate Press, 1980.

Harvest of Memories: RM 134 and Shamrock. Regina: Focus Publishing, 1990.

History of the Golden Prairie Community. Medicine Hat, AB: Val Marshall Publishing, 1968.

Mankota: The First Fifty Years. Mankota, SK: Mankota Book Committee, 1980.

Maple Creek and Area: Where Past Is Present, vol. 1. Altona, MB: Friesen, 2000.

Memories of Cluny. Winnipeg: Inter Collegiate Press, n.d.

Prairie Crucible: The Roads of History. Altona MB: Friesen, 1991.

Prairie Echoes: A Story of Hatton and Surrounding Area. N.p., 1983.

Range Riders and Sod Busters. North Battleford: Turner-Warwick, 1984.

Richmound's Heritage: A History of Richmound and District. Richmound Historical Society, 1978.

Sceptre. Past to Present, 70 Years: 1909-1979. Sceptre-Lemsford Historical Association, n.d.

Treasured Memories. N.p.: Burstall History Book Committee, 1983.

Val Echo: A History of Val Marie. Val Marie: Val Echo Publishing, 1955.

Journal Articles

Anderson, Carl. "'Dominion Lands': Policy, Drought, and the Better Farming Commission." *Saskatchewan History* 61, no. 1 (2009): 4–21.

Bonsal, B.R., X. Zhang, W.D. Hogg. "Canadian Prairie Growing Season Precipitation Variability and Associated Atmospheric Circulation." *Climate Research* 11 (April 28, 1999): 191–208.

Hande, Darcy. "Saskatchewan Merchants in the Great Depression: regionalism and the crusade against Big Business." *Saskatchewan History* 43, no. 1 (1991): 21–38.

Jones, David C. "We'll all be Buried Down Here in This Drybelt." *Saskatchewan History* 35, no. 2 (1982): 41–54.

———. "School and School Disintegration in the Alberta Drybelt of the Twenties." *Prairie Forum* 3, no. 1 (1978): 1–19.

MacPherson, Ian, and Thompson, John H. "The Rural Prairie West, the Dirty Thirties and the Historians." Unpublished address delivered at a joint session of the Canadian Historical Association/American Historical Association, Winnipeg, 1986.

Marchildon, Gregory, and Carl Anderson. "Forgotten Farmer-Minister in R.B. Bennet's Depression Era Cabinet." *Prairie Forum* 33, no. 1 (2008): 65–98.

McManus, Curt. "History Public Memory and the Land Abandonment Crisis of the 1920's." *Prairie Forum* 33, no. 2 (Autumn 2008): 257–79.

Neatby, Blair H. "The Saskatchewan Relief Commission, 1931-1934." *Saskatchewan History* 3, no. 2 (1950): 41–61.

Powell, T.J.D. "Northern Settlement, 1929-1935." *Saskatchewan History* 30, no. 3 (1977): 81–98.

Russell, P.A. "The Cooperative Government's Response to the Depression, 1930-1934." *Saskatchewan History* 23, no. 3 (1971): 81–102.

Wheaton, E., et al. "Agricultural Adaptation to Drought (ADA) in Canada: the case of 2001 to 2002." *Saskatchewan Research Council* (May 2007).

Secondary Sources

Archer, John. *Saskatchewan History*. Saskatoon: Western Producer Books, 1979.

Balkwill, Dan. *The Prairie Farm Rehabilitation Administration and the Community Pasture Program, 1937–1947*. MA thesis, University of Saskatchewan, n.p., 2003.

Barnhart, Gordon. *Peace Progress Prosperity: A Biography of Saskatchewan's First Premier*. Regina: Canadian Plains Research Center, 2000.

Berton, Pierre. *The Promised Land: Settling the West, 1896–1914*. Toronto: McClelland & Stewart, 1984.

Bicha, Karel Dennis. *The American Farmer and the Canadian West, 1894–1914*. Lawrence, KS: Coronado Press, 1968.

Bliss, Michael, and L.M. Grayson. *The Wretched of Canada*. Toronto: University of Toronto Press, 1971.

Bracken, John. *Dry Farming IN Western Canada*. Winnipeg: Grain Growers Guide, 1921.

Broadfoot, Barry. *Ten Lost Years: Memories of Canadians Who Survived the Great Depression*. Toronto: Doubleday, 1971.

Breen, David. *The Canadian West and the Ranching Frontier, 1874–1924*. Toronto: University of Toronto Press, 1983.

Carter, Sarah. *Lost Harvest: Prairie Indian Reserves and Government Policy*. Montreal: McGill-Queen's University Press, 1990.

De Toqueville, Alex. *Democracy in America*. Trans. George Lawrence. New York: Harper Perennial, 1968.

Egan, Timothy. *The Worst Hard Time*. New York: Mariner Books, 2006.

Friesen, Gerald. *The Canadian Prairies: A History*. Toronto: University of Toronto Press, 1987.

Gray, James H. *Men Against the Desert*. Saskatoon: Western Producer Books, 1978.

Jones, David C. *Empire of Dust: Settling and Abandoning the Prairie Drybelt*. Calgary: University of Calgary Press, 1987.

———. *Feasting on Misfortune: Journeys of the Human Spirit in Alberta's Past*. Edmonton: University of Alberta Press, 1998.

———. *"We'll all be buried down here": The Prairie Dryland Disaster, 1917–1926*. Calgary: Alberta Publications Board, 1986.

Loveridge, D.M., and Barry Potyondi. *From Wood Mountain to Whitemud: A Historical Survey of the Grasslands National Park Area*. Ottawa: Parks Canada, 1983.

Martin, Chester. *Dominion Lands Policy*. Edited by Lewis H. Thomas. Toronto: McClelland & Stewart, 1973.

Potyondi, Barry. *In Palliser's Triangle: Living in the Grasslands, 1850–1930*. Saskatoon: Purich Publishing, 1995.

Quiring, Bret. *Saskatchewan Politicians: Lives Past and Present*. Series editor: Brian Mlazgar. Regina: Canadian Plains Research Center, 2004.

Sharp, Paul. *The Agrarian Revolt in Western Canada: A Survey Showing American Parallels*. Regina: Canadian Plains Research Center, 1997.

Smith, Henry Nash. *Virgin Land: The American West as Symbol and Myth*. New York: Vintage, 1950.

Stegner, Wallace. *Wolf Willow: A History, a Story and a Memory of the Last Plains Frontier*. New York: Penguin, 1990.

Thomas, Lewis H., et al. *The Prairies to 1905: A Canadian Source Book*. Toronto: Oxford University Press, 1975.

Waiser, W.A. *Saskatchewan: A New History*. Calgary: Fifth House, 2004.

———. *The New North West: The Photographs of the Frank Crean Expedition, 1908–1909*. Saskatoon: Fifth House, 1993.

Ward, Norman, and David Smith. *Jimmy Gardiner: Relentless Liberal*. Toronto: University of Toronto Press, 1990.

Wardill, William. *Sand Castles: A Story of Dryland Settlement*. Eatonia: Seagrass Specialties, 1996.

Widdis, Randy. *With Scarcely a Ripple: Anglo-Canadian Migration into the United States and Western Canada, 1880–1920*. Montreal: McGill-Queen's University Press, 1998.

Wilkes, Fred. *They Rose from the Dust*. Saskatoon: Modern Press. 1958.

Wright, J.F.C. *Saskatchewan: The History of a Province*. Toronto: University of Toronto Press, 1950.

Index

HAPPYLAND

Schuler district, 57

Schuler-Hatton-Leader corridor, 131

science, 22, 221

science of farming, 21–22, 52

scientific basis for agricultural economy, 177

Scotland, 239

Scots settlers, 132, 184

Scotsguard, 10

Scott, Walter, 22, 38, 41, 63
  manic depressive, 39
  philosophical ideas about what it meant to
    farm, 39
  on philosophical virtues of crop failure, 40
  vision for a rural wheat-growing Eden, 73

scurvy, 121, 135, 197

second homestead, 68–70

secret hoards of grain, 146

Sedley, 167

seed, 37, 76, 80

seed drills and direct seeding, 52

seed grain indebtedness, 209. *See also* debt

seed relief, 23, 48, 74, 122

seizing grain grown with seed relief, 143–45,
  147

seizure of land and property, 81, 143, 145, 147

self-esteem and the expression of one's rights,
  154

self-reliance, 154–55

Senate, 10
  evacuation, 49–50, 88

sentiment that accompanied settlement
  destroyed by 1930s, 214–15

settlement
  two distinct phases of western settlement,
    224

settlement camps, 239

settlement era
  ended in the droughts, 231

settlement obligations (of settlers), 20, 105,
  166

settlement past
  cities and towns moving away from,
    244–45

"settler" (word rarely used now), 244

settlers
  average example of settler who fled, 212
  as burden to the municipality, 227
  concerned with survival, 77

contempt by those providing aid (1920s),
  143

crucial component in nation and province
  building, 62–63

disposal of crops while owing for such, 78

emblem of democracy and progress, 17

freedom, 154, 232

hard work would overcome all (belief), 227

image of the Proud Settler, 130, 227

not much respected by cattle ranchers and
  cowboys, 153

one-time gift of steers and dairy cows, 36

petitioned against Pope Commission
  recommendations, 44

poor English and little education, 38

position on priority list, 179

problems their own fault, 164

return to England, 174–75

settlers, RM and province (1914–1937)
  conflicts between, 171

settlers and provincial government
  conflicting aims, 232

"settlers in sheepskin coats," 18

settlers "walking out" of drylands, 13–14, 64,
  70–71, 217. *See also* evacuation

settlers who fled south and west plains, 13–14,
  165, 167, 211–12, 226

sex, frontier substitutes for, 29

sex, ubiquity of (illicit and premarital), 10,
  29, 131

sexual mores, 131, 133, 197, 229

Shamrock, 10, 134
  history, 242
  intolerant of indigents who didn't want to
    work, 141
  lakes and rivers dried up, 135

Shamrock district, 116, 129

Shamrock Primary School, 137

Shaunovan, 239

Shaunovan settlers
  request for relocation money, 211

short-grass prairie, 216

Shortreed, F.R., 85

Sifton, Clifford, 224
  courting the cattle rancher, 16–17
  success in settling Saskatchewan, 18

Simpson, Tom, 26, 30

"Sixty years of Progress," 238

Sliding Hills, 114–15, 202